Leadership of Schools

Chief Executives in Education

ANGELA THODY

CASSELL

Cassell

Wellington House
125 Strand
London WC2R 0BB

PO Box 605
Herndon
VA 20172

First published 1997

British Library Cataloguing-in-Publication Data
A catalogue record for this book is available from the British Library.

ISBN 0-304-33359-X (hardback)
0-304-33360-3 (paperback)

Typeset by Action Typesetting Ltd, Gloucester

Printed and bound in Great Britain by Redwood Books, Trowbridge, Wiltshire

Contents

Foreword

This book is about the days of the chief education officer, studying how these have changed from past to present, and what this may mean for the future. The study is the result of 'following the leader', shadowing and reflection. Through this rigorous pursuit of leadership, Angela Thody captures both significant shifts of role and function and implications for the future governance of education. It is lively, human and wonderfully readable – a thoroughly researched study, both distinctively unique and well related to earlier studies in Britain and abroad. It also adds a challenging speculative view of a century hence that provokes alternative visions.

Publication is timed for a new phase of British government, one in which the review of local democracy and the powers of central authorities will be of critical importance in setting future directions. All the key issues are in this book, for in the role of the chief education officer are to be found everchanging but constantly contradictory pressures – of central and local power, of professional and political perceptions, of institutional and client community interests, of cultural, social and economic priorities, of the past and the future.

Leadership of Schools also marks a turning point in this series. The five women and five men who have each presented significant studies of key issues in education management have all inevitably been exploring the interface of management and leadership, however variously defined. It is a pleasure, therefore, to have this book as the inaugural volume for the widened and newly titled series, Management and Leadership in Education, and to be joined by Professor Peter Ribbins in editing future contributions.

John Sayer

Acknowledgements

Grateful thanks to the eight chief education officers (CEOs) who allowed me to observe them, to the councillors and officers who talked with me, to my husband who brought the quantitative data under control, to my daughters who brought the index and my stress levels under control, to the Universities of Leicester and Luton who supported the study financially, to Don Jones who commented on the history chapter, to research students Anne Punter and Vi Chau Ke who chased references and counted CEOs, to John Sayer of Oxford University who guided the manuscript and to Naomi Roth of Cassell who encouraged me.

Glossary

CEO	Chief Education Officer. The senior executive of the education department of an English local education authority.
CE	Chief Executive of all the departments of an English local authority. The line managers of CEOs.
CO	Chief Officer. The senior executive of any department of an English local authority.
Chair	Elected politician who leads the Education Committee of an English local authority.
Councillors	Elected local politicians who direct English local authorities.
Governors	Members of a school's governing body. Each school must by law have a governing body consisting of elected parents and teachers, nominated party political representatives, and co-opted persons from the local community.
Leader	Elected politician who leads the majority party which controls an English local authority.
LA	Local authority. The principal unit of local government in England and Wales.
LEA	Local education authority. The name of the department within each local authority that is responsible for education.
Members	Another term for Councillors.
Officers	Appointed staff who administer English local authorities

CHAPTER 1

The life in the days

'I'll walk you back to your car', offered the chief education officer (CEO) to my profound relief. The inner city, 2300 hrs, in November 1986 was not my usual beat. Not so unusual though for the CEO of the education department of an English local education authority (LEA), attending a late-night community protest meeting about the neglect of the interests of one racial group at the expense of another. Being the executive's shadow, I followed whither he went, noting the surroundings, the events, the people and his role in it all. I was in the first months of non-participant observation research on strategic leadership. One CEO had been observed. The second observation was in progress. Still to come in this investigation were nine years and seven more CEOs. Five of these were observed between 1986 and 1988 and four between 1994 and 1995.

The chief education executives observed for this study were all at the same level of seniority. Their position was equal to that of chief executives of businesses or of other public or private services. All those observed were the leaders of education services (chief education officers) a role which makes them the equivalent of North American school board superintendents or chief education officers, of Australian sub-state area leaders, and of sub-systems leaders in countries in which central governments delegate to agencies or to regional or local governments.

This chapter introduces the investigation, first reporting on a meeting which is a typical event for a CEO. This typicality is then set within the study as a whole, its objectives, methods and processes, thus providing a brief introduction to the research methods. The Appendix provides a more detailed review of these methods.

A first concept

On that dark November evening at the community protest meeting, tempers were fraught. The CEO began by operating what I later found to be a CEO's central role, that of a listener. A chief education executive does not necessarily have to do anything but does have to be present. To cope with the range of issues raised by the many contacts, these CEOs appeared constantly to be in what one might term listening mode. The body was always on the incline, the head was held at an angle to deflect any impression of confrontation and the eyes swivelled, both to enable the speaker not to feel daunted by continuous eye contact and to ensure that any one hovering outside the immediate conversation was both noticed and reassured of the senior executive's later attention. The look was of concentration and interest with the body positioned slightly diagonal to the contact producing an impression of readiness to move off quickly in order to do something about the speaker's needs. Doing something meant that these CEOs moved into transmission mode, passing on as quickly as possible the information gleaned, to whomever it was most relevant.

At this late-night community centre event, the listening revealed that, in addition to the racial concerns, there were objections to the community centre becoming too much of a further education centre and a specific complaint about the need to support a steel band. The CEO neatly wove the points into last-minute alterations to the preplanned speech. The CEO's subordinates back at the office had anticipated some, though not all, of the supplementary questions heard that night.

The CEO passed from listening into mode two of operation, as a speech-maker representing the public face of an LEA. Lunge, parry, defend, deflect, salute, respect the rules and show preparedness to face challenges from unexpected directions – the CEO's speech offered the group all these. First was the promise of a new beginning for a policy for the centre, then deft praise of the local political representative (present in the audience). This was followed by an outline of the local policy on community education and of the need for equitable provision in all areas of education. Blame was firmly placed on central government's failure to support local requests to provide courses for adults without traditional qualifications. The senior executive stoutly defended his subordinates in what appeared to be a speech unlikely to reach the hearts of the audience and to pass over their heads in esoteric language and in references to equity for others. Further observation of the meeting revealed the need for such a bland defence. Tempers were running high. My notes that evening recall, 'Wow – this is a political minefield!'

The senior executive did not need to tread on mines. They exploded spontaneously. One participant offered to kick in the CEO's door in order to make him listen. Accusations were made of local officials obtaining 'perks' in the form of investigative visits to Bangladesh (organized so that the officials might better understand the cultures of large minorities within the authority). There were demands for fee remissions for facilities and courses and for the rapid purchase of a minibus. Pointedly strong remarks noted the area's insufficiency of primary school places. A calm CEO sat centre left. 'Let me hear your ideas', he was able to interject above the hubbub. 'You are misinformed about what to do', he insisted. 'Partnership is what we want to achieve', was the CEO's hopeful conclusion.

Partnership concluded the evening. The crowds left. The community centre committee and staff chatted at a post-meeting reception with the CEO. He returned to listening mode, clearly attempting to assess the extent of the meeting's representativeness. The verbal flow drifted into snatches – the neglect of Afro-Caribbean groups, the impossibility of satisfying all, the 'what can we do?' and the 'we're pushed into a corner'. Eventually, we all pushed off home.

Questioning strategic leadership

That evening encompassed many of the responsibilities of those at high levels of strategic leadership: planning for the whole area, finding and managing resources (human and financial), minority protection, educating adults and school-age students, accountabilities to local and central politicians, curriculum development and estate management. The superficial treatment of the many elements, and the late finish to the day, encapsulated the multitude of issues that had to be covered briefly in these CEOs' days, at a rapid pace and through long hours. The audience represented all the groups to whom CEOs have to be responsive, the service providers (teachers, LEA subordinates, support staff) the community stakeholders (parents, unions, students, governors, community groups and business groups) and the politicians (local and central). All these aspects became the framework for the research and for this book.

Through the swirling word clouds of that evening, arising from those myriad responsibilities, emerged my first concept of a strategic leader as the hub of a wheel. The hub is the strong part. Its place reflects the setting of the plan of the vehicle, derived from the engine. Information about how the plan is working at the rim is transmitted through various spokes to the hub. The hub then retransmits the vibrations along other spokes back to alternative parts of the rim which makes use of the information while some of the transmissions go to the engine. This analogy leads to a central question of this book. Are senior executives, like wheels, essential to the operation of the vehicle?

Management pyramids in all organizations are being flattened as the middle layers are reduced in numbers. What then will happen to the senior levels? Strategic planning is now regarded as a team game, not one for the solo, visionary leader model of the 1980s. What then should senior executives be doing? In sympathy with these trends, English and Scottish local education authorities are no longer obliged to appoint a CEO though all of them seem to be continuing to do so (Dobie, 1996, p. 10). Will the role eventually disappear and, if so, will it have to be reinvented if the style of strategic leadership which it embodies remains necessary? If CEOs are reinvented, will they be in a new form ? These are the central questions on which this book focuses.

Revealing strategic leadership

A wheel analogy is not particularly academic terminology nor are 'swirling word clouds', 'spontaneous explosions' and 'political minefields' used above in the report on the late-night meeting. They essay to be expressive phrases but are they suitable for an academic text about strategic leadership? The main question for me was how to convey the fascination and allow readers to feel part of the action, as I had been myself, while producing a text that had academic validity.

My objective was to add descriptive and analytical material to the few studies of the powerful in education management not only because of intrinsic interest but in order to understand how to influence policy-making processes and how further to characterize leadership, the nature of which 'continues to be enigmatic' (Walford, 1994a, p. 3). Amongst leadership studies, the roles of CEOs are of current interest: their resignation rate has increased during the last decade; studies have begun, in Canada, linking CEOs to outcomes (Musella, 1992) and in England in 1995, Chris Woodhead, the director of OFSTED,[1] announced that differential outcomes of LEAs were to be investigated. Any differential outcomes might be traced back to the effects of different senior executives. One can draw an analogy between senior education executives and managers of football teams, a profession with rapid turnover as managers face dismissal if their teams fail. From that analogy arises a question central to this investigation: 'Players play, coaches coach, chairmen chair, so what's left for the manager to do? ... the dwindling role of the motor mouth on the bench' (Novick, 1995, p. 76). Though written as a description of football managers, with a slight adaptation of language one could have the same discussion about the role of the CEOs studied here. Teachers teach, central government directs, councillors chair – so what's left for the motor mouth in the office?

First, though, I had to locate the motor mouths willing to be closely observed. Five were found between 1986 and 1988 and four in 1994–95. The senior executives were at different career stages: one was just appointed at the time of the observation; one had been two years in post; two were on the verge of retiring after many years' service. The others were well established but had differing lengths of service at the time of the observations. Only one was in post during both periods of research. Others retired before the second shadowing and I found replacements.

Each of these senior executives was a CEO in a local authority with educational responsibilities (LEA) and was thus the most senior manager in the education service. Their role was to manage the locally maintained sector of educational provision.[2] For comparisons with executives in other businesses and public sector services, the size of these managers' responsibilities would encompass a minimum of 100 sites and a maximum of 500 sites. Personnel employed as teachers would be approximately 10,000 in the largest LEAs and in addition there would be approximately 3000 school support staff, advisers, inspectors, administrators and central services staff, such as educational psychologists, drivers, welfare officers, grounds maintenance workers, peripatetic music teachers and school-crossing patrol wardens. In 1986–88, these executives also had responsibility for further and higher education colleges. All these responsibilities, in both of the periods of the observations, were spread over extensive geographic areas. Buildings had to be planned, monitored and decommissioned. Supply chains to schools had to be organized with children, books and equipment to be delivered on time. Marketing had to be led to demonstrate the success of the organization. The research had to find a way to convey all these responsibilities and their similarities to those of executives anywhere.

The research was:

- **qualitative**, observing and recording all the details of this group of senior executives' activities. Semi-structured observation by a non-participant researcher (myself) was used. I was at virtually all events during a total of 36 days, divided between the two periods, for each cohort, 1986–88 and 1994–95. The detailed recording was to illustrate subtleties of strategic leadership not amenable to demonstration from questionnaires, interviews or documentary evidence. A senior manager must, for example, 'learn … to introduce ideas slowly and informally during conversations … use the "planted question" in committee, he must be "politician himself"' (Hornsby, 1984, p. 110).
- **quantitative**, collating and analysing some of the elements of the senior executives' activities in order to clarify the myriad complexities of this level of strategic leadership (Konnert and Augenstein, 1990, p. 11) and to develop some comparisons.
- **set in the executives' real work environment** uncontrolled by the researcher. The observations were undertaken in the situations in which these executives spent most of their time and with which they were most familiar.
- **partial**, emerging from the researcher's view of the people observed.
- focused on **executives' tasks** and the time and processes involved in accomplishing these in order to ascertain contributions to strategic leadership.
- **exploratory,** avoiding conceptual structuring at the fieldwork stage and allowing categories for analysis to emerge from the data.
- **generalized,** providing a portrait of strategic leadership rather than of individual leaders. It abstracts the behaviour of these leaders from their singular, local contexts and sets the whole within the common context of 1980s' and 1990s' systems changes.

Like North American superintendents, with their responsibilities to elected school boards, these English senior managers have an additional responsibility. They are answerable to an elected, political council. The responsibility itself is not dissimilar to that of a chief executive to a board of directors but the local politicians have a loyalty to a party line and to their voters in addition to their accountability for the financial health of the organization and to satisfying the companies' customers. The political affiliations of the LEAs within which the executives in this research worked, covered the spectrum. One had a secure Tory majority and two had secure Labour majorities. Two had marginal Tory majorities and two had marginal Labour majorities. Two were 'hung' with a balance amongst the Tories, Labour and Liberal Democrat parties or a balance between Tory and Labour with the Liberal Democrats or Independents therefore able to determine the vote.[3] All the LEAs were in middle England; four were large shire counties, one was a large city and one a large town.

The aim of this book is to look for the routines of strategic leadership rather than the new and the special. Seeking those routines from non-participant observation produced extensive data: reducing these to quantitative tables could destroy the fascination of the detail; reproducing them as qualitative narrative could overwhelm with the busywork of ethnography (Theobald, 1990). My objective is to locate the middle ground between detail and outline and between academic and novelistic language.

The choice between the academic and the novelistic is illustrated by comparing these two extracts. The first is from a novel about a retired CEO. The second is from a report of a research project on superintendents in the USA.

> Aspirate-dropping politicians, educational psychologists, parents hot under the collar, lunatic school teachers had all added to the tally of ludicrous error but then so had he. His whole career was shot through with misjudgement, mismanagement, support of wrong causes, failure to assist decent men and women, and yet he was still praised as one of the most successful directors of education in the whole country since the war. He could not see why he had made such a name, except that favourable publicity or circumstances had helped him and his pleasant but utterly serious committed manner and approach had led people, political masters or paid subordinates alike to act more sensibly.
>
> (Middleton, 1986, p. 70–1)

> The superintendent moves between the nomothetic to idiographic dimensions to transactionally and transformationally interact with board members, principals, parents … to persuade these individuals to accept the goals of the organisations as defined and visualised by the superintendent. The superintendent acts to persuade these individuals to participate in the formulation of … goals additional to his own.
>
> (Griffin and Chance, 1994, p. 81)

The first approach, characterized by Atkinson (1990, p. 38) as 'naturalistic', would be difficult to sustain throughout a book without also adding to it the story elements of a novel as, for example, does David Lodge (1989) in *Nice Work* (a novel about a senior business executive shadowed by a university researcher). This I have not done. I have, however, used sparingly the novelist's descriptive techniques to add interest and readability to the items such as that of the second extract, 'more suited conventionally to realistic and factual texts' (Atkinson, 1990, p. 38).

In seeking answers to questions about strategic leadership, non-participant observation can describe those parts of the roles of strategic leaders which other approaches to researching the powerful have not reached. Among the many studies of leadership in education management – estimated as 10,000 by 1991 (Walker, 1994, p. 3) – few have been conducted by non-participant observation. Those that have used this method have been virtually all of school principals, both in England and elsewhere. Only one study of Canadian superintendents by non-participant observation has been located (Duignan, 1980) and one of Australian regional directors of education (Macpherson, 1985a). Of the few studies of English CEOs, none used observation. The seminal and substantial Kogan trilogy studying CEOs used interviews and questionnaires (Bush and Kogan, 1982; Kogan and van der Eyken, 1973; Bush *et al.*, 1989). Other studies have used primarily documentary sources (Hornsby, 1984), brief commentary by or about CEOs (Binns, 1957; Brighouse, 1986; Wood-Allum, 1987) or are biographies of famous, individualistic CEOs (Fisher, 1965; Jones, 1988; Ree, 1973; Seaborne, 1968). The latter style 'may even do a disservice, these fun books with their tales of heroes and myths of the mighty by suggesting that leadership is only for the new and the special' (Handy, 1994, p. 206).

Rather than looking at the special, this book describes, and comments on, chief education executives realistically at work in their daily contexts. Before returning readers to that real work from Chapter 3 onwards, Chapter 2 provides a conventional academic introduction to the contexts of CEOs' activities.

Notes

1 Office for Standards in Education, the central government agency charged with organizing inspection of schools.
2 In 1995, of the 24,000 publicly funded schools, approximately 23,000 were locally maintained.
3 The parties are roughly designated: Tory, right wing; Labour, left wing; Liberal Democrats, centre.

CHAPTER 2

The contexts of the days

Leadership is not a subject that has national boundaries. Hence this chapter commences by reflecting on the commonalities of strategic leadership in the late twentieth century. I aimed to generalize rather than to particularize the data so that it could offer validity for all strategic leadership studies, hence the focus here on similarities. In most countries there have been marked centralizing tendencies, particularly since the mid-1980s, and these have been combined with their opposite, that of delegation of power to schools. These two trends appear to decrease the power of sub-system strategic leaders who sit between the centre and the schools. This chapter outlines how these trends have developed in England both to familiarize readers with the national context of the study and to enable readers to assess how far other nations' developments provide a similar context for their education executives. The chapter concludes by describing the senior executives' physical contexts, i.e. their office environments, so that readers can envisage the *bricolage* with which they chose to surround themselves. All these contexts should help readers travel with me in time, place and perceptions.

Leadership contexts

Expectations of leadership

The two cohorts of senior executives whom I observed, operated in a period of conflicting expectations and understandings of leadership. Some writers envisaged leadership as enigmatic and therefore not susceptible to transmission as guidance to senior executives (Walker, 1994, p. 3). To others, leadership was visionary and transformational and able to provide clear guidelines for action. A leader must be a risk-taker, with strong values, coping with ambiguities and mentoring others in their organizations (Peters and Waterman, 1982; Mortimore, 1988). Further interpretations have taken realistic views: 'If I knew how miserable and terrible it was going to be I probably wouldn't have signed up but who the hell knows that before you sign up for the war?' asked one of the executives in Tichy and Devanna's (1990, p. 264) study of American executives. In the background have been those rewriting our understanding of the organizations in which leaders operate (Morgan, 1993; Gleick, 1987).

The decade 1986-96 has not provided certain definitions of how leaders should behave. Nor were they years of certainty for the job security of senior education managers who seem not to be highly regarded despite their hard work, efficiency and client responsiveness (Blundell, 1988). Removing CEOs seems to be the most often suggested political solution to prevent LEAs overspending. Likewise, the political solution for an LEA in difficulties has become the dismissal of their CEOs as happened to Derek Esp (Lincolnshire) in the 1980s and Pat Black (Cumbria) in the 1990s, amongst others. Chief Education Officers themselves saw the job as less than a commitment for life. There was, for example, interchange with academic careers (Tim Brighouse, John Tomlinson and Margaret Maden) and with new educational agencies (Kathleen Lund, Hillingdon, to head the City Technology Trust[1]). There was also accceptance of a greater variety of backgrounds amongst appointees to senior education leadership posts than was the case before the mid-1980s. More women gained CEO positions (there was only one at the beginning of this period but 20 by the early 1990s, from a total of 119). A few from ethnic minority backgrounds were appointed such as Gus John (Hackney) and Bebb Burchell (Lambeth). Some had much less lengthy experience than previously demanded such as Geoff Lennox (Derbyshire) who leapt from assistant education officer to CEO. More were from non-teaching backgrounds such as Roy Atkinson (Northamptonshire) who was an educational psychologist, Geoff Lennox (Derbyshire) and Ann Sofer (Tower Hamlets) who were councillors.

Despite the uncertainties and changes, public perceptions of senior education leaders seem to retain some of the certainties of old. Reporting the arrival of a new CEO in its county, a local paper recorded the first parents' meeting attended by the new director. 'Our big hope educationally lies in the hands of the county's new education director ... Ms Strong, apparently strong by name and nature ... although [she] said nothing ... she went down a storm with the crowd. She listened very well and everybody was most impressed' (Mercury, 1994, p. 29). It seems the CEO didn't even have to do anything to be perceived as valuable!

The importance of leadership studies

The decision to research strategic leadership through a field study of senior executives in their natural habitats was taken because there was nothing else similar. There is a general belief that English CEOs and those in analogous positions elsewhere in the education service, are powerful in strategic leadership (David, 1977, p. 33–8; Ozga, 1986, p. 44; Walford, 1994a). Researching the powerful is seductive *per se* but limited largely because of the difficulties of gaining access (Walford,1994b). Such difficulties have inhibited research by non-participant observation. Consequently, there are no such studies of English CEOs nor of any chief officers in local government. There are very few observation studies of those in equivalent roles in other countries (Australia: Macpherson, 1985a; Canada: Duignan, 1980) or of strategic leaders at this level in other sectors (Mintzberg,1973). I believed that this type of research could tell us something about policy- making processes that could not be found from other sources and that observation of naturally occurring events would be helpful in 'encountering alien worlds and [trying to] make sense of them' (Agar, 1986, p. 24).

Strategic leaders from English local government have never been a popular topic for any type of research (Browning, 1972, p. 4; David, 1977, p. 29). This study aimed to present primary, detailed empirical evidence from new sources and perspectives which Bush *et al.* (1989, p. 90) concluded was greatly needed after their seminal research arising from interviewing English CEOs. Their interview series, which began in 1973, is a major source of reference on the topic (Bush and Kogan, 1982; Bush *et al.*, 1989; Kogan and van der Eyken, 1973). Their research for the 1989 book, coincidentally, was concluding as this study began so this research updates it. Concurrent with the Kogan trilogy was the only other direct study of CEOs, that by David (1977). This concerned developments in LEA policies and who was involved in changing them, producing a typology of CEOs as an outcome. Indirect evidence on CEOs can be gleaned from the National Foundation for Educational Research (NFER) research on LEAs in the early 1990s (Brown and Baker, 1991; Edwards, 1991) and from Middleton's 1986 novel about a retired CEO, which offers some reflections on the daily round of CEOs' activities which have been little described or discussed in other research studies.

The cohorts observed

All ten CEOs whom I approached were deemed to be effective according to the education management 'grapevine of anecdote'.[2] Of these, eight were willing, nearby and in areas whose spread enabled the research to cover areas of different political persuasions, urban and rural environments and geographical locations around central England. It was fortunate that those who accepted my presence worked in a variety of LEAs as I intended the research to have generalizable validity. The 1986–88 cohort were in three counties and one city. In 1994–95, they were in two counties, one town and one city. These covered the political spectrum from secure Labour to secure Conservative or with varying shades of 'hungness'. Such a range parallels that of other local education studies (Brown and Baker,1991; David, 1977; Edwards, 1991) and offered the chance to test Hendy's (1987b) contention that urban politics are sharper (this did not seem to be the situation in my study). Other ways of differentiating the contexts of these education leaders would be to select from a range encompassing varying attitudes of CEOs (Brighouse, 1986, p. 257; David, 1977) but these would require pre-tests beyond the capacity of this research and would have pre-empted the conclusions on how the CEOs operated.

Rejected leadership contexts

I chose to exclude contexts such as character descriptions of each of the leaders or details of the educational provision in their areas. I was not looking for contextual explanations of behaviour. To even attempt these from a small group of leaders seemed presumptuous and to require immensely detailed information with which to justify correlations. David (1977) disputes the value of this approach because it rests on the assumption that personality is a determinant of administrative behaviour. Researchers then prove this by producing copious data on personality; the outcomes are a self-fulfilling prophecy. None the less, there are writers who accept that personality and other local context information are vital and are behaviour determinants (Clarke and Stewart, 1986, p. 8; Griffith, 1966, p. 522-3; Konnert and Augenstein, 1990, p. 9; Greenwood et al., 1980, p. 95). Others produce it as background but use very little for correlations (Bush and Kogan, 1982; Bush et al. 1989; Kmetz and Willower, 1982; Kogan and van der Eyken, 1973; Martin and Willower, 1981). Townsend gives contextual detail about the Canadian he observed but he concedes that 'some readers will find [it] boring' (Townsend,1991, p. 47). If his one context was boring, the eight needed for this study might have been extremely boring! Readers will have to judge whether it would have helped their understanding of strategic leadership to know that the CEOs had different personalities. When dealing with intransigent politicians, for example, one character would remark explosively: 'Councillor X is ... barking mad', whereas another CEO would impishly note: 'What larks, Pip. Here we have fun'. The way they each coped with the politicians in question was the same. It was only the words that differed.

There was also the difficulty of deciding what contextual detail would have been relevant. Greenwood et al. (1980), for example, identified eight subtle gradations of internal management structures as determinants. To locate these for this study would have required a separate research project. The variations may be even wider than these eight since Browning (1972) concluded that no English local authorities are identical. Such a conclusion can become an escape from making generalizations. Greenwood et al. (1980, p. 161) and David (1977) accepted that the most common differentiators of LEAs, i.e. the types of area governed (metropolitan or shire) and their party political complexion, were significant determinants of behaviour. These factors have been used in this study to differentiate the quantified information produced in the following chapters. Readers should thus be able to judge for themselves if there are relationships between context and outcomes.

The context of centralization

Impressions of centralization

In 1987–88, I recorded the daily visits of a man watering the plant arrangements in the office of one of the CEOs. In 1995, in the same authority, the CEO's successor had no plant arrangements; there were a few, haphazardly scattered plants watered by the CEO personally. Between these two observations were massive spending cuts enforced by central government. The disappearance of the 1980s' plant arrangements and their minder seemed symbolic of all that had gone. The 1994 office building looked distinctly dilapidated compared with seven years previously. Paintwork needed replacing or cleaning. Equipment looked battered with overuse. Corridors were untidy. Carpets needed more regular vacuum cleaning.

For all English LEAs, there was a diaspora between 1986 and 1996, pushed by central government. The 1994–95 LEAs had fewer administrators than did their 1986–88 counterparts. Deputy CEOs had become almost defunct; retiring post holders were not replaced. Whole sections dealing with further education and with school finance, disappeared or were decimated. Advisers were virtually extinct.[3] Services previously provided by officers were consumer-led businesses. Regional agencies led education and industry links and employment issues. National agencies handled funding, teacher training, curriculum direction and inspection. Central government took leadership of the curriculum from LEAs. Central government took pedagogical decisions from the teachers and advisers. Governors took over school direction and administration from the LEAs. All schools became autonomous.

With so many changes during the period of my observations, it is tempting to agree that it 'is doubtful if any previous time was so packed with incident or produced so much change' (Bush and Kogan, 1982, p. 4). This quotation, however, refers to the 1970s. It is also tempting to aver that there was a revolution in local educational administration between 1986 and 1996, but Sylvester thought that was true in 1957. Central regulation seems very strong now but in 1966 Griffith viewed school building controls as detailed and unassailable and Smith (1965, p. 3) was concerned that power had shifted too much to the centre. Central powers over the structures of secondary schooling were characterized as very powerful in 1974 (Saran, 1974, p. 260). The 1944 Education Act left unchanged many of the powers and duties of LEAs and added to the established control and direction of central authorities. Griffith in 1966 (p. 51) noted LEAs' lack of powers to determine anything other than minor, marginal issues. Crosland, Minister for Education during the 1960s, regarded LEA freedom as rhetoric rather than reality (Boyle and Crosland, 1971, p.127) as did Griffith (1966, p. 100).

It is perhaps fairer, therefore, not to view 1986–96 as inordinately centralized but instead to view the post-1944 period (if not the whole twentieth century) as a period of centralized leadership and to recognize that LEAs were also affected by factors outside the control of central government, such as demographic change and rising societal and parental expectations of achievements and equity. This is not to underestimate the effects of all the changes between 1986 and 1996, but it is to see these years set in the context of continuations of established centralizing trends rather than as aberrations in an otherwise localized pattern.

There is a strong yearning to depict England in the pre-1980s as a partnership of equality between central and local government (Hall, 1984). The 1960s are often depicted as years of local freedom(Heller and Edwards, 1992, p. 106) because of increased national funding for education and its distribution to local authorities as general grants which they could allocate as they wished amongst local services. In reality, LEAs have always been administrators of central policies (Thody, 1976) and, as such, they themselves have been accused of the same dictatorship as that of central government (Edwards, 1991, p. 23). It is within these perceptions of centralization that I observed the CEOs over the nine-year period.

Structures of centralization

Like all democratic polities, the central direction of English education is shared between politicians and administrators. The politicians are MPs elected to Parliament by a majority of a local constituency. This local connection makes it important for CEOs to liaise with MPs. Senior MPs from the majority party in Parliament are selected by the Prime Minister as ministers and junior ministers for education. The minister for education is a major political post and always has Cabinet rank. The title is at present Secretary of State for Education and Employment. Education legislation is discussed both in full meetings of Parliament and in non-specialist legislation committees. There is a Parliamentary Committee on Education and this specializes in investigations into aspects of education. The administrators are civil servants in the department with responsibility for education. They are regarded as neutral advisers with permanent posts whichever party is in power in Parliament. In 1986, the civil servants for education were in the Department for Education and Science (DES). By the time these observations ended in 1995, the department had twice been renamed becoming, first, Department for Education (DFE) and, secondly, the Department for Education and Employment (DFEE).

Her Majesty's Inspectors of Schools (HMI) are central government employees, theoretically independent of the DFEE but less apparently so in practice. They provide information for ministers on the state of education. School inspections are franchised to teams of inspectors privately contracted through OFSTED, the Office for Standards in Education. The development of the OFSTED system occurred during the period of these observations, one of the many changes dictated by central government.

Expressions of centralization

The outward and visible sign of the inward and spiritual changes brought by central leadership was the alteration to the names of the organizations within which I conducted the observations. During 1986–88, all were Local Education *Authorities*. By 1994–95, most had renamed themselves as Education *Services*. The nomenclature signified the end of LEAs' position to direct and the beginning of the consumer-dominated era. Whatever the local name, however, central controls remained the same. Such centralization has its parallels around the world though specific impacts will vary. The specific impacts on this group of CEOs are described below.

Major effects from central directives were evident in budget issues. At the end of observations of cohort one in January 1988, a CEO was trying to impress on councillors the seriousness of having to find £10 million in reductions following cuts in central funding and the centre's refusal to allow local authorities the power to raise income from other sources. By the time the cohort two observations began in 1994, one CEO had retired, unable to make the necessary budget cuts. Another had managed to persuade the LEA to reduce the overspending on schools from £12 million to £1 million. The 1994–95 group were all coping with arguments over allocations among services of much reduced income. Fewer local government finance officers remained, having set up financial delegation to schools. Alterations had been made to the formulas whereby funds were delegated to schools and LEA finance departments had managed to bring under control the workload of moving to the new system. In one LEA, the CEO went personally to congratulate the officers for whom financial delegation had now become so routine that they no longer had to work overtime to cope with the demands of the annual allocations and of 'glitches' in the management information systems for schools. There were, however, some 'glitches' in central dissemination of information and money, such as when a CEO could not tell a governors' forum what money the Department for Education would be allocating to governor training as the information had not arrived.

There were signs of some relaxation of central financial direction by 1995. The leader of one local authority, in cohort two, announced to the press that the LEA was avoiding increased class sizes by allowing an overspend of £1 million. This would mean

> challenging and pushing our legal powers to the limit and could bring us into disagreement with the government but we will not distribute help according to a formula that does not reflect need. The legal position is not entirely clear ... there is little room for manoeuvre but there are indications that what the government might have dropped on two years ago, they would not now do so – but that's a political, not a legal opinion.

Throughout this statement, the CEO was present but did not comment other than to provide some detailed information on service cuts when requested.

On some issues, CEOs firmly supported central government. During the 1995 observations, school governors threatened to resign *en masse* unless central government allocated more money to schools. 'We would advise governors,' remarked one CEO, 'that resignation won't produce more money. They should stick with it and try to ensure that however scandalously inadequate our resources, their job is to manage as best as possible, as we've had to do in local government, not running away from it'. On the vexed issue of OFSTED inspections, one CEO stated: 'I really think it's working to raise standards. The process is having an effect but don't quote me on that' (since all this is anonymous, I hope I may be forgiven for repeating this remark). One CEO was using central government agencies as a gateway to influence. The CEO was a member of the Further Education Funding Council part of whose remit was to pronounce on Grant-maintained Schools' applications to establish provision for Years 12 and 13, provision that could compete with that of LEA maintained schools.[4] This type of central involvement was that used by CEOs in the past to sway central policies. It was, and is, invited and accepted by central government.

Generally, it was the politicians in both 1986–88 and 1994–95 who were anti-central government, not, apparently, the CEOs, thus reinforcing my impressions of CEOs as akin to French regional inspectors acting as neutral interpreters of the centre to the localities. CEOs' published views revealed a more anti-central government stance. The publication, *Education*, regarded as a voice for local education authorities, included a weekly column written by CEOs. Between 1986 and 1996, many of these were anti-central government (Lockhart, 1996; Walton, 1987, 1990: Westerby, 1987; Wood-Allum, 1987) although a more balanced view was emerging by 1995 (Du Quesnay, 1993; Harris, 1995).

Opposition to central government was endemic amongst the political leaders of the LEAs. I noted that when observing CEOs in both Labour and Tory authorities in both cohorts, had I not known in advance the political complexion of the chairs of their Education Committees, it would not have been possible to guess these from their attitudes to central government. The politicians encountered in both cohorts, in all the LEAs whatever their parties, seemed likely to have supported the Education Committee chair who said in 1995: 'We will follow our own priorities, not serve the ends of the Department for Education.' As a corollary to this, the CEO quietly reported that the LEA would just be able to meet DFE staffing demands and to submit the capital plans as required. CEOs were more realistic than the politicians; 'I'm not sure we're going to be much different if Labour gets in next time – it's always just us against them' commented one CEO. The expected neutrality of CEOs and their LEAs was underlined by one of the 1994–95 cohort who reported to the departmental management team the central government's advice that any indication of unfairness in school ballots to opt out would result in that ballot being declared void. 'Unfairness' was deemed to mean the LEA dispatching biased propaganda to parents. The LEA must, therefore, avoid this, noted the CEO.

CEOs were responsible for interpreting central government policies to the service providers and stakeholders in their areas but neither cohort had any contacts during the observations with central government departmental personnel. In addition, CEOs spent less than 1 per cent of their time with MPs and HMIs. Despite this lack of contact, there were several examples of CEOs having to disseminate and explain central policies without the benefit of clear guidance from the centre.

During 1986–88, CEOs found themselves determining local versions of what counted as teachers' hours of work (e.g. How many minutes before the start of the school day did teachers have to arrive? Was a training day to be a full calendar day? How many training days should part time or supply staff attend? What should be assessed for the award of merit pay? How should responsibility allowances be apportioned?). The CEOs used phrases which neatly encapsulated their role as spokespersons for the centre: 'The Secretary of State feels …'; 'in view of the Secretary of State's powers, we haven't got much to debate'; 'it all depends on what the Secretary of State wants'; 'decisions are not possible until the Secretary of State decides'. Teachers, governors and councillors looked to the CEOs to disseminate understanding of central government policies. One of the 1986–88 cohort had two lengthy meetings, first with school principals and then with governors to explain central policy on teachers' incentive allowances and hours of work. The CEO regretted being unable to answer all their questions because the 'Secretary of State is not getting the information through'. Pushed by the unions to determine matters, the CEO responded with: 'I don't think I can take it any further. I have to work within the 1,265 hours and accept that.'

A CEO regretted not being able to produce answers to questions concerning the teachers' training days in a handbook for distribution to teachers and governors but the LEA did not want to use resources for this until the Secretary of State had reached his final decisions and the handbook could be definitive. On small school closures, a CEO had to gather information from the press after a minister's announcement of a change in policy. Later that day, the Schools Sub-committee was to discuss this. The CEO asked his deputy to phone a contact at the central department for details. On another occasion the chair of the Education Committee agreed to arrange an informal meeting with a junior minister. Both of these were useful ways to obtain information but neither was open and satisfactory for everyday information on policy interpretation.

In these circumstances, the LEAs felt to me like the local offices of a national organization though without the benefit of a shared logo and a consultative mission statement. Observing the same issues being debated in different authorities, I questioned the justification for having local interpretations of central policies although a CEO felt that discretion was vital to correct policies. The CEOs spent a large amount of time negotiating with teachers' unions locally and the outcomes were not significantly different in different authorities. As disseminators of central policy, CEOs were, perforce, less than efficient because central government did not provide enough information to them and because the nature of the system pushed local government to seek variegated solutions where national policies could have been more equitable.

My perception of LEAs as franchisees from central government was reinforced by the minor administrative matters for decision which reached CEOs as link persons to central authorities and as part of the detailed implementation of central policies. In 1987, for example, one CEO set up a working party with the Deputy Chief Constable to organize police consultation on the curriculum as required by the 1986 Education Act. A 1995 Afro-Caribbean Unit needed to know how to respond to Home Office enquiries. The same unit had to be apprised of enquiries from MPs. The government's decision to require local authority services to be subject to competitive tender resulted in the privatization of the careers services in two LEAs of cohort two. One of the CEOs concerned then had to resolve the complications arising from LEA employees transferring to the new company; the start date for the new company would mean effective losses of two weeks' pay and there were delicate negotiations on this point led by the CEO. Other CEOs were learning to work with the new Funding Agency for Schools (FAS)[5] as sufficient schools in their areas had opted for grant-maintained status to trigger the joint authority with the FAS. There were detailed administrative points to be settled about sharing financial information as a consequence. The outcome of all this was, as one CEO remarked: 'It's getting to be more and more paper.'

The introduction of the National Curriculum in 1987 prompted one of the first cohort's CEOs into overt opposition to central government. Together with several other CEOs, he laid plans to defeat the National Curriculum on its passage through the House of Lords. Were these to be unsuccessful (as they were), the CEO stated that 'I've got some views on how we might defeat it ... but I'm keeping them up my sleeve for the moment'. The National Curriculum was well established by the period of the second round of observations and opposition was saved for other issues. On the issue of grant-maintained school status, for example, some of the CEOs uttered anti-central government sentiments but mainly CEOs adopted the position of implementing the views of whichever party was in power locally. One CEO in the first cohort summed up the CEOs' role when opting out was first discussed in 1987: 'I'm not making a political point, it's just the practicalities' about which there was officer concern. There was no overt CEO opposition but there was, for example, assistance to a school's governors in 1995 who changed their minds part way through organizing the balloting process for opting out. The CEO was unsure of the legal position but made clear that the LEA would facilitate a return to the LEA. 'After all, the governors can't be sent to the Tower so we just have to see them through the uncomfortable way back,' remarked the CEO of the repentant governors.

Planning the local education service, a requirement placed on CEOs by the 1944 Education Act, became difficult as central policies changed rapidly. In 1987, all small schools were up for closure, a policy then amended to be those in certain situations only. In the same year, one CEO encouraged the councillors to hold back on planning further and higher education provision until the government's decisions on allowing colleges to become independent were known. One CEO considered that national priorities for money to be spent launching the new GCSE in the mid-1980s had distorted the LEA's local priorities for primary school developments. Central policies to allow parental choice of schools conflicted with LEA policies to stop schools competing with each other and 'poaching' pupils. New schools could only be established where there were not surplus places, a policy reversed by central government in 1994. The LEA plans to close schools in the 1990s were overthrown by central government allowing many such schools to opt out into grant-maintained status.

Did the changes wrought by central legislation affect the CEOs' contacts? During the 1994–95 observations, I noted occurrences which indicated that not all the CEOs' contacts had reoriented their pathways to take account of developments. Schools were autonomous but that did not stop a principal coming to a CEO for advice on how to finance a sports centre, how to deal with the roll-over budget and various personnel issues. A grant-maintained school sought advice on inspection. An anonymous person from a local grant-maintained school thoughtfully passed on to the CEO a letter from the Funding Agency for Schools which seemed indirectly critical of the LEA. There were also enquiries to a CEO about further education matters, long after the colleges became independent. In general, though, queries about further education were not routed to CEOs in either cohort. CEOs in the 1986–88 cohort had deputies responsible for further education who were virtually autonomous. Two of the CEOs admitted their ignorance of further education and called in the deputy to deal with it. By the time of the 1994–95 observations, further education had been removed from the LEAs.

It was clear that some contacts were aware of the new positions accorded them by central government and that they, accordingly, bypassed CEOs. CEOs in the 1986–88 cohort spent 17.36 per cent of their time with school principals and teachers. Their 1994–95 counterparts spent 10.16 per cent of their time with the same group. Contacts with school governors declined marginally from 2.63 per cent of time in 1986–88 to 2.56 per cent in 1994–95. A 1986 CEO was informed by the political leader of the education committee, that the LEA would be given enough money from central government to provide 12 more teachers, provided that two were placed in each MP's constituency, according, therefore, to political rather than educational need. 'Preposterous' was the CEO's comment to the local politician offering the deal. 'Not … likely' was the comment to me. In contrast to this resistance to outside intervention in local decision-making, a 1995 CEO was not informed about, nor invited to, a meeting of primary school principals and governors apparently to be held in the LEA offices. Exclusion from governors' matters also affected a 1987 CEO. He was incensed to discover that an MP had written directly to governing bodies without consulting the CEO. He translated his anger into objections to the MP and into making governors aware of his displeasure. His 1995 counterpart simply noted a similar exclusion privately.

There was also one permanent exclusion to organize which revealed the effect of centrally directed changes on LEAs. A 1994 CEO had to decide whether there should be an employees' retirement party. Usually this would involve only a small number of people around 65 years old. In 1994, there were 196 employees retiring, many of them early leavers.

The local government system

Centralizing trends have, therefore, dictated changes in the English local government system. Its basic elements, similar to those of other democratic countries, remain unchanged. Each LEA has a political and an administrative section. The politicians are termed, 'councillors' and the administrators are 'officers'. In theory, the politicians are the strategic leaders and the administrators are the implementors. In practice the job descriptions are much less clearly delineated than this, as later chapters illustrate.

The political element consists of councillors, elected for a limited term on a simple majority system, to represent areas of each authority's territory. Councillors are usually elected as political party representatives and these parties are the same as those which operate in the national polity. Councillors are part time although the workload for the chairperson of an authority[6] (who is the leader of the majority party), the party spokespersons (in a hung authority, each party's leader may take turns at being the leader), or the chairpersons of the principal committees, creates almost a full-time job for which councillors' employers usually give them some paid leave of absence. Councillors receive expenses and attendance allowances and some, such as those who serve as leaders or chairs of committees, receive fees.

Each authority organizes its political decision-making through a structure of formal committees, informal working groups and party caucuses, the patterns of which will vary slightly in different authorities. The formal committees are sub-groups of the Council, the decision-making body which consists of all the councillors. The council as a whole would meet usually about eight times a year whereas committees meet more frequently. The lead committee is that for policy and resources. There is then usually a committee for each local authority service, including education. These subdivide into smaller committees. Education, for example, might have sub-committees for monitoring schools or planning. Committees and sub-committees vary in size but are composed to match the political complexion of the Council as a whole. Working parties, set up for specific, short-term objectives such as school closures or devising religious education syllabuses, are likewise politically representative and often include administrators as well as politicians. CEOs, or their representatives, attend council and committee meetings but cannot vote. They do not speak unless asked to do so. Council and committee meetings are open to the public and to the media. Each local political party also has its caucus. This comprises councillors from that party only. Meetings are private and are held to discuss party tactics for meetings of council and committees. CEOs do not attend caucus meetings but they do brief the leader of the majority party, or the leaders of all parties in a hung local authority, prior to their caucus meetings.

Administrators in English local government are termed 'officers'. They are full time, paid and appointed for their expertise. Councillors will be involved in selecting holders of senior executive posts (such as the CEOs observed in this study). These executives, however, generally cannot be dismissed if there is a change in the political balance after an election. Senior executives in English local government are viewed as neutral and willing to serve councillors of any political complexion. Occasionally, CEOs are appointed on limited contracts but this is not yet the norm. Officers have their own career ladders; CEOs, for example, would be likely to have entered the service at around age 30, after experience as teachers. They would then progress through grades of assistant education officer and then to deputy education officer before reaching the top strategic position from around age 45 onwards. There are no standard qualifications expected of those who hold these posts but it would be usual for such leaders to hold university degrees and professional accreditation.

Between 1986 and 1995, there were three types of English authorities with responsibility for education: counties, some towns, and cities. Each is divided into functional departments. They vary in size, their boundaries having been set according to a combination of historical precedent, urban morphology, economic regionalism, geography and political lobbying. These three types of authorities are the largest units of local government in England and such authorities also had responsibility for other major services, such as planning, social services, libraries, police, museums, transport, trading standards and roads. Education was the largest of the local services with the largest budgets and the largest departmental staffs, which gave the CEOs in this study a powerful position within their local authorities.

CEOs' power was mitigated, throughout the years observed, by the requirement that each local authority must plan corporately so that education plans had to fit within the overall strategies of their authorities. This requirement appeared to sit lightly on some CEOs, as Chapter 5 illustrates. CEOs' influence was mitigated by the requirement that power be devolved to schools from 1986 onwards which transformed LEAs into servicing, rather than directing departments. This devolution was instigated largely by central government although some LEAs had already allowed their schools some freedom. CEOs' power was further mitigated by having to lose parts of their empires. During the 1980s, central government required most services previously provided by local government to be put out to tender. In competition with the private sector, many local authorities 'hived off' existing sections and turned them into companies, bidding to undertake the work as companies separate from the parent local authority. Examples include school meals, school maintenance and the careers service.

Throughout the years observed, therefore, the LEAs were instructed by central government to dig their own graves, training school personnel to take over the roles previously performed by local officers while also handing over to schools the grave-digging fees. They dug with remarkable grace, elegance and forbearance.

Since these observations ended there have been further changes in local government organization (from 1996). Some of the larger authorities have been subdivided. The subdivisions have taken over some of the parent authorities' educational responsibilities. More CEOs have, therefore, been created. The final chapter of this book speculates on the effect of this development.

Office contexts

The CEOs observed between 1986 and 1988 spent 15.85 per cent of their time alone in their offices; those observed between 1994 and 1995 spent 13.42 per cent. Both cohorts also held one-third of their meetings there. The ambiences of their rooms were, therefore, important not only to the comfort of the leaders themselves. Those joining meetings there could feel disadvantaged in a room which they did not own. The messages the offices conveyed mattered to the success of gatherings.

The first message conveyed was that of the occupants' desire for the anonymity usually attributed to the administrative, adviser role. Secondly, there appeared to be a desire for impeding people's access to the offices. Thirdly, there were marked indicators of equality with other officers.

These messages began with the difficulty of finding the offices. Whether the office buildings were purpose-built for local authorities or not, the CEOs' offices were not readily accessible to external stakeholders nor were they obviously marked or differentiated from those of other officers. Three of the eight offices were at the end of long corridors so that I felt as if I were approaching the monarch's throne room. Five could only be reached by most callers through the secretaries' rooms. Senior staff indicated their status by entering their leaders' rooms directly through alternative doors. The CEOs' offices were larger than those of other staff but only two could have been described as being on a grand scale.

Despite the difficulty of locating the leaders' rooms, everyone was warmly welcomed. Not only this but there was a casualness about the entrance of other senior officers and politicians. They barely knocked but wandered in and out and made themselves at home. Meetings could commence while the CEOs were working at separate desks or still moving around the room with papers. CEOs accepted the traffic. Sandwiches were shared. Coffee was produced. Papers mulled over. Jokes passed around. Clearly all felt at home in the surroundings.

A study of Canadian superintendents' office surroundings revealed that their

> primary message was a commitment to students – pictures by and of students hung on their walls – and to their professional associates – modest gifts with organisational and professional meanings ... For most, personal artefacts, things made or given by their children, family photos and the like also were displayed as if to say 'there's more to life than just work'.
>
> (Lawton and Scane, 1991, p. 202).

This description fits the offices of those whom I observed. I noted that the student artefacts selected by these CEOs were markedly modern whereas the furnishings were generally traditional. Only in one office did the furniture appear to have been designed for the room and to be a matching set throughout. Most of the furniture was standard office issue with nothing *outré*.

None of the offices was luxurious thus signifying 'non-materialistic values' as did those of their Canadian counterparts (Lawton and Scane, 1991, p. 202). The display items, books and magazines indicated interest in the literary, visual and performing arts although there were few books other than official-looking reports. This too these English education leaders had in common with the Canadian superintendents. It was concluded that the lack of books might 'reflect an administrative dependence on condensed, pre-digested information and on a valuing of oral sources' (Lawton and Scane, 1991, pp. 202-3). Such a conclusion seemed appropriate for these English leaders too.

The arrangements of the surfaces and chairs conveyed the message of a degree of status mixed with a welcoming equality. All the offices except one contained the *sine qua non* of the 1980s' executive, the coffee-table and easy chairs for informal meetings. There were usually one or two filing cabinets with wood facias. All offices except one (which was very small) had a more formal, large, meeting table with chairs, and all had a desk.

Most of the CEOs sat behind their desks though they generally emerged from them as soon as anyone entered the room. They remained behind their desk barriers only if a visitor were just fleetingly passing through or if there were some displeasure or distance to be indicated (very rarely). Two pushed their desks against the wall so that their chairs were unprotected and could be instantly swivelled to participate in what was to happen in the room. One of these never used the desk other than to store papers, habitually working at the coffee-table, often companionably with the councillor who was the chair of the Education Committee. All but one desk had sparse but not spartan desk furniture. All but one were tidy. None appeared to have entered the technological age. If there were e-mail terminals, they were not visible and most of the phones were not overly 'high tech'. Four sited their desks so that they faced entrants to the room. One CEO moved me from the chair I had first selected as my observer post because I then blocked his view of who was coming in. He liked to have instant access to information on visitors.

The wall decorations chosen by these CEOs seemed symbolic of their place in time. There was an even balance between the ancient (antique maps, for example) and the futuristic (such as students' abstract paintings). Most had some souvenirs of their travels abroad on behalf of their LEAs. Strategic leaders in motion between the past and future seemed an appropriate position from which to launch their daily routines, the subject of the next chapter.

Notes

1   This organization guides the City Technology Colleges. These colleges, for pupils aged 11+, are part funded by industry and part by central government. Each has a specialism, e.g. performing arts or technology. They were established from the late 1980s.
2   This was personal enquiries amongst colleagues working with and in LEAs. A refined version of this was used to select ten Canadian CEOs for Hickcox's (1992) research. He received nominations from 74 CEOs for colleagues they rated most effective. The most frequently cited were asked to participate.
3   LEAs employed senior teachers to advise schools on their curriculum developments. Local authorities reduced their advisory services when central government devolved the LEAs' powers to control finance to schools in the late 1980s to early 1990s.
4   The 1988 Education Act gave schools the right to opt out of LEA control and into direct control from central government. The right caused much controversy as opted-out schools received more funding than did those locally maintained and their leaving an LEA caused a decrease of central government grants to that LEA.
5   Funding Agency for Schools. This is a central government agency which distributes funds to grant-maintained schools which are outside LEA control. Once the number of grant-maintained schools in an area exceeds a certain percentage, FAS becomes jointly responsible with the LEA for school planning in that area.
6   Colloquially referred to as 'the council'.

CHAPTER 3

The days begin ... and end

The CEOs began most of their days with warming-up exercises in the offices whose descriptions closed Chapter 2. This chapter begins with recollections of those commencement exercises. These illustrate the detail of data collected, the contexts in which the executives worked and their many roles. A table summarizes every daily activity of two CEOs, one from 1987 and one from 1994. The aim is to demonstrate the outline format in which the raw data was recorded and to begin comparisons of the two time periods during which data was collected. Thirdly, there are vignettes of the CEOs at the end of their daily work and from these can be seen the many types of people with whom they interact.

The days begin

That a week begins on a Monday was not usual for CEOs. Several arrived with work in progress from weekend home activities. A fairly minimal weekend might entail four hours short-listing through 59 applications or reading government reports. One of the 1986–88 cohort looked at his Monday work pile and said 'This is when one pays for not working over the weekend'. What these CEOs paid was roughly the same for all of them. On the 36 days recorded, work away from home regularly began between 0800 hrs and 0830 hrs. There was no difference in the mode or median start times for the two cohorts. There was one start at 0730 and three after 0900 (all from the 1994–95 cohort). Several of the group indicated, either directly or indirectly, that they had already been working at home before leaving to travel to the office, one habitually starting at 0530.

Warming-up exercises

The most usual activity in the pre-0900 period could be described as analogous to 'warming-up exercises'. A typical list of dispatches for the first 15 minutes can be judged from this record of 9 September 1986:

- approving a dinner menu
- reviewing a short list for a post
- setting up a senior team meeting to discuss the short list
- reading letters from fellow CEOs concerning a forthcoming meeting
- checking that travel insurance had been arranged for a visit to France
- confirming the date of a meeting for Industry Year Committee
- 'line moving activities' i.e. redirecting mail, minutes, reports, journals to other staff
- reading a circular on courses offered by the Institute of Local Government (INLOGOV) at the University of Birmingham
- making notes on aspects of legal issues of which the Industry Year Committee need to be apprised
- drafting a few thoughts on a presentation to a meeting with the teachers' union (the only item which merited a comment, 'now that really is important')
- deciding that problems concerning the authority's outdoor pursuits centre should be dealt with by other officers
- signing letters to a local MP and to the director of a polytechnic
- chasing up a major industrialist with a personal invitation to the Industry Year Committee
- contacting a deputy director to ask him to speak about a written memo he had sent about curriculum review
- arranging a meeting about a recalcitrant chair of governors who was causing grief to a school's principal and governing body.

To this type of varied list, two of the CEOs in each cohort customarily added a glance through the newspaper, or the *Times Educational Supplement* (*TES*) or *Education*. One such reading caused a flurry of activity when the Secretary of State for Education announced (in May 1987) that the government had decided against insisting on the closure of all small schools. This topic was already on the agenda for that afternoon's Schools Sub-Committee and the CEO made phone calls to discuss consequent policy change with the chair and sent photocopies of the article to the subordinates concerned.

Decisions would be taken very rapidly on the contents of the in-tray. Twenty-two items were dispatched during the first hour of one day in 1986. 'That's rather slow for him' remarked one of his subordinates. 'I hesitate to leave documents on his desk because I know they'll be quickly returned to me with something further to do as a result.' This might be, as one of the CEOs made clear, because the paperwork was abhorred as it was boring. 'Paper is the enemy' remarked one, 'bloody mountains of it. You could spend your life shifting it.'

This pile of 'on desk' activities awaiting attention at the beginning of the day was not all of the mail received. The daily sacks of letters were usually sifted twice before reaching these CEOs and items redirected elsewhere if possible. The surviving letters invariably concerned issues which had, or might have had, implications beyond the remit of a single subordinate, which needed a policy decision before a subordinate could continue or which required further research or meetings. Secretaries selected, for priority attention, any letters that had likely political implications. The volume of letters from schools increased as the school term wore on; the longer the term, the greater the number of letters as principals became stressed. The volume also rose after governors' meetings.

An occasional, apparently inappropriate item arose such as the need for the CEO to issue a reminder that confidential material should not be placed in corridors while building contractors were altering offices. The CEO remarked, 'I haven't got time to think about that now but isn't there an alternative?' One felt that such minor matters should be directed from elsewhere but, on reflection, where would 'elsewhere' be for such reminders - or, indeed, for other minor matters with which the morning warm-up exercises were concerned? In any system, there are unplaced responsibilities and new occurrences; those in the system will pass these upwards. Hence, there was apparent trivia very occasionally.

Only once was the quiet, early morning time used for a sustained period of writing instead of the warm-up exercises. A CEO in the first cohort prepared a speech for the Education Committee. During the one and a half hours, only three phone calls were momentary distractions from this preparation of an anti-National Curriculum alert. 'If I don't say anything, the councillors might do something silly,' he remarked to me.

Alternative beginnings

Alternatives to the paperwork routine revolved around subordinates, such as a briefing for an assistant director's appointment. The pre-0900 period was the time for those without appointments to drop in for a chat. Chats often concerned items that could have a direct bearing on the public image of the organization or that might cause concern amongst the politicians. A CEO would need to be apprised of these since councillors might contact him for discussions. It was noticeable that these executives gave much more alert and determined concentration to items likely to be immediately politically significant than to other items. Any desultory chatting metamorphosed into more of an interrogation if a CEO sensed political implications.

Direct access over the phone or by visit could usually be guaranteed in this hour before the secretaries were habitually on duty and while the warm-up paper exercises presented a relatively unenticing distraction for senior officers who are strategists. Significant others were aware of this morning gateway. CEOs rang each other during this period. The local press representative rang for a comment on an article in the *Times Educational Supplement* in the midst of early debates about grant-maintained schools. A local school principal had sent a letter to the editor of the *TES* in reply. The *TES* editor had sought sanction from the CEO to place the letter prominently and to amend the letter slightly so that the criticisms were more muted. A distraught parent using the early morning route received half an hour's personal counselling. Any later in the day and the call would have been transferred to a subordinate or marked for response later.

An alternative form of the warm-up written exercises was the 'follow up the night before' mode. Many days concluded with meetings, usually far too late to conduct any more work afterwards. Consequently, the following morning's first activity was the routing of items arising from the meetings to others for action. This may be to dignify the activity with an importance it did not possess as one of the CEOs remarked: 'Most of this could have been dealt with by the caretaker.' This same CEO clearly preferred the spoken to the written word since the warm-up exercises were almost entirely interpersonal, led by whichever officer happened to drop in. Personal interactional warm-ups were the preferred format of the two of the group both of whom had been longest in office at the time of the shadowing (they both retired shortly afterwards). Two others in the group added physical exercises to the early morning process; both preferred to visit than to be visited and the days commenced with nipping to other offices for chats about past and forthcoming events. The morning's letters and reports were drafted together with the subordinates visited.

It was noticeable that conversational starts to the day were concerned with what might be termed 'the core business' for these executives, i.e. issues directly related to teaching and learning. The exchanges would invariably include comments on curriculum or pedagogy. The paperwork warm-ups seemed more related to support for teaching and learning – the management of resources to make the core business effective.

Meetings begin

The early morning 'grasshopper' routine invariably led into a meeting with some members of the senior team. On the morning described in the opening chapter, for example, a significant, lengthy, eight-minute, informal meeting followed the desk warm-up exercises. The outcome of the meeting was that one of the deputy directors was charged with investigating nursery assistants' involvement with midday lunch supervision. More formally, the departmental, or senior management teams had meetings. During such meetings, a typical range of pre-0900 topics would include:

- motivating staff to apply for school principalships
- reports on staff appointed
- final agreements of the format of a document to be sent to councillors to gain their approval for departmental restructuring
- commentary on how they would manage the process of dispatching grants to students in higher education at the start of the new university year

- argument about the best way to develop the privatization of the school cleaning system
- a health and safety induction course
- area meetings which the CEO wanted organizing for school principals and their chairs of governing bodies
- social deprivation
- the equalization of educational opportunities.

During the observations of the second cohort, those termed senior staff now included the newly 'privatized' direct services provided by LEAs under contract to schools. Hence one day's beginning included a confidential session with catering and cleaning directors. On days when the CEO arrived later than usual, a senior team collegial activity would be the first item in the day, sometimes appearing to be dispatched with greater speed than when preceded by the warm-up exercises. These exercises would usually follow the first meeting of the day if displaced from their pre-0900 spot.

An occasional alternative (which occurred on 16 per cent of the days recorded) to personal or paper warm-ups followed by senior team activities was early travel to meetings with the day commencing off site (those who did this lived at a considerable distance from their offices so meetings *en route* saved time). Breakfast enlivened the 0730 start of one of the 1994–95 cohort. This was at a local school that was seeking industrial sponsorship in its bid to become a technology school. Nervous dinner ladies, transmuted into croissant-servers, set the scene together with flower arrangements in a style popular in the 1950s. The CEO, in a public relations role, milled about purposefully locating the school's principal, a local inspector, the chair of the Training and Enterprise Council and school staff who received a word of praise for their efforts. The CEO spent the majority of time corralling local industrialists in order to encourage their financial support. The public (and political) significance of the role was marked for another of these CEOs who attended an early morning press briefing given by the leader of the council and concerning budget overspending and its relation to class sizes. The CEO's role was not an active one, being confined to providing a three-minute contribution (in half an hour) on details of service cuts. Enacted here was very much the traditional role of the CEO as technocrat adviser to political leadership but the 'adviser' was not always the public cipher to the political activist. One morning meeting found the CEO centre stage at a gathering of school principals, community agency and local representatives, delivering a ten-minute speech on the values of school links with Europe.

These three examples are all from the 1994–95 cohort. The one early start external meeting for the 1986–88 cohort was more parochial, directly involving only those within the education service. One CEO took the politicians (the council leader and the chair of the Education Committee) to visit two schools, one of which had been remodelled and one of which was in need of the same. The CEO prompted the school staff to demonstrate their needs, chatted with all staff and some children, and ensured that the politicians realized how their policies had taken effect. The CEO walked ahead of the party, very much the monarch with the politicians in his wake as courtiers. The school was the world of the educational administrator to which he introduced the politicians. 'I don't know much about children,' happily remarked the political leader being led by the educational leader.

Shortly after 0900, the main business of the day began with much longer meetings scheduled or visits away from the office.

The CEOs' typical days

On almost every day of my shadowing, one of the CEOs remarked, 'Of course, that wasn't a typical day'. Only one noted that there had been a 'typical week' while I was there. Despite these views, there is a reasonable degree of similarity about what happened on the days observed, irrespective of the different types and sizes of authorities being directed, the different years or the times of the year at which the observations took place. Similar degrees of commonality have been found in observation studies of school principals.[1] Manasse (1985), for example, concluded that there was not even variation in daily activities amongst those principals deemed to be effective and those not so described. Perhaps the perception of the observer differs from that of the subjects, or CEOs are not aware how others like themselves behave. Alternatively, these CEOs could have meant that because of the enormous variety in any one day, it seemed difficult to characterize a single day's generality.

In using the ordinary business of the day as its data source, research by accompaniment results in copious and detailed information. To reduce this to manageable proportions, some non-participant observers have used daily summaries (Hall *et al.*, 1986) such as in Table 3.1. These have the advantage of allowing 'the reader to formulate his or her own hunches about the perspective of the people who have been studied' (Silverman, 1993, p. 146), of establishing the credentials of the research and of demonstrating quickly the outline of a typical day. I selected foreground items only (Sydor, 1994) to avoid swamping analysis (each day's records averaged 20 closely written pages). The omitted background items serve the same purpose as extras on a film set. The crowd scenes may not appear in the final edit but they create requisite atmosphere for the actors to play against.

Throughout these days, the pace was unrelenting. Every spare minute was used. Meetings were chaired at speed and with efficiency to ensure that all items were covered. The activities usually kept to their allotted times. Rarely did these CEOs linger after a meeting for a cup of tea or a chat unless it was the last meeting of the day. I felt somewhat surprised by this, having expected more informal negotiations to be apparent. Such informalities, however, were mainly confined to sessions with other staff of the CEO's own department rather than with any outsider groups. Returning to the offices after meetings, all these CEOs immediately began replying to letters, collecting messages, making phone calls or processing minor jobs without noticeable pause.

Table 3.1 Daily activity records

23/10/87: Large city LEA *Secure Labour majority*	*9/2/1995: Large city LEA* *Secure Labour majority*
0800 Prepares papers for the day; reads reports 0840 Discussions with secretary on day's activities. More papers delivered for reading 0855 Phones a school governor. Discusses funds allocation for a school, which Councillors will be involved, arranges contact with Charity Commission	0830 Prepares papers for the day 0835 Collects accompanying officer. Car travel to meeting at Teachers' Centre
0905 Deputy CEO[2] drops in to discuss pay negotiations with nursery nurses. Tactics explored for later meeting. Discussion of councillors' attitudes. 0910 Phone to exchange views with the chair of the Education Committee on councillors' attitudes to the pay negotiations and how she will influence these. 0919 Discussion with officer from Central Policy Review Unit[3] concerning how the LEA will develop racial harassment policies; CEO co-operative but warns that his officers are short of time for the additional work; CEO reports schools' anti-racist activities 0937 Deputy drops in for instructions on a school contract 0938 Discussion on racism continues 0945 Meets deputy – discusses attendance at anti-apartheid conference, contacting the Deputy Chief Constable to arrange a working group re 1986 Education Act,[4] holiday dates, a TV training course being part funded by the LEA for principals' training, links with local industry to improve school leavers' employment prospects, world student games which the town is to host. 0956 Phone – chats about last week's council meeting with an officer 0958 Makes three phone calls while dealing with letters and papers. Discusses local government finance, finds papers wanted for local MPs briefing, discusses issues re tertiary education	0900 Meeting with primary school principals and assistant director for primary education re line management for nursery school principals; issues relating to the National Curriculum implementation; discussion on nursery principals needing their own representative group instead of using the primary principals' group; requests for publicizing LEA plans for nursery education; campaign, 'Raising the Profile' of primary education, CEO passes on the chair of Education Committee's views on the budget

Table 3.1 continued

1018 Chief primary adviser[5] comes for advice on obtaining central government grants, for discussion on moving the science training centre and altering the premises
1023 CEO goes to find information on the regulations for the new premises – tutorial rooms must be found
1025 Discussion continues
1030 CEO meets finance officer – asks him to attend a working group on revenue budgets on CEO's behalf, asks for a document to be written in accessible language so that the CEO can explain it to councillors, discusses deployment of the officers' team at council meetings, decides that information needed on other LEAs' spending in order to encourage the councillors here to be bold and to accept that budget cuts must be made
1046 Secretary drops in with information concerning presentation of merit awards. He asks her to see if the Education Committee chair wants to attend
1049 Phone call re school contract
1051 Paperwork – prepares MPs' briefing
1053 Deputy to discuss merit award ceremony
1055 Briefing paper continues

1000 Meeting with adviser from Curriculum Support Team – discuss her personal development plans and the movement of the CST to another location
1010 Car travel back to office

1030 Corridor chat with asistant director from the earlier meeting with primary heads. 'Hidden agenda' of personality clashes debated

1040 Letter writing. Phone calls. Reading

1130 Meeting with new primary phase adviser for induction. Discuss schools she has visited, facilities for her job, suggestions for a replacement school principal, how to deal with a problem school, training ideas for teachers

1131 Plans diary commitments with secretary. Responds to chair of Education Committee – enquiry about meeting MPs. Discuss the sensitivities of whether or not the chair should be invited to a secondary principals' meeting
1146 Dictating letters re social worker's involvement in a particular child's case, principal's funeral, setting up meeting of officers, arranging a governors' conference, Audit Commission,[6] teachers' union conference

1205 Officer with research proposal to follow up on racial harassment. CEO advises him not to extend his workload
1208 Deputy brings an offer from an outside polytechnic[7] to share expensive software with local polytechnic. CEO offers to expedite
1210 Returns to paperwork interspersed with attempted phone calls
1230 Officer delivers contract for discussion. Document finalized
1250 Goes to lunch. Ponders budget strategy and campaign to oppose the 1987 Education Bill[8]

1230 Lunch
1240 Letters continue
1300 Walk to Town Hall with deputy
1305 Chat with officer to arrange meeting
1315 Education Policy Working Group on the budget. Presentation by school principals to councillors on effects of budget cuts. CEO participates with responses to questions

Table 3.1 continued

1430 Meeting with an officer to discuss outcomes of working party on TVEI[9] and how this should be reported to councillors. Officer also clerks a governing body and reports on problems with this – the school governors disagree with the local authority over the information to be sent to applicants for principalships and over how the school will fit into the LEA's policy on regrouping tertiary provision. Officer warns of a local warns of a local principals' delegation to oppose LEA policy on this – CEO says they will be disciplined if they publicly disagree with LEA policy 1455 Sits and thinks	1440 Budget discussions continue after school principals leave 1450 Walks back to office with deputy 1455 Arranges with deputy which activities he will undertake while CEO is away. Discusses the department's management team
1510 Visits deputy to report TVEI issues. Delegates to him the role of making contact with councillors on this 1515 Preparing agenda for industry issues – TVEI, contracts, partnership – for a meeting with project leaders 1546 Phones to discuss the software offer 1552 Continues paperwork	1505 Meeting with deputy and legal officer to discuss legal implications of governors' threatened resignations.[10] Decision to collect information on what was happening elsewhere. Drafts memo to be sent to clerks to governing bodies 1550 Visits librarian to obtain information on teachers' pay award
1620 Meets primary phase adviser to discuss project on problem solving for which the LEA has a special grant awarded. Explains presentation of results to parents. Adviser reports on the lesbianism of a teacher appointed to AIDs advisory post – there might be PR implications 1640 Several phone calls on the contracts 1650 Officer with information from the chair of Education Committee on issues arising from the restaffing of tertiary colleges. CEO advises officer to meet staff not to communicate by paper 1700 Briefing of local MPs, joined by chair of Education Committee. 1987 Education Bill discussed and matters relating to individual MPs' constituency areas 1752 Full meeting ends. Some leave. Others remain for social chat. Further discussions on 1987 Bill 1820 Checks progress on the school contract 1830 Leaves work	1600 Chats over budget issues with deputy 1615 Phone calls and letters 1625 Reads press cuttings about a previous meeting. Finance officer drops in with information about the teachers' pay rise. 1630 Deputy and finance officer discuss budget projections 1635 Finance officer is due to have his annual career review – termed 'stocktaking' – but he is not in the mood with all the issues relating to budget cuts, teachers' pay rises to be accommodated and governors' threatened resignations so they agree to hold it over to another time and to discuss current issues instead. They search through the budget to locate areas for cuts 1735 Discussion on tactics for a meeting to be held that evening for governors 1745 Tea break 1800 Letters 1830 Governors' meeting to inform them of budget issues. CEO listens as officers lead the meeting 2030 Leaves work

The CEOs' days end

The long day

Formal meetings were common in the last two to three hours of most days, These often took place after what others would consider to be the normal end to a working day. An average day at work for the 1986–88 cohort of CEOs was 11 hours and 20 minutes and for the 1994–95 cohort, 10 hours and 39 minutes. The average for the two was 10 hours and 42 minutes. In addition, most did some work at home before or after the day's end. The long hours were often commented upon. One officer remarked 'Christ, you must have some bloody stamina, I couldn't keep up with him for one day let alone four days for observation'. Comments, in like vein, were recorded for several of those observed.

The average day reduced by 41 minutes between the first and second cohorts. The one person who was in both cohorts worked an average day that was 69 minutes shorter in 1994 than it had been in 1987. It is tempting to attribute this to the diminished responsibilities of LEAs since 1986. The person who spanned both cohorts was, however, new in 1987 and had increased his efficiency/productivity rating by 1994. He processed more activities in the same time in 1994 than he did in 1987. The second cohort also included two executives who were suffering a degree of ill health. The LEAs managed by the second group included a small town whereas those in the earlier group were all large in counties or cities. None the less, it will be interesting to see if the hours diminish further in those LEAs within which subordinate organizations took over some areas of their educational responsibilities in 1996.

Despite their extensive schedules, all these CEOs remained alert and energetic throughout, in some cases positively bounding with enthusiasm into yet another late-night meeting. The least popular meetings were mainly public relations events at which the CEOs had to speak with those important to a scheme but did not have to negotiate serious decision-making.

Evening meetings

Evening meetings for the 1986–88 cohort included a discussion with officers on the short-listing for an assistant education officer's post and the organizing of the interview process during which the CEO was clearly pushing for a particular candidate not favoured by the others. The following day concluded with meeting the appointed candidate and debriefing unsuccessful candidates. (The successful candidate was the CEO's original choice: 'Now you scc how far a CEO can influence appointments', the CEO remarked to me privately.) External affairs led one of these CEOs to attend a small schools' research group conference (at which he gave the introductory speech) and to participate in a session for the chairs of community centres. At this latter meeting, the CEO met attacks with time-honoured techniques of inclusion – 'We're not in a game of them and us, we're all in this together'; 'I think your point's very valid but …' – and of apportioning blame to absent politicians – 'At the end of the day, it will be a political decision'. The tactics proved successful. One of the chairs remarked: 'What you said just now put things in a different context. If we'd known what was in your mind, we'd have been more supportive.' Lobbying local MPs with explanations of how forthcoming legislation would affect the locality provided an apparently fruitless end to one day; MPs agreed that the law would be 'catastrophic' but that even the 'guerrilla tactics' proposed by the CEO for their parliamentary activities would not halt the 1987 Bill (they were right). Evening work also entailed public food. One of many dinners eaten by these CEOs in the course of duty was to meet candidates for the directorship of one of the LEA's colleges – 'trial by knife and fork' as the CEO defined it. Finally, all the CEOs were invited to multitudes of school events; one such was to a book exhibition at a primary school celebrating reading week. The somewhat anxious fluttering around the CEO from governors and the school principal demonstrated the CEO's monarchical position. The CEO demonstrated the children's monarchical role by determinedly centring on their work and ensuring staff received praise for their efforts.

The 1994–95 cohort had similar evening meetings. CEOs in local government have roles outside education since the advent of corporate management within local authorities from the mid-1960s. A clear expression of this was in a CEO's attendance at a business leaders' dinner related to the whole town and all its services. Each chief officer of the local authority's departments was charged with being the eyes and ears of the authority to report back to the chief executive the following day. Corporate demands also rounded off the day for another of these CEOs with discussions on how far the education department had proceeded in implementing the corporate plan on change. 'No bad thing, really,' commented the CEO, who reported the institution of regular, structured meetings with assistant directors as 'beneficial'. Late-evening meetings specifically related to education were the committees of the LEA. At a Schools and General Purposes Committee, for example, the CEO introduced:

- a parents' petition on nursery schooling
- a good news item on community education
- privatization of parts of the adult education service
- education on drug abuse
- increases in admission limits for two schools
- approvals for playing field developments
- a report on the impossibility of building programmes for nursery schools
- discussions on a path across a primary school playing field
- discussions on school holiday dates.

Warming-down exercises

When there were no meetings, the last hour of each day was spent in the corollary to the morning's exercises, which now served the purpose of 'warming-down' and relaxing the mental muscles before proceeding to home mode from work mode. A letter or two might be drafted or signed, a phone call made to a councillor, the early evening edition of the local newspaper might be perused. The range of topics was similar to that of the early morning. For example, there might be a brief foray into professional development courses for teachers or the agenda for a meeting on theatre in education. A subordinate or deputy would occasionally drift in for a gossipy chat about a meeting or to pass on information. One such, ostensibly coming for a career stocktake, used the time instead to find out what intelligence had been collected on school principals' reactions to the possibility of altering the formula on which funds were distributed amongst schools. A lively exchange followed over sandwiches. The mode, as in all these end-of-day sessions, was deliberate yet desultory.

Equivalent warming-down exercises also occurred after meetings as the CEOs rarely dashed away but remained quietly chatting with the key players who usually stayed after the majority had left. If back at the office, staff or councillors often used this time to call in and ask the CEO's advice on how to proceed on an issue. Here the CEOs operated in 'counsellor' mode, listening as a mentor while the caller usually proposed the solution that their boss endorsed. Should a letter be sent out now to a parent threatening removal of her children from the local school? How could money be found from the budget to pay the increased salaries of the nursery nurses? One CEO neatly encapsulated such informal chats as 'keeping the troops on course'. They were also central to the information power of the CEO: 'If you want to know about anything happening in this authority, ask the CEO,' remarked the mayor of one authority. Officers and politicians recognized this centralized source of information since it is mainly through the person at the top that all the elements of the organization meet. The CEO is the only person likely to have involvement in all of the elements.

The unusual in the days

The remainder of this book classifies all the elements encountered throughout the CEOs' days into various domains for analysis. There were some quirky oddments, however, that did not fit the domains, that were unexpected to me as the observer, that provided a little light relief to the CEOs or that illustrated the range of issues which come to a CEO for action, information or resolution. These might be seen as distractions from a strategic role.

Middleton's fictional retired CEO noted one such when he recollected a celebration party for a local poet: 'The meeting seemed an oddity, amongst the many to which county officials lent their presence' (Middleton, 1986, p. 178). Such an oddity, in this research, was the occasion when one of the CEOs was photographed so that his head could be sculpted as a gargoyle for a building being restored by the local authority. For another (of cohort one) there was the day which opened with an irate letter from a parent anticipating the CEO's personal attention to the matter of a dead hedgehog in a school swimming pool. The same day ended sombrely with the CEO penning a note of sympathy to the family of a teacher who had a heart attack in a school swimming pool. There was a persistent correspondent whose determination to push the wholefood cause often enlivened the daily post. There was a memo to school principals with advice on whether or not children should be allowed to wear political badges in school when a national election was imminent. There was the response to be written to a parent demanding the ejection of fairy tales from primary schools since the stories frightened their child. A newspaper cutting on a lad expelled from exams for being drunk signalled to the CEO an item which councillors might raise. Another CEO had to decide under what budget heading to classify the repair to the broken leg of a grand piano loaned to another authority. A sunny morning found one CEO measuring an Iron Age fort with disaffected students.

Reviewing the day

The beginnings of the days observed indicated a pattern of activities common to both cohorts. The early morning activities cleared the remnants of each previous day, began new routes of activity, checked the coming day's events, collected information needed for the day and, thereby, touched on most areas of the role's responsibilities. It certainly emphasized the need for mental agility as one of the group remarked, 'It's going off in all directions and I can't keep track of it'. Early morning CEOs can be portrayed as rapid response forces, reacting with accurate placement of fire once they have the necessary information for troop deployment. However extensive the number of short tasks completed before the planned meetings of the day began, the air was of calmness, quiet deliberation and of some enjoyment of the day to come. 'It's good fun and in spite of it all you feel that youngsters are still being educated somewhere in the system,' remarked one of the 1994 cohort.

The fun of exercising mental agility continued through the rest of the day and into the night. With little apparent tiredness, these CEOs concluded the days with long meetings. A little relaxation with warming-down exercises completed their activities.

The non-existent leader

Despite all these activities, my unexpected, initial impression was that, superficially, CEOs do not exist. Having begun the research vaguely aware of them as rather mystical, distant, important and singular persons, I discovered that they appear to be amalgams of other people. They are conduits, links, hubs; they guide and reformulate ideas and locate where they should go from one group to another; they look, nod, watch, listen, give silent signals; they receive others' views, they respond, create reactions and push others to develop.

When speaking to councillors, these CEOs transmit the views of teachers. When speaking to teachers, the CEO becomes the councillors' representative. When speaking to parents, these CEOs become councillors, teachers or central government apologists. When speaking to governors, CEOs emerge as parents, councillors, central government or teachers. There is not a CEO's view. The CEO appears as the servant of all the other groups.

The construction of this impression may be due to the nature of observational research. Recording daily events makes difficult the revelation of the strategic leaders' thinking behind daily routines of activities. It is not easy to piece together the elements that comprise a policy theme. Nor can it be for the CEOs who are charged with maintaining those policy themes through the daily round – and that is the subject of the following chapter.

Notes

1   Their patterns of work are broadly similar whether the leaders are in primary, secondary or tertiary educational organizations (Davies, 1984, 1987; Hall *et al.*, 1986; Harvey, 1986; Lyons, 1974; Martin and Willower, 1981); whether they are in governmental administration or schools (Duignan, 1980); or in different countries (Bezzinna, 1996; Edwards, 1979; Kmetz and Willower, 1982; Manasse, 1985; Willis, 1980). The findings remain unchanged over time (Lyons, 1972; O'Dempsey, 1976; Thody, 1994) and between fiction and fact (Lodge, 1989).
2   One of three deputies. By 1995, there were no permanent deputies in this LEA, following budget cuts.
3   This unit is responsible for policies throughout the local authority, not only for education.
4   Under this Act, a school's curriculum had to be approved by the local Chief of Police. The requirement was largely made redundant by the introduction of a National Curriculum for all state schools in 1988.
5   Each LEA employed substantial numbers of advisers, both generalist and specialist, whose role was to advise the CEO on policy, visit schools (mainly on request) to see teachers and to organize training events for the LEA's teachers. Very few remained after the budget cuts of 1995.
6   Acting on behalf of central government.
7   Polytechnics were large institutions of higher education offering largely degree and other advanced vocational courses. They became independent of the LEAs in the late 1980s and were granted university status in 1993.

8   This introduced the National Curriculum. Between 1902 and 1988 curriculum issues were largely directed by the LEAs.

9   TVEI (Technical and Vocational Educational Initiative) was a major, 1980s, central government encouragement, through targeted funding, to develop technology teaching in schools and to encourage links with industry. LEAs had to bid for funds from the central government for this initiative and had to match the funds awarded with a similar amount from their own resources.

10 The possibility of school governors resigning *en masse* everywhere in the country was being discussed at this time. Governors objected to what they perceived as the government's failure to fund schools adequately, leaving governors with no choice, it was claimed, other than to set budgets which anticipated deficit or to resign in protest. Setting deficit budgets would mean that the governors would have to be dismissed and the LEAs then became liable to take over the governors' roles in schools.

CHAPTER 4

The round of the days

This conference calls the attention of local authorities to the serious restriction of the opportunities of many local government officers for education, rest, recreation and social activities, as a result of their officers being required to attend evening meetings of Council and Committees.
> (Resolution passed at the 1936 conference of the National Association of Local Government Officers: Hill, 1938, pp. 55–6)

Unusually long hours are demanded of chief officers, including weekend and evening meetings.
> (Cole, 1956, p. 119)

He had an 'exacting personal timetable', working until 11 p.m. on Sundays, meeting officers between trains to fit in discussions, requesting them to be at his house at 11 p.m. on Saturdays.
> (Description of Stewart Mason, CEO Leicestershire, 1947-71: Jones, 1988, pp. 145, 186)

My work load decreased when I moved from the CEO's post to being the Chief Executive of the Authority.
> (CEO from cohort one of this research)

He works from 0730–2300.
> (Report on Tim Brighouse, CEO Oxfordshire: TES, 1989b, p. 10)

I hate breakfast meetings but I'll turn up if I have to.
> (CEO in cohort two, 1995)

Long working hours were an anticipated and observed feature of the lives of these CEOs. Beyond this, I discovered that the patterns of their days were not quite as expected. Meetings were longer and more frequent. Collaborative sessions gave these CEOs time for reflective planning even if no hours were set aside for personal contemplation as time management experts suggest should be the case. The routine short interactions with which meetings were interspersed sustained policy thrusts through the multitude of daily tasks, injected humanity into administration and relieved the potential stress of the executives. They exhibited high-level competences to achieve all these. What I observed was far from being the 'solitary, poore, nasty, brutish, and short' life (Hobbes, 1651, p. 186) that is the state of nature for executives which Mintzberg's (1973) seminal analysis has accustomed us to expect. If it had been, would the CEOs in both cohorts have appeared as enthusiastic as they did, bearing well 'the burden and the heat of the long day'[1] and illuminating the conclusion of CEO Tim Brighouse that he loved every minute of his job (*TES*, 1989b, p. 10).

In retrospect, life was not perceived as sweet by all of those I observed. Reflecting on the long hours and the records I produced, one of the 1986–88 cohort wrote: 'I suppose I must have thought my daily activities were pretty important back in 1987 but glancing at them now they seem trivial. Looking back, my feelings about the late 1980s lie on a line from disappointment and frustration through to tedium' (personal letter to the author, 28 June 1995). The analyses, in the remainder of this chapter, of how these CEOs spent their long hours, should help readers decide if they agree with those perceptions or not.

The hours of the days

I have to agree with one of the CEOs in cohort two, who remarked: 'This is an anti-social job with many evening commitments and work to be done at home and at weekends. The trouble with doing so much is that I don't have time to look after my personal interests.' Personal interests included lunch which most of these CEOs experienced minimally. Only one routinely went home for lunch. Most had working lunches or very rapid breaks (seven minutes from entering to leaving the cafeteria were recorded on one day). One regularly took a full lunch-break (and reportedly time for golf on occasions too but not during the observations). Time working at home was not recorded in these observations but this would certainly have increased the totals considerably. One, for example, reported starting each day at 0530. All took papers home and two reported visiting other officers at their homes in the evenings. The quotations which opened this chapter indicated that such long hours have been expected since the 1930s although Henry Morris (the 1930s Cambridgeshire director) apparently found time to attend choral evensong during the afternoons and did not arrive for work until 0930 (Fisher, 1965, p. 14). We do not know, however, if he worked evenings and weekends to compensate, nor how much holiday he took.

National and international comparisons

Between 45 and 75 hours each week have been noted for other CEOs' work with the outcomes for their organizations being apparently no different whatever the hours worked (Brighouse, 1983, p. 102). On taking office as a CEO, Fryer noted that his retiring predecessor was, for the first time, not taking home a pile of papers for the weekend (Fryer, 1988b, p. 523).

Table 4.1 Total hours worked

	1 County Tory margin 1986	2 County hung 1986	3 County Tory 1987	4 County Tory margin 1987	5 City Labour 1987–88	6 County Labour margin 1994	7 County hung 1995	8 Town Labour margin 1995	9 City Labour 1995	All 1986–88	All 1994–95
Average hours, mins at work per day	10.38	12.23	11.31	10.52	11.12	10.36	11.09	10.06	11.11	11.20	10.39
Total hours, mins observed	45.17	80.33	57.38	32.37	44.50	29.10	30.40	40.26	19.35	260.55	119.51

Fryer recorded himself as working two evenings and all day Saturday every week besides his expected five days (Fryer, 1988a, p. 3). Such weekend activity no doubt contributed to some of the exhaustion recorded by CEOs in education (Gedling, CEO Dorset, 1986, p. 71).

Around the world, these CEOs' equivalents also worked well beyond their salaried hours. Australian regional directors of education worked days of 'longer than twelve hours without significant breaks' (Macpherson, 1985a, p. 195). One woke at 0500, lay worrying until 0600 and then reviewed the day ahead until its regular commencement time. Canadian superintendents kept to a more reasonable 8.2 hours of working time each day but at a rapid pace often operating through lunch and refreshment breaks (Duignan, 1980, p. 20). Other Canadian research showed superintendents labouring between 40 and 80 hours weekly (Allison, 1991a). During their daily hours, Canadian superintendents generally achieved 38 different activities, each averaging 12.68 minutes. Some were very short; 39 per cent were less than five minutes and 65 per cent lasted less than ten minutes. Their work was mainly reactive. They were frequently interrupted and their work was 'characterised by abruptness and discontinuity' (Duignan, 1980, p. 20). Discontinuity arose partly from the nature of the work and partly from the need to travel to alternative locations.

Travel

It was through observing CEOs that I learnt advanced driving skills. Shaving the last flicker from the green traffic light, I would hang on grimly behind a CEO fast disappearing into the twilight distance. Travel between meetings was timed to a nicety. A close knowledge of the road plus a willingness to become a racing driver were, therefore, prerequisites for holding these strategic leadership positions. I needed good eyesight, intense concentration and an ability to disregard likely obstructions. Following the executives occurred only at the end of day when we would separate after the last meeting. During the day, I was driven by the CEOs themselves. I revelled in this opportunity for personal high policy discussions, diverted my gaze from the speedometer and wondered if Wordsworth had a car whose speed resulted in his 'forty cattle feeding appearing to munch as one' as he flashed past.[2] Meanwhile, I framed the first recommendation from my research: strategic leaders need chauffeurs.

There was no money for chauffeurs nor first class rail travel. These CEOs worked on trains and thought in cars; every moment was utilized but the travel environment was not luxurious. CEOs chauffeured others; they collected political leaders and delivered them to school visits. The aim was to ensure that the political leaders were in a receptive frame of mind after a restful drive. The CEOs did not get a rest. They even taxied young officers who lacked their own transport.

Table 4.2 Car travel time * and activity periods

	1 County Tory margin 1986	2 County hung 1986	3 County Tory 1987	4 County Tory margin 1987	5 City Labour 1987–88	6 County Labour margin 1994	7 County hung 1995	8 Town Labour margin 1995	9 City Labour 1995	All 1986–88	All 1994–95
Car travel hours, mins	5.0	3.25	3.48	2.45	0.15	1.07	1.30	3.19	0.45	15.13	6.41
% of total time in car travel	11.04	4.24	6.59	8.43	0.56	3.83	4.89	8.20	3.83	5.83	5.58
Activity periods in car travel	8	13	5	8	1	3	2	9	2	35	16
Average mins of car journeys	0.17	0.16	0.45	0.20	0.15	0.23	0.45	0.22	0.23	0.26	0.25

* This does not include home to first meeting travel, nor home from last meeting travel, whether or not such meetings were away from the LEA offices.

Canadian superintendents spent a similar amount of time travelling as did their English counterparts: 8 per cent of the Canadians' daily time was spent travelling. This was divided into two sessions daily, each averaging 20.9 minutes (Duignan, 1980). Those in this English study who led urban authorities had the advantage of being able to reach their imperial perimeters more quickly than those in the English counties. They could

> get anywhere within about fifteen minutes ... Not just twice as many meetings in a day, but often twice as much ground covered in those meetings. No need ... for niceties – to allow time for unwinding after a longish drive held up by cows or tourists ... it is wham bang straight down to business
> (Hendy, CEO Stockport, 1987, p. 227)

In comparison, Cornwall's CEO 'needed to leave very early in the morning and travel ... miles' (Fryer, 1988a, p. 3).

The most restful travel for all these CEOs was that between meetings in the same building or to other local authority offices or council chambers near by. Often a pleasant chat with a colleague enlivened the route. Such travel occupied just under 20 minutes a day for each of the CEOs, less than one per cent of their time. At its end lay the fascination of senior staff policy meetings or entry into the public world of crustaceous council or committee rooms, with their proclamations of local democratic history. Here were the symbols of the origination of local power.

Locations

The walls of those council meeting rooms presented a cacophony of long since silenced local politicians weighted down with various grades of precious metal chains, elaborately gilded gowns and differential abilities of artists to depict them. The chief living politician sat within the arcs of paintings facing the horse-shoes, or circles, of councillors. Slightly below and/or to the side of this chief politician, sat the CEO whom I was observing, flanked by attendant officers with specialist knowledge. The outer circle was the public gallery featuring, usually, no one. Only twice during my observations, were the seats fully occupied with banners and lobbyists attempting to influence policies on lunch-time supervision or on school closures. Occasionally a press representative yawned by.

The CEO's physical position made the role status difficult to assess. Visible – unlike a civil servant in Parliament.[3] Invisible – taking no part in the formal proceedings unless requested to do so. An insider – the confidant and informant of both politicians and officers, joining in the passing of verbal or written notes during council meetings like children in a classroom. An outsider – able to work through a pile of in-tray exercises while waiting to be called on to speak. A VIP – close to the day's god and with comprehensive information to which no one else could be party. A nonentity – exiled from those with power to take decisions, separated from

Table 4.3 Locations of encounters as a percentage of total time in contact with other people

	1 County Tory margin 1986	2 County hung 1986	3 County Tory 1987	4 County Tory margin 1987	5 City Labour 1987–88	6 County Labour margin 1994	7 County hung 1995	8 Town Labour margin 1995	9 City Labour 1995	All 1986–88	All 1994–95
Own office	14.22	41.52	30.46	43.93	61.85	48.06	21.24	30.17	30.78	36.01	32.62
Other LEA offices	3.78	–	5.18	–	16.09	0.65	4.23	19.27	1.53	3.89	8.50
Committee council rooms	32.40	28.53	32.49	15.90	19.65	25.41	–	13.57	49.77	27.84	18.76
Corridors, car parks	1.32	1.80	1.00	0.75	2.41	1.02	–	–	7.20	1.45	1.33
Schools	30.10	12.41	16.45	17.50	–	–	–	15.80	–	16.01	5.84
Teacher centres	4.13	11.32	–	13.45	–	–	6.88	5.85	10.72	5.96	5.08
Offices outside LEA	7.17	–	–	–	–	10.07	6.39	4.96	–	1.36	5.82
Other	6.88	4.42	14.42	8.47	–	14.79	61.26	11.15	–	7.48	22.05

Table 4.4 Locations of encounters: number of activities in each location

	1 County Tory margin 1986	2 County hung 1986	3 County Tory 1987	4 County Tory margin 1987	5 City Labour 1987–88	6 County Labour margin 1994	7 County hung 1995	8 Town Labour margin 1995	9 City Labour 1995	All 1986–88	All 1994–95
Own office	10	36	37	16	26	19	4	31	10	125	64
Other LEA offices	1	–	5	–	6	4	2	4	1	12	11
Committee council rooms	7	11	8	2	3	4	–	3	4	31	11
Corridors, car parks	2	4	2	2	2	3	–	–	6	12	9
Schools	7	3	3	2	–	–	–	2	–	15	2
Teacher centres	1	3	–	2	–	–	2	2	2	6	6
Offices outside LEA	1	–	–	–	–	1	1	1	–	1	3
Other	1	2	4	1	–	1	5	1	–	8	7
Totals	30	59	59	25	37	32	14	45	24	210	115
Total hours, mins of encounters	33.34	63.50	47.55	23.45	24.53	22.52	27.16	26.41	13.33	193.57	90.22

subordinates who had in-depth knowledge of greater magnitude. An expert listener – assessing what was likely to be politically acceptable. A writer – taking notes like a court clerk.

The theatres of council chambers and of committee rooms were the main venues for lengthy meetings though their importance declined between cohorts one and two. For the 1994–95 cohort, venues outside the old power parameters of the political offices had risen in importance. Such venues included the offices of the TECs,[4] of various private businesses, of other public buildings (such as magistrates' court buildings) and of conference centres. Schools featured less prominently for the second cohort but corporate connections had risen in popularity with an increase in meetings elsewhere in the local authority than in the education departments.

Meetings

The general picture of the distribution of these CEOs' time, both here and elsewhere, was of far less variety, fragmentation and brevity than Mintzberg's seminal study of CEOs revealed in 1973. This more structured pattern of distribution of time in different types of meetings changed scarcely at all between the two cohorts. There was variation amongst the patterns for each executive but it did not seem related to types of organizations in which they worked.

Planned, formal meetings subsumed the bulk of the time. The CEOs had virtually no control over the timing or length of these. They included meetings of the full council, the Education Committee and its sub-committees. Meetings between the CEOs and their subordinates, included budget planning, departmental strategy planning, the regular, weekly departmental management team meetings and working parties. The importance of the latter was underlined by Peter Gedling, CEO for Dorset:

> While it is time-consuming to serve on working parties, I have chosen to chair the curriculum working party and the advisory committee on management development – two particularly important groups ... Rather than commit myself to set meetings of working parties, advisory committees and so on, I prefer to join groups for an occasional session and thus to keep in touch with as many interesting developments as possible.
>
> (1986, p. 71).

Long, planned formal meetings also included consultative meetings with teachers' unions, with principals and with governors. Briefing meetings for the local parties' education spokespersons and for local MPs were in this category. Interviewing for new staff and disciplining existing ones were definitely to be classified as formal. Also in this group were meetings with heads of other local authority departments as part of corporate management and meetings with outside agencies and of the boards of newly privatized local government services. Finally, there were the CEOs' equivalents of a monarch opening charity events: school concerts and exhibitions, formal dinners and

Table 4.5 Types of encounters as a percentage of total time in contact with people

	1 County Tory margin 1986	2 County hung 1986	3 County Tory 1987	4 County Tory margin 1987	5 City Labour 1987–88	6 County Labour margin 1994	7 County hung 1995	8 Town Labour margin 1995	9 City Labour 1995	All 1986–88	All 1994–95
Planned/formal	89.93	68.21	60.05	57.83	44.32	65.88	80.15	63.58	58.34	66.27	67.84
Planned/informal	0.33	23.94	23.37	26.80	38.50	24.29	18.39	22.10	21.21	21.23	21.50
Casual/chance	8.68	6.43	11.11	7.18	12.01	6.55	0.00	2.98	18.18	8.84	5.23
Casual/arranged	1.06	1.42	5.47	8.19	5.17	3.28	1.46	11.34	2.27	3.66	5.43

Table 4.6 Types of encounters: number of activities of each type

	1 County Tory margin 1986	2 County hung 1986	3 County Tory 1987	4 County Tory margin 1987	5 City Labour 1987–88	6 County Labour margin 1994	7 County hung 1995	8 Town Labour margin 1995	9 City Labour 1995	All 1986–88	All 1994–95
Planned/formal	17	24	13	8	7	7	8	10	5	69	30
Planned/informal	1	17	14	4	11	6	5	9	6	47	26
Casual/chance	11	16	24	10	15	16	–	9	17	76	36
Casual/arranged	1	2	8	3	4	3	1	16	1	18	21
Totals	30	59	59	25	37	31	15	45	23	210	114
Average hours, mins of encounter	1.07	1.05	0.49	0.55	0.40	0.43	1.57	0.36	0.35	0.55	0.48
Total hours, mins of encounters	33.34	63.50	47.55	23.45	24.53	22.52	27.16	26.41	13.33	193.57	90.22

troop-rallying addresses to advisers, local inspectors and teachers.

During these long meetings, the CEOs' active participation was rarely extensive. Their questioning was sparse but the tone of enquiries gave the impression these CEOs were seeking reminders rather than new information. Such a tactic (if tactic it was) meant that they appeared in possession of vast amounts of detailed information yet it was unlikely that this was possible. It also appeared that they asked questions to keep their staff alert, to make them aware of what outsiders might ask them and for which they had to be prepared. In meetings with outsiders, one saw his role as 'putting the record straight – clarifying our position which can be so easily misunderstood'. One of them explained that attendance enabled him to assess the value others attached to issues, to keep quickly up to date without extensive reading, to assess what tactics might be needed for further action and to indicate the importance the education department attached to particular groups of people. The attendance of the CEO symbolized importance.

The presence of several of the senior executives from the education department presumably symbolized the greatest importance. Such multiple attendance was reserved for committee or sub-committee meetings of the politicians and in these meetings, the leading executive could be quite involved. During a 1986 sub-committee, for example, the CEO made 39 interventions, totalling 36 minutes, 17 seconds from a meeting time of 1 hour and 44 minutes. About half of these interventions were self-initiated, i.e. were not directly requested by the chair of the sub-committee. The other interjections were in response to questions or where information or clarification were needed. In addition, the CEO made ten asides to his subordinates and the chair as he made arrangements for others to speak in his place. This division between self-initiated and requested interventions was about the same at another sub-committee in 1986. The Finance and General Purposes Sub-Committee met for 3 hours and 5 minutes during which the CEO spoke for 37 minutes and 47 seconds with 16 asides totalling 3 minutes and 45 seconds. In this meeting, more of the issues had been delegated to the deputy which may have accounted for the different proportions of participation time between this and the other sub-committee. That same deputy, who replaced his predecessor on the latter's retirement, reduced his participation in meetings by introducing the device of a written report in order to shorten agenda items.

The planned, informal meetings involved much smaller groups than the formal meetings listed above. There were policy chats with deputies over lunch, individual staff appraisal sessions, welcomes for new members of staff and budget explanatory and planning reviews. The largest group in this category were meetings with officers to decide how to persuade councillors to adopt policies and meetings with party leaders to do exactly the same. Responding to political leaders' requests for advice on the maintenance of party discipline was an important feature of these executives' activities.

They did not just advise on strategic plans but also on how to persuade others to adopt the strategic plans.

Casual, chance meetings were those when subordinates or political party leaders dropped in, usually briefly, or were encountered in corridors or *en route* to other meetings. The exchanges were used to keep information flowing on policy progress, to provide advice on the next stage of a policy, to maintain morale, and to enhance sociability. Casual, but arranged meetings occurred when the CEOs called on a subordinate to provide information later that day or as soon as possible thereafter. These usually concerned matters which reached crisis point during a week.

International comparisons indicate that this strategic leadership role was played the same way elsewhere. The Canadian superintendents who participated in Hickcox's 1991 study (published in 1992) used about five hours a day for meetings. Their predecessors in the late 1970s were measured as having 12 unscheduled meetings per day, each lasting about 10.3 minutes and using 25 per cent of daily time. Scheduled meetings were fewer, but longer. There were two daily, averaging 54.6 minutes each or 24 per cent of the time (Duignan, 1980). Allison's group of Canadian superintendents (1991), regularly scheduled meetings and a 'multitude of timetabled meetings is clearly the staple of a CEO's working life' (Allison, 1991a, p. 28). One of the Australian regional directors of education observed by Macpherson (1985a, p. 195) spent 62 per cent of his time in meetings.

Alone

'One needs a grasshopper mind to do this job' remarked a CEO in cohort one as he leapt from phone to letters to reading and to sorting, interrupted by people dropping in for the brief beneficence of the CEO's attention. Such commentary was expected and was in line with the views of others: 'With so many meetings to attend, it is only too easy to fall behind with personal correspondence ... there is a huge amount that I would like to read but there is virtually no time during the day and I am determined to lead a reasonably balanced life at home' (Gedling, CEO Dorset, 1986, p. 71). There were some very short sessions alone lasting between three and five minutes which scarcely gave time to read the first letter in the waiting pile. There were, however, many longer periods for virtually uninterrupted work. Most of these CEOs had one or two periods during the observations when they had at least one or two hours to plough through the waiting mail, reports and newspapers.

International comparisons indicate that most CEOs spend about the same amount of time at their desks as this English group did. Canadian superintendents in 1980 allocated 20 per cent of their time to desk work (I have to assumed that this meant they were alone) (Duignan, 1980). Their 1991 counterparts reduced this, spending

Table 4.7 Solo time (desk work, lunch, travel)

	1 County Tory margin 1986	2 County hung 1986	3 County Tory 1987	4 County Tory margin 1987	5 City Labour 1987–88	6 County Labour margin 1994	7 County hung 1995	8 Town Labour margin 1995	9 City Labour 1995	All 1986–88	All 1994–95
% of total time spent solo	25.87	20.75	16.86	27.18	44.50	21.60	11.09	34.01	30.81	25.67	24.60
% of solo time spent at desk	54.91	69.79	49.06	47.18	71.68	29.37	50.98	63.03	63.54	61.75	54.55
% of total time spent at desk	14.21	14.48	8.27	12.83	31.90	6.34	5.65	21.43	19.57	15.85	13.42

relatively little time alone in their offices, reading, writing or thinking. One spent not more than one hour a week alone in his office. From two to four hours would be typical (per week) with the time spent going through correspondence ... On the other hand, several indicated that they took reading and writing chores home with them, spending an hour or two at night, or more typically time on the weekend on these more thoughtful tasks.

(Hickcox, 1992, p. 4)

Australian regional directors of education passed 39 per cent of their time alone (Macpherson, 1985a, p. 195).

Contacts

'Administrators ... periodically move back and forth, and in and out of many ... groups which assemble, disband, and reform in order to pool and dispense wisdom' (Gronn, 1984, p. 90). Such is an excellent description of how CEOs move from listening to transmission mode amongst various groups. These strategic leaders were not solo decision-makers. Their activi-

Table 4.8 Contacts as a percentage of all time spent in encounters: 1986–88

	1 County Tory margin 1986	2 County hung 1986	3 County Tory margin 1987	4 County Tory 1987	5 City Labour 1987–88	All 1986–88
Education officers	12.40	33.11	32.11	48.28	28.81	28.83
Deputies	11.63	14.19	12.84	5.17	5.08	10.50
School principals	12.40	10.14	4.59	12.07	5.93	8.90
Teachers and support staff	6.98	2.03	3.67	5.17	0.00	3.38
Local inspectors/advisers	6.20	3.38	0.00	6.90	7.63	4.62
Secretary	11.63	14.86	8.26	3.45	26.27	14.06
Service providers	0.00	0.00	1.83	3.45	3.39	1.42
Other chief officers	5.43	2.03	2.75	1.72	1.69	2.85
Officers of other departments	0.00	0.00	0.92	0.00	2.54	0.71
CEOs from other LEAs	5.43	1.35	1.83	0.00	2.54	2.13
Councillors	4.65	6.08	6.42	3.45	0.85	4.45
Chair of Education Committee/ party education spokespersons	11.63	1.35	11.93	1.72	5.08	6.58
Unions	2.33	3.38	4.59	1.72	1.69	2.85
Pressure groups (not unions)	0.00	1.35	0.00	0.00	0.85	0.53
Media	0.00	0.68	0.92	1.72	2.54	1.07
Parents	0.78	0.00	0.00	1.72	0.00	0.36
Pupils	4.65	1.35	0.00	0.00	0.85	1.60
Governors	2.33	0.68	0.92	1.72	0.85	1.25
MPs	0.00	0.68	0.92	0.00	0.85	0.53
HMI	0.00	0.68	0.00	0.00	0.00	0.18
Academics	2.33	1.35	0.00	0.00	0.00	0.89
Business people	0.78	0.68	0.00	1.72	0.85	0.71
TEC personnel	0.00	0.00	0.00	0.00	1.69	0.36
Representatives of religions	0.00	0.00	3.67	0.00	0.00	0.71
Other	0.00	0.68	1.83	0.00	0.00	0.53

Table 4.9 Contacts as a percentage of all time spent in encounters: 1994–95

	6 County Labour margin 1994	7 County hung 1995	8 Town Labour margin 1995	9 City Labour 1995	All 1994–95
Education officers	37.70	25.71	43.51	28.57	37.32
Deputies	6.56	8.57	0.00*	14.29**	5.07
School principals	3.28	8.57	5.34	8.16	5.80
Teachers and support staff	0.00	2.86	3.05	0.00	1.81
Local inspectors/advisers	4.92	0.00	6.11	2.04	4.35
Secretary	16.39	8.57	15.27	8.16	13.41
Service providers	4.92	5.71	2.29	2.04	3.26
Other chief officers	3.28	8.57	3.82	2.04	3.99
Officers of other departments	1.64	2.86	0.00	0.04	1.09
CEOs from other LEAs	1.64	5.71	0.00	0.00	1.09
Councillors	4.92	8.57	3.05	10.20	5.43
Chair of Education Committee/ party education spokespersons	6.56	5.71	4.58	8.16	5.80
Unions	0.00	0.00	2.29	2.04	1.45
Pressure groups (not unions)	0.00	0.00	0.76	0.00	0.36
Media	0.00	0.00	0.76	2.04	0.72
Parents	0.00	0.00	1.53	0.00	0.72
Pupils	0.00	0.00	0.00	0.00	0.00
Governors	1.64	0.00	0.76	2.04	1.09
MPs	0.00	2.86	0.00	0.00	0.36
HMI	0.00	0.00	0.00	0.00	0.00
Academics	0.00	0.00	0.00	0.00	0.00
Business people	0.00	0.00	2.29	2.04	1.45
TEC personnel	0.00	2.86	2.29	2.04	1.81
Representatives of religions	1.64	2.86	1.53	0.00	1.45
Other	4.92	0.00	0.76	4.08	2.17

* No deputies
** No permanent deputies. This was a senior officer preparing to take over while the CEO was on holiday.

ties constantly involved others in complex patterns of communications (Konnert and Augenstein, 1990, p. 52). The Tables 4.8, 4.9, 4.10 and 4.11 summarize these attachments, detachments and reattachments. Discussion of each follows in Chapters 8 and 9.

The value in the hours?

Amidst policy and leadership studies with their emphasis on a grand, strategic planning role, it is easy to underestimate, or to ignore, the importance of the routines and regularities of CEOs' days. A cohort one CEO remarked that, 'Eighty per cent of what I do is relatively unimportant. Only about twenty per cent needs someone of experience to cope with it'. Another reflected that if you added up all the time spent each week for management, there would be little left for education. He was appointed for his

Table 4.10 Contacts as a percentage of all time spent in encounters: 1986–95

| | All | All | Canadian superintendents (Hickcox, 1992)* |
	1986–88	1994–95	1991
Education officers	28.83	37.32	9.88
Deputies	10.50	5.07	10.76 (whole SMT)
School principals	8.90	5.80	12.85
Teachers and support staff	3.38	1.81	4.10
Local inspectors/advisers	4.62	4.35	na
Secretary	14.06	13.41	4.10 (all office staff)
Service providers	1.42	3.26	na
Other chief officers	2.85	3.99	na
Officers of other departments	0.71	1.09	na
CEOs from other LEAs	2.13	1.09	na
Councillors	4.45	5.43	16.50 (Board/committees) 9.32 (Members)
Chair of Education Committee/ party education spokespersons	6.58	5.80	3.09
Unions	2.85	1.45	1.85
Pressure groups (not unions)	0.53	0.36	nr
Media	1.07	0.72	nr
Parents	0.36	0.72	0.97
Pupils	1.60	0.00	nr
Governors	1.25	1.09	na
MPs	0.53	0.36	3.21 (Ministry officials)
HMI	0.18	0.00	na
Academics	0.89	0.00	nr
Business people	0.71	1.45	na
TEC personnel	0.36	1.81	na
Representatives of religions	0.71	1.45	nr
Other	0.53	2.17	nr

* From diary records, not observation (nr = not recorded; na = not applicable)

management skills, being asked to sort out the administration which his predecessors had failed to do.

Practitioners recognize the value of routine administration, as do theorists and researchers (Hodgkinson, 1978, p.90; McCabe, 1992, p. 12). 'Economical and efficient administration is essential in order to release creative energy' wrote a 1970s' CEO (Bush and Kogan, 1982, p. 98) and training advice for CEOs stressed the importance of routine 'to create and sustain systems of human co-operation' (Fisher, 1957, p. 251). Kenneth Brooksbank, CEO for Birmingham, 1968–78, was as highly regarded for his administrative skills as for his strategy: 'nothing escaped him … He left one of the most efficient, streamlined administrative machines possible' (*Education,* 1990a, p. 161). This was no light achievement when the 'burden of administration is growing every day and routine stifles opportunities for reflection … every detail, however small, must go through the office' (Lawrence, 1972, pp. 166–7).

Table 4.11 Contacts as a percentage of all time spent in encounters: 1986–95 (in comparative rank order)

1986–88	All 1986–88	All 1994–95	1994–95
Education officers	28.83	37.32	Education officers
Secretary	14.06	13.41	Secretary
Deputies	10.50	5.80	School principals
School principals	8.90	5.80	Chair of Education Committee/party education spokespersons
Chair of Education Committee/party education spokespersons	6.58	5.43	Councillors
Local inspectors/advisers	4.62	5.07	Deputies
Councillors	4.45	4.35	Local inspectors/advisers
Teachers and support staff	3.38	3.99	Other chief officers
Unions	2.85	3.26	Service providers
Other chief officers	2.85	2.17	Other
CEOs from other LEAs	2.13	1.81	TEC personnel
Pupils	1.60	1.81	Teachers and support staff
Service providers	1.42	1.45	Business people
Governors	1.25	1.45	Representatives of religions
Media	1.07	1.45	Unions
Academics	0.89	1.09	Other local authority depts' staff
Business people	0.71	1.09	Governors
Representatives of religions	0.71	1.09	CEOs from other LEAs
Other local authority depts' staff	0.71	0.72	Media
Other	0.53	0.72	Parents
Pressure groups (not unions)	0.53	0.36	MPs
MPs	0.53	0.36	Pressure groups (not unions)
Parents	0.36	0.00	Pupils
TEC personnel	0.36	0.00	Academics
HMI	0.18	0.00	HMI

Such detail requires the humanitarian injections of a CEO to help others cope with the bureaucracy (David, 1977, p. 44). These injections were the numerous, short meetings with officers which punctuated every day. These were not interruptions. They were the heart of the job. They were also valuable for the humanity of the CEO personally. Brief, personal interactions relieved the potential stress of the lonely strategic leader. The CEOs in this study always welcomed those who dropped in for a brief chat and engineered opportunities themselves to go and enjoy a short gossip, collecting and transmitting information verbally while admitting that the boredom of paper work needed the relief of these wanderings. Duignan recorded similar activities for Canadian superintendents in 1980. They made two such tours daily, lasting 16.9 minutes totalling five per cent of their time. They were still wandering ten years later when Hickcox noted their preference for personal contacts with employees, students and parents (Hickcox, 1992, p. 14). The modern public sector strategic manager thus presents a different picture from the 1950s' official, a 'sedentary institution … We picture him, rightly, at work in his office chair. He works from his desk' (Wheare, 1955, p. 14).

Management by wandering about facilitated mental delegation. It enabled work to be off-loaded to subordinates from the vast range of wants and desires confronting the CEO daily. The record of one day in 1987 indicated the variety of these wants and desires. The art and design lobby put views on an exhibition, a councillor requested advice on speech-making during an LEA trip to Germany, a teachers' union lobbied for class size reduction, the local paper reported on single sex schooling, one of the political parties sought advice on budget cuts suggestions, a national association asked the LEA to become a subscribing member, a parents' group wanted to establish a nursery school and a councillor popped in to say: 'Just happened to be passing by and thought I might drop in to ask if anything's been done about that school crossing patrol wanted at my local school.' All these contacts occurred before 0950 on one morning. A full day's list is too extensive to include here. Many of these were passed on to subordinates in the CEO's short contacts with them later in the day.

Most of the CEOs I observed appeared to revel in this traffic of ideas though occasional disgruntlement surfaced: 'I'm a bit fed up with this politicking' remarked one though the next minute he was adding to it with a series of phone calls chasing the right place to get action and clearly enjoying the gossiping about personalities and politics that ensued.

These short interactions relieved the stress of the lonely job of strategic leadership although stress did not appear to afflict these particular incumbents. They presumably became used to 'flirting with fear' (Middleton, 1986, p. 71) and the 'terror of near failure' (Macpherson, 1985a, p. 195). The CEOs were unlikely to reveal this to an observer though occasionally it emerged as the observer became familiar; the CEOs shared personal opinions on 'hidden agendas' or asked the observer's advice on issues that were not raised with any of the staff encountered. The CEOs in this study all faced the difficult task of making major budget cuts with their concomitant challenge of choosing who should suffer most. There was also the prospect of themselves losing their own positions if the budget failed to match the financial strictures of the local authority. On a micro-level, all faced potentially stressful, daily ethical dilemmas (Walker, 1994, pp. 19-21) such as how much criticism to give a failed interview candidate at a debriefing, whether to follow up minor abuses of travelling expense claims and decisions on how much information to pass on to parents or unions.

Policy and leadership studies note the lack of time apparently accorded by CEOs to strategic planning. Educational leaders have long been enjoined to set aside time to think and this is regarded as impossible within their crowded activity schedules (Hill, 1938, p. 115: Konnert and Augenstein, 1990, p. 55; Sylvester,1957, p. 186). When, however, observation studies seek to discover leaders' thinking and planning time, it is uncovered during their evenings, early mornings, driving and holidays, and while they are performing administrative tasks, or attending meetings, that only require minor attention. A second layer of concentration is meanwhile producing plans and visions (Macpherson, 1985a; Thody, 1991b). In addition, strategic leaders' constant interactions produce ideas and reflections on policy, only fleetingly recorded as brief observations or memos to themselves for later contemplation (Sylvester, 1957). Planning has also been seen as a co-operative activity in local government for some time (Browning, 1972, p. 5). These CEOs, like leaders in other spheres, are not meant to be solo thinkers. Consequently, there were meetings about setting strategic missions and operational targets. Amongst the group in this research was one person who spent a whole team day working on strategic planning and there were other shorter, similar events for the rest of the two groups. Chapters 5 and 6 discuss this further.

   Theorists' rethinking on goals in the 1990s should also make us less critical of CEOs who do not set aside time specifically for reflection; goals are beginning to be viewed as restrictive 'straitjackets' (Isenberg, 1994, p. 129). More prosaically, perhaps reflection time is not so very valuable when few decisions are momentous and 'the immediate cost of an error of judgement is not great' (Duignan, 1980, p. 24).

Closing thoughts

These CEOs' days were less fragmented than earlier studies of such managers led me to expect. The many planned formal and informal meetings framed the day. The numerous, routine, short interactions which intercalated with the meetings maintained policy initiatives, motivated staff and relieved the CEOs' own potential stress. These CEOs needed high-level competencies to achieve all of these successfully. Through 'the wear and tear, getting and spending, learning and forgetting that ... rattled on daily' (Middleton, 1986, p. 71), the CEO must retain and emphasize whatever strategic vision has to be implemented. How this is achieved is the subject of the following chapter.

Notes

1   *Morality*, Matthew Arnold.
2   *Written in March*. The speed of senior executives' driving was also noted by Macpherson (1985a) in his study of Australian regional directors of education.
3   In both houses of the British Parliament, civil servants sit behind the Speaker's chair and cannot be seen from the main chamber.
4   Training and Enterprise Councils. These were regional agencies with responsibility for encouraging vocational education.

CHAPTER 5

Daily leadership

Each organization had a variety of policy objectives:

- Service diversity – it aimed to maintain customer loyalty by offering a full range of products.
- Equity – it aimed to enhance the quality of provision for all clients equally.
- Special services – it aimed to offer additional opportunities to consumers with needs and abilities that differed from the norm.
- Individualization – it aimed to provide each customer with appropriate services.
- Good employment practice – it aimed to ensure that qualified staff were appointed, that they were motivated to perform well and received a fair day's pay for a fair day's work.
- Effective and ethical marketing – it aimed to offer services in areas in which marketing executives indicated greatest demand but without breaching the canons of equity.
- Financial health – it had to ensure that spending was kept within its budget agreed both by the board of directors and the organization's financial backers.

Such were the long-term policy objectives of all the organizations within which these two cohorts of CEOs worked. Since the organizations were English local government educational organizations, some readers may feel more comfortable if words such as 'voters, students, parents, teachers, councillors, Policy and Resources Committee and central government' were substituted for 'clients, consumers, customers, staff, marketing executives, board of directors and financial backers' whereas others will recognize in the terminology the acceptance of the market and business-conscious context that came to dominate public services in the 1980s and 1990s. The organizations' major objectives remained the same whatever the words used. Within each of the organizations included in this study, the long-term aims had been translated into varying shorter-term plans naming, for example, particular services to expand or contract, specific percentages of the budget to reduce or precise extensions of staff training provisions to be made. In addition, the marketing managers (the party political councillors) would each be pressing for policies to benefit particularly the different areas which each served so that they could retain their jobs.

It was the role of the CEOs observed in this study to maintain these long- and shorter-term objectives through the daily round of activities. This part of policy-making is usually hidden to outsiders, those 'elements of chance, ignorance, stupidity, recklessness and amiable confusion ... the hundreds of small tableaux, the little dramas, that result in a policy statement or a bit of strategy' (Shrivastra, 1983, p. 21). Observations of these give rich, anatomical data (Gronn, 1984) which helps to remove the secrecy associated with policy-making and to debunk its reputation as a high-powered process different to everyday decision-making (Self, 1977, p. 207). Direct, continuous observations reveal details of everyday life not usually noted (Delamont, 1988, p. 4). Such observations can fill gaps in our understanding of policy processes, understanding which is important to discover how best to influence the processes (Walford, 1994a, p. 3).

To enhance this understanding, this chapter first follows the progress of a policy line through the interstices of daily activities over four days. This reveals, *inter alia*, how issues can become dominant for short periods and then disappear, creating temporary distortions in workloads and policy directions. Discussion of this phenomenon forms the second part of this chapter. Finally, the leadership of a single department within an organization affects, and is affected by, the other departments as organizations strive to achieve corporate strategy. This chapter concludes by describing how the departments in this study were fitted into the whole organizations by their CEOs.

A policy is revised

Disputes arose concerning the music service provided by one of the LEAs during one week of this study. It enabled me to follow the CEO attempting to maintain all the long-term objectives described at the beginning of this chapter and the shorter-term objectives of reducing the costs of this service to meet general budget cuts imposed by central government, which local politicians had translated into specific service reductions on the advice of the CEO whom I was observing. The issue also provided an excellent example of local government being attacked for implementing policies made unavoidable by central government decisions. Local administrators and politicians were the 'whipping boys' for central politicians.

As reported below, it appears that the CEO did nothing other than follow through the music problems. In practice, the events observed spread over four days in 37 separate activity periods, each interspersed throughout a day with a myriad other items to which attention had to be given. The issue used 12 per cent of the CEO's time. Reflecting on this, he was surprised that it was so little 'but I suppose time speeds up when you are enjoying your-self,' he wryly added. It seemed, to both him and me, that the issue dominated the week. It became the leitmotif, reappearing like a Greek chorus whenever a lull threatened.

The organization's policy was to maintain a small service offering group and individual musical instrument tuition, peripatetic music teaching, specialist music curriculum advice and the organization of orchestras and choirs to offer expanded musical opportunities for students of all ages in the LEA's schools. The amount of local discretion and money involved was very small. Only 8 per cent of the area's students used the service; some schools benefited disproportionately from music provision, thus breaching the equity objectives. Responding to stakeholder attacks to alter decisions on the music service could only mean that other services, unprotected by artic-ulate pressure groups, would have to lose money regained for music. Available money could not be increased, only moved.

The progenitor of this dispute was central government's reductions in finance for public provision and requirements for locally managed services to become competitive businesses. Amongst the few services over which LEAs have discretion,[1] this area selected the music service as one of those to be changed. Subsidies were lessened and charges were to be made to parents for their children's personal instrument tuition. The service was reduced and redundancies loomed. A local campaign was organized to attack councillors who had agreed the policies. Councillors were meanwhile accusing the service of nepotism as it appeared that the partners of full-time employees of the music service were well represented amongst those with part-time contracts.

The issue began quietly with a proactive CEO discussing how best to market the service in order to encourage more participants. This quickly became submerged, during discussions between the CEO and some subor-dinates, in revelations about those campaigning against the reductions. The opposing group were accused of issuing a scurrilous cartoon lampooning the elected politician who was chair of the Education Committee, for parsi-mony towards the music service. Lengthy phone calls and meetings between the CEO and his political colleague ensued in order to lessen the personal annoyance suffered by the politician. The CEO demonstrated his support for the policy line by castigating the music service and its lobbyists for 'suici-dal policies' including unwillingness to provide paid tuition to non-locally maintained schools.[2] The phone wires began to burn with frequent use and colourful language as the issue escalated. The CEO issued strong advice to the music providers to organize civilized advocacy and to ensure that there could be no grounds for any criticisms of the service which angry politicians might find useful. Behind the scenes investigations were instituted by the CEO to find the originator of the cartoon. The CEO chased up a finance officer to refresh his memory on the music cuts and to discuss how reduc-tions might be made. Over lunch with the senior inspector and a finance officer, the CEO alerted them to the issue and discussed the reductions again. Speculation and advice on tactics concluded the lunch. The CEO later chatted informally with a union official who offered his good offices to try to persuade the music staff to withdraw their attacks. Thirty minutes later, a subordinate's phone call alerted the CEO to the next stage in the cartoon argument which enabled him to appear knowledgeable when, 30 minutes later again, he had to brief an annoyed chair of Education Committee. The CEO followed with a detailed phone discussion on meeting tactics, the origin of that cartoon again and attempts to distract the local newspaper from becoming involved. One more phone call produced the ammunition the CEO needed for a speech. Then came the CEO's delicate job of refereeing a one-hour meeting between the chair and the music providers. This ended day one.

The following day commenced with the CEO's tactical discussions with a subordinate officer. The post produced protests from the lobbyists together with a visit from a subordinate for an exchange on the outcomes of the previous night's meeting and yet more about the cartoon. In due course, the CEO relayed this to the chair by phone. Meanwhile, the CEO was obtaining information concerning the allegations of nepotism. Officers accordingly came and went with past employment records of part-time music staff. The CEO later drafted letters replying to those received earlier in the day from members of the public, politely correcting misrepresentations of the LEA's policy. To avoid other misrepresentations, the CEO requested oversight of a speech to be delivered by the music service leader and arranged a meeting for the following day with the subordinate administrators responsible for this policy area. The CEO then briefly returned to a proactive role, a discussion with a subordinate about arranging direct debits for parental payments for tuition. This facility might encourage more parents to pay, thought the CEO. Reactivity quickly returned as the practicalities of insurance cover, travel allowances and redundancy payments had to be debated with officers, leading the CEO into the organization's long-term policies on employment matters.

Formal presentation of the issue was one of the items at the Education Sub-Committee which concluded the day. Formality rapidly disappeared as the music service accused politicians of betraying the service. The CEO gave gentle leadership with cautious warnings that the matter was not for discussion as it was the outcome of central government policy. This attempt to deflect anger failed. The CEO closed the issue by ordering the music staff to desist from their efforts or face disciplinary action.

Day three opened with preparations with a subordinate officer for the public meeting to be held concerning the music issue. The CEO reported his activities to solve the problem informally through the unions. The officer reported on possible slide presentations and speech formats. An hour later, the head of personnel dropped in to report informal enquiries from music staff about pensions. In return, the CEO reported on his trawl through staff records for evidence of nepotism. This trawl continued for a further 20 minutes interrupted by budget debates on moving money to the music service. There were brief enquiries from a concerned officer about progress on the nepotism search. The secretary brought in an urgent request from a councillor for the CEO to chair the potentially fraught public meeting later in the week. '... off' muttered the CEO. The CEO allocated further time to assessing possibilities for financing the service while co-ordinating phoned information from the chair, an officer and other LEAs about how charges were allocated elsewhere. Armed with this information, the CEO coped with more budget implications brought in by an officer. Together they mulled over the tactics for Committee and how they might meet the objections of all the groups involved. 'We have to get the parents back on our side,' commented the CEO, 'and that will be difficult'.

On the last day of my observations, the music issue did not surface until mid-morning when the CEO discussed tactics for the forthcoming public meeting with an officer on the phone for few minutes. By lunch-time, a detailed strategy meeting was under way. The CEO received a verbal report from finance officers about discussion with staff on redundancies. The staff had moved out of total rejection into making suggestions for income generation and alternative use of music staff. A long phone call followed in response to a councillor's request for full clarification on how the budget might accommodate changes. Three minutes were used later in reporting the councillor's request and, together, the CEO and the officer speculated on the councillor's power to keep the party in line for decision-making. The day ended in an irascibility of erratic, short meetings. Councillors, chair and officers crossed and recrossed each other's paths through the CEO's phone routes. The officer was briefed for the evening's meeting. Music staff, it was learnt, were refusing to teach. My observation ended as the CEO chased the officer who would chase the recalcitrant staff with warnings of legal requirements of their presence. The public meeting after I left resulted in some minor cuts restored.

A week later, at an Education Committee meeting, these were formally agreed. Politicians

> capitalised £18,000 of instruments purchased for 1994/5 and 1995–6 (i.e. transferred them to the Finance Committee budget), took out £20,000 of staffing costs and put them in another budget which [was] underspending, and effectively agreed to a further £12,000 worth of unachievable savings. In all, therefore, £50,000 of the [originally planned] £186,000 cut was massaged out of the system, [at a cost of] approximately £10 per letter and phone call by the protesters. It is nice to see democracy in action.
> (personal letter from the CEO to the author, 3 February 1995)

Throughout this dispute, the CEO was in the middle, the conduit between the lobby, the music service, the administrators and the councillors. Each group was kept informed of what the others were doing and each group was advised on appropriate tactics with impartiality. In most such disputes observed, CEOs supported everyone's views, defending each group to the others. In this case, the CEO was firmly with the councillors' perceptions. The policy was agreed and had to go forward. When the politicians changed their minds, the CEO began to reorganize accordingly. Throughout the dispute, the CEO was effectively defending central government policies but no one remarked on that.

The Greek chorus effect

In several of the organizations observed, central government policies indirectly or directly created similar effects to that described above concerning the music service. Each of these threaded through the observations, demanding immediate reactions, meetings to be arranged, numerous phone calls, memos and letters to he drafted and politicians to be consulted. Each issue popped on and off the stage like a Greek chorus dolefully reminding the principal actors of the underlying miseries of life and interrupting the other story lines. Observations of Canadian superintendents spotted this effect too, naming it the 'chain reaction phenomenon' (Duignan, 1980, p. 20) in which one letter or event would precipitate an unplanned series of activities that would last throughout a week. Policy leadership at this level clearly demonstrates, 'low, co-ordinate rationality ... decisions are pushed and pulled between contextual and top-down forces' (Schoemaker, 1993, p. 116).

Greek chorus topics in these cohorts all arose from unexpected changes in the top-down forces of central government policies and clashes of these with local contexts. They included disputes over what and who should be paid for providing supervision of students during lunch-time breaks, over teachers refusing to attend training for the implementation of new examination systems, over interpretations of what constituted teachers' duties for inclusion in their contractual hours and over what constituted a 'small school' for purposes of deciding when 'small' was small enough to justify closure.

In all of these issues, the CEO was the prime mover of action. No one else was in a position to handle all of the multitudinous strands of the issues which led into various sections of the CEO's department. No one else had the same responsibility to liaise with external groups and to maintain good relations with local politicians. No one else had quite the same freedom of action to mobilize quickly. This central position was also significant to the CEO's role in corporate policy-making.

Corporate policy-making

The sovereigns were momentarily discomforted. Their nation states, constituents of a confederation, were instructed to move rapidly into becoming, not just a federation, but a unitary state in which their freedom to make their own policies was to be subsumed into policies made for, and by, all the states in the group. The sovereigns were annoyed. Their nation states were the largest in the confederation and had the most money yet they were to be treated equally with the smaller and poorer ones. The sovereigns would serve on the body which decided the policies for the unitary state, but they would have only one vote, just like the smaller states. The sovereigns could participate in directing the thrusts of policies for states other than their own but, in return, would have to accept others directing what they were to do. While the sovereigns remained the decision-makers, they could decide no policies for their own states until the group as a whole had set the general guidelines. Money previously used for their states, could be used for the others. Some sovereigns were so angry about these changes that they abdicated but the instructions were explicit and unavoidable. Unite and act collectively. The remaining sovereigns quickly learnt how to operate within the new system, discovering how to persuade sovereigns of smaller states to their points of view. Thirty years later, the unitary state seemed more like a federation with some states more dominant than others.

Such is a brief history of the development of corporate management within English local authorities since the 1960s. Fitting education's policy-making into the corporate strategy of the whole organization became an objective following local government reforms of the 1960s and 1970s. Previously, education (and other local government services) had operated separately and the change to corporateness was initially much resented. From the late nineteenth century, education departments in local authorities had behaved as *ad hoc* bodies (Peschek and Brand, 1966, p. 33), even though corporate management had existed always through the Clerk to the Council who was closely in touch in every department (Hill, 1938, p. 29) and even when corporateness was enforced through local authorities having to decide how to share the general grant from central government amongst their services from the late 1950s. One CEO records that he had to 'fight every item' with the other departments, not a happy picture of local authority corporateness (Bush and Kogan, 1982, p. 120). This unhappiness was also recorded by a 1950s' CEO who recounted disputes amongst departments and the problems of being both customer and colleague of other sections of the local authority (Binns, 1957, p. 142). Some CEOs reacted to this by keeping education as separate as possible from the rest of their local authorities. Stewart Mason, for example, Leicestershire's CEO, 1947–71, 'displayed little patience with any department in County Hall which threatened to limit his freedom' (Jones, 1988, p. 186). This must have been common since Senior's (1969) Memorandum of Dissent on the Redcliffe-Maud Report on the future of local government described education departments as alienated and segregated. There was a continuing defensive posture (Jennings, 1983, p. 31). I located just one voice from the past in favour of corporateness. 'The Education Department needs at all points and at all times the complete co-operation and goodwill of other local government services ... with some it must be continuous and accompanied by the most complete understanding' (Sylvester, 1957, p. 188).

By the time of my observations, corporate policy-making no longer attracted controversy (Bush *et al.*, 1989, p. 39); each local authority had a policy committee of councillors to lead this, on the advice of the appointed chief executive of the whole organization and a committee of the chief officers of the local authority services, including the CEOs whom I was observing. Corporate planning and monitoring processes were well established, having become 'part of the furniture'.

It seemed to me, however, that the furniture was kept in the front parlour for special visitors. The observer attended regular meetings of the leaders of all of the local authorities' departments. At these, the CEO appeared to act out a stylized ritual of accepting the corporate dimension but it did not relate to what went on back in the education departments. Comments made about other departments and about corporate organization in the privacy of the education departments, were not complimentary. General mirth greeted one CEO's ironic statement that 'I'm starting a positive corporate campaign – I'm going to visit some of the other departments occasionally'. Neither CEOs nor their subordinates appeared much in contact with other departments; other departments' considerations very rarely formed the subject of conversations though there were rather more contacts with the chief executives of each local authority, which could be seen as a reasonable way to conduct corporateness as the chief executive is aware of the activities of all departments.

During seven days observation of one of the 1986–88 cohort, the only mention of other departments' affairs, or of policies pertaining to the organization as a whole, was at the regular, fortnightly meeting of the chief officers of each of the departments. The CEO stayed for an hour, at one of these meetings, leaving early to attend a meeting with school principals. He spoke on all but two of the items, totalling just over 15 minutes of active participation. Amongst other matters on the budget, the CEO asked if he were still free to advise the politicians on the Education Committee what should be growth items. On being assured that this was the case, he remarked: 'no different from some years ago then'. He participated briefly when enquiries were made about whether a local school could provide crèche facilities for the children of staff in the authority's offices. An item on educational guidance for adults was introduced by the CEO but this was to ask if other departments had any interest in, or connections with, the issue. The Three Year Capital Programme report from a working party passed on the nod with a brief enquiry from the CEO about the place of information technology in the plans. There was a lengthy and lively discussion which did produce a corporate negative – politicians' proposals that chief officers should all have a compulsory retirement age. The last item was the CEO's attempt to sort out who was involved in the inner-city regeneration project (his own part in this was the meeting reported in Chapter 1 of this book).

I attended the equivalent of this corporate meeting during one of the 1994–95 cohort observations. The tone and topics were similar although there was the addition of the organization's bids for European Union funding which did require multilateral co-ordination. This took the form of departments considering each other's proposals for projects to include in the bids. Other agenda items seemed more bilateral than corporate or at a level of importance to be better dealt with through paper exchanges.

Corporate activities of a formal kind did not seem highly valued by the CEOs. One asked to send a deputy on a corporate visit to Germany on which both the chief executive and the leader of the council were going. The CEO also asked if his staff could be excused the task of arranging the visit since they were overworked. In the second cohort, an evening dinner mixing all the chief officers with local business leaders was regarded as an unnecessary chore by the CEO who felt he could not readily contribute an opinion on urban economic renewal. Like the other chief officers at the dinner, his role was to be 'the eyes and ears of the chief executive' and to report back to him the next day. This was done but not with quite the good grace reserved for solely educational matters.

Efforts to promote corporately the economic development of the areas governed by these organizations did not attract wholehearted support from these CEOs. 'Waste of time' grumbled one as we meandered off to a town hall meeting of the great and the good in business developments in 1987. The comment was repeated by 1994–95 counterparts on the way to meetings to discuss projects to regenerate areas with economic problems. Papers for such meetings rarely seemed to have been absorbed in advance by these CEOs who read the papers in the meetings. Once briefed, however, they leapt in with intense and sometimes disconcerting questions.

Informal meetings between the CEOs in this survey and representatives of the central policy departments of their organizations also demonstrated a lack of attachment to corporatism. There was an visit by an administrator from the central personnel department to check on the education department's involvement in the organization's anti-racial harassment policy in 1987. His questions were met politely with assurances of support but also with reminders that the education department had its own, successful policy on this matter already, that education administrators could not cope with much more work and that the centre's corporate policy of consciousness-raising was too long-term to be quickly successful. None the less, the CEO offered a contact officer within his department for liaison with the central unit. Race relations were a corporate issue in another of the 1986–88 cohort organizations. Here the CEO was due to report activity on this issue to the regular corporate meeting but he 'didn't get around to it'. The 1994–95 cohort included one whose organization had a corporate policy of revitalization. According to the CEO, this was not being taken seriously by any department, although the CEO later stated that it had encouraged changes and that it had done so sensitively by facilitating each department's commitment to it through allowing their influence upon the items chosen for the policy.

My impression that corporate management was followed more by rote than reason was supported by the 1986 Widdicombe Report which recommended strengthening central policy-making at the expense of the individual departments. Bush *et al.* recorded an interview with a CEO in whose local authority a consultant had 'found that there really wasn't enough central direction'. The executive commented that the chief executive 'doesn't tell me how to run the education department. He is supportive ... and he makes comments from time to time without my asking' (1989, p. 114). Corporate management appeared to be more of an abstract god than a concrete one (Hendy, 1987b). Separate departments remained important (Edwards, 1991, p. 7) to the extent that there were 'real life conflicts' (Morris, 1994, p. 21). In one of the 1986–88 cohort, for example, conflicts surfaced between the finance and the education departments and had required much effort to overcome on the part of the CEO. Another in the same cohort noted that the chief of the finance department never visited the education department and 'doesn't know what's going on here'. None the less, this CEO did realize that he had to defend and explain education department expenditure to the head of finance.

Competition amongst departments arose because staff have strong functional professionalism and loyalties (Rhodes, 1988, p. 190) and education department staff in particular are perceived as arrogant (Goodwin, 1995a, p. 9). This surfaced amongst these cohorts sometimes. 'We have a dialogue with our political mates perhaps better than other departments' commented one CEO in 1994. The same person noted that other departments felt aggrieved when education staff had benefited most from a redeployment policy.

This is not to claim that corporate planning does not exist, but it seems more like corporate administration and management than policy and strategy. Education departments did not ignore corporate planning mechanisms, but appeared to have retained their sense of separateness from the other departments and a mode of semi-autonomous imperialism. Education is still the largest department, often employing about half of a local authority's personnel and being responsible for about two-thirds of its expenditure. The size of an education department compared with those of the other services was underlined at a ceremony in one authority when long-service awards were presented to employees; the CEO presented ten people for their awards; other chief officers had only one to present.

Before denying the existence of corporate management, I reflected on the possibility that corporateness, and one department's place within it, might not have been readily susceptible to revelation from observation. I was excluded from two chief officers' meetings and attended only two others (one during each cohort) since no others occurred during the observations. Yet Liverpool's CEO reported in 1995 that he spent approximately half his time on corporate duties (Cogley, 1995, p. 10) because he had to obtain the support of the city's other heads of services for his initiatives. One of the 1994–95 cohort reported spending 20 per cent of time on corporate matters. When this figure was queried as too high by the central personnel department, the CEO reminded the department that half of this was the weekly meeting of the organization's heads of departments. Ten per cent for other corporate issues did not, therefore, seem an excessive estimate of time spent on matters appertaining to the whole authority.

Corporateness was encouraged by this recognition that the education department needed the support of others. One of the subjects of this survey admitted to having been too protective of the education department and having latterly changed policies to seek allies amongst the other departmental heads. This policy change was evidenced in enthusiastic participation in a major corporate event when all the chief officers of the different departments and staff representative of all levels had a planning day. During both cohorts, there were meetings amongst all the departments' chief officers to discuss their own pay and conditions of service. Such events indicated that there was a close corporateness in some circumstances as reported by Goodwin (CEO, Coventry from 1994). She saw 'an urgent need to establish the service as part of the city's corporate identity. We are learning to take our role as a corporate player seriously' (Goodwin, 1995, p. 9).

Evidence from these observations does not support strongly the view that CEOs were committed to corporate planning. A final comment on this was from one of the 1994–95 cohort who stated, 'we don't want to get this for empire building of course, but we'd like to get it before the corporate lot do'.

From daily leadership to policy

A policy was revised, showing a CEO responding reactively to events. Departments faced their responsibilities towards corporate strategies which again demonstrated reactive strategy-making. The scope for a degree of policy proactivity is discussed in the following chapter.

Notes

1   LEAs are required by law to provide schools for the years of compulsory education from age 5 to 16, and curriculum and special needs support. These subsume the majority of their income. Teachers', administrators' and other staff salaries were determined nationally so there was no discretion about what LEAs could pay employees. Their discretion extended to deciding which peripheral services to provide from amongst, e.g. additional music or other curriculum enrichment opportunities, adult education and pre-school education.

2   In the early 1990s, of state-provided schools in England and Wales, approximately 1000 were maintained directly by central government (GMS – grant-maintained schools) and 23,000 were maintained locally (LEA schools). The GM schools had opted to leave local control, thereby gaining increased finance and increased attractiveness to parents. There was, therefore, bad feeling in some areas between the local and GM schools. Some education professionals were unhappy about co-operating with GM schools and some LEAs refused them access to local services even when they were willing to pay for them.

CHAPTER 6

The days' policies

With my evostick and my sellotape, I try to bring together the political planning and priorities with the department's aims.

(CEO, cohort one, 1987)

The processes used by senior managers have been little researched, outside of documents and meetings in the public domain (Cookson, 1994, p. 16). These can give the impression that the roles of strategic leaders are mainly concerned with helping to set grand visions, mission statements or objectives (which all late twentieth-century organizations are deemed to need in order to be successful) and with monitoring final outcomes of policies. Imagining visions is, however, the work of minutes. Turning visions into grand plans is the work of hours of long team meetings. Implementing the plans is the rest of the time. This study mainly concerns the rest of the time.

During the majority of the time of these CEOs, policies were investigated for feasibility, resourced, implemented, monitored in progress, reported and evaluated. The process sounds neat and tidy but there were many policies operating concurrently, each policy was proceeding at different rates with varying start and finish times, and the unexpected could intervene. How did those charged with policy leadership maintain the objectives? This chapter relates first, the visionary objectives. Secondly, there are tables outlining what topics were most discussed and at what stages of policy-making the CEOs concentrated their efforts. Thirdly, the incremental nature of policy-making is described, concluding with a proposed conceptualization of the CEO's role.

Expectations of vision

A Canadian study concludes that 'the superintendency is about transformational leadership' (LaRoque and Coleman, 1991, p. 103). An Australian expert notes the current obsession of leadership studies with this transformational role (Gronn, 1996). History determines that it is the transformers amongst English CEOs who are remembered, whose achievements became the expectations for all their successors (see Chapter 9) and who were early expected to play a role in long-term planning (Hill, 1938, p. 118). Theory requires transformers with immense abilities; the American superintendent, for example, 'should know everything that is going on in the district ... be concerned with systemwide missions and goals' (Konnert and Augenstein, 1990, p. 50). Research discovers such transformers as American superintendents with 'clarity of vision and organisational goals' (Griffin and Chance, 1994, p. 75). These visionaries are leaders with strong personal values in theory and practice (Macpherson, 1985a; Thom, 1993; Walker, 1994, p. 23) who are committed to deep, structural change (Bryman, 1992). The measure of Canadian CEO effectiveness has been defined as an ability to be transformational (Musella, 1992, p. 5). Fictional CEOs are credited if they are transformational (Middleton, 1986) or castigated if they are not (Middleton, 1976). Historical CEOs discover its joys:

> Some men have a natural gift for anticipating the needs of the future and when the truth of their common-sense ideas has dawned upon others, they are said to have worked with vision. There is much more joy in being a ragged-trousered pioneer of ideas which are twenty-five years 'before their time' than in being a Beau Brummel of common practice.
>
> (Hill, 1938, p. 116)

It is generally felt that executives who are at this level of leadership should, and do, have considerable influence on policy decisions (Bush and Kogan, 1982, p. 100; Gronn, 1996, p. 9).

Evidence for vision can be found from this and other research. For example, one of the progenitors of devolved school financial management now common in Britain, New Zealand, Australia, in parts of the USA and in experimental groups in Singapore, was London's scheme of Alternative Uses of Resources. Eric Briault, the then CEO, recalled that 'it was my particular invention ... I planned and worked out that AUR scheme' (Bush and Kogan, 1982, p. 185). Farmer, CEO for Coventry, had a more generalized vision: his organization should

> recognise that salvation ... lay in its own hands, in accepting the idea that its continuing usefulness depended on the provision of cost effective, user friendly services for its schools with advice and leadership based on sound educational values and local democratic accountability. Above all it needed to demonstrate the advantages of working together ... against the dangers of a free-for-all in a culturally diverse city.
>
> (Goodwin, 1995b, p. 9)

Brighouse, CEO for Birmingham, envisioned more specific goals: base-line assessment of four- and five-year-olds, a university of the first age as an enrichment programme for 11- to 13-year-olds, Primary Guarantee that children would each have five special experiences over their primary years of schooling (such as field trips) and Secondary Guarantee including improved examination results and entitlement to careers' preparation and computer literacy. A good source for ascertaining these CEOs' visions was the weekly journal, *Education* (regarded as the voice of LEAs. It ceased publication in April 1996). In this, CEOs wrote a regular column. Here could be found visions for improving the lot of the least academically able, the greening of the curriculum and the empowerment of stakeholders in designing the curriculum amongst many others (Atkinson, 1988, p. 123; Walton, 1987, p. 205; Wood-Allum, 1987, p. 357).

From those general visions, the process unrolled. In one of the cohort two organizations, the CEO admitted to having 'a bit of a bee in the bonnet' about science education. The push behind the policy was to make that authority one of the best in the field. The next stage was to set up working groups to investigate the vision and its implications: 'these are the strategic thinking opportunities for which I like to make time' stated the CEO. From these, which aimed to 'stir up as much discussion as possible', a major planning document would emerge which would be launched at a big meeting.

Strategies, once launched, did not remain static. An LEA views itself as providing education services from cradle to grave hence an adult guidance service is an important part of that vision. In one of the LEAs observed a decision was needed on whether to reduce the size of this service to meet budget cuts; debate ensued about the repercussions of breaking the cohesion of the service and of causing additional work for other services. No decision was taken – the debate just moved the issue a little further along the line. One of the CEOs in this research had effected his vision of linking education and industry through a partnership committee. This was hijacked as the basis for corporate liaison with business representatives. The CEO then reoriented the vision by beginning the process of reducing the committee to an advisory body only and establishing a new one to fulfil the original aims. The CEO did not suggest this directly but picked up on the views of others who wanted the committee reduced in power for other reasons. These he supported and the new policy line began to inch forward. In contrast, one CEO's vision could not be rescued. In cohort one, a CEO had launched an initiative to develop the curriculum in conjunction with teachers' consultative committees. The outcome was a ferment of discussion throughout the area with all interested parties but it was overtaken by the advent of the National Curriculum.

The CEOs in this study took care to develop visions in consultation with their staff. One such major consultation occurred at a planning day during the 1994–95 observations. At this meeting the CEO gave the leadership to officers who made presentations. There were interjections from the CEO who provided comparative evidence to motivate staff to action. 'Our record is a disgrace compared with other education authorities' was the rallying cry from the CEO. This networking of information into policy discussions was a principal role for the CEO who brought information from other areas and contacts. Chairing the discussion, the CEO traversed all the areas requiring discussion and particularly emphasized the need for good publicity about whatever was decided. Also stressed was the importance of selecting visions without initially considering the financial consequences. Several strategies for selection relating to different aspects of the education service spanned the day. Each followed the pattern of being led by a subordinate officer with the CEO chairing the ensuing discussion.

Consultation could not guarantee acceptance. One CEO lamented that it was disappointing to find that staff never referred to the plan they had so enthusiastically joined in creating, that it had not empowered staff as had been hoped, that staff undertook activities that were not in the plan and did not refer to it when prioritizing. Perhaps staff felt over-strategized. In another LEA, I was informed privately by a subordinate member of staff that 'we have too many strategy meetings. Once a month is too often'. However often they are, their role is considered vital if local government is to survive. 'Under local management of schools, the majority of functions are already devolved to governing bodies [of individual schools]. The remaining functions are strategic and do not lend themselves to devolution' (Northants, 1994, p. 21).

All the CEOs in this research were classified as transformers by those with whom they worked. I was told, for example: 'Of course, our CEO is quite unique'; 'You won't find another CEO who leads like this one'; 'A great ideas person'; 'A quite exceptional person'. I would not dispute any of these views but it was interesting to note how the same comments were quickly made about the successors to those who retired from my cohorts. There is an expectation of transformation, perhaps almost a wish for it. Leadership is about proactive, visionary change management.

Continuous, proactive change must be, however, exhausting both for those leading it and for their followers being chased to implement it. Continuous, proactive change can be expensive: 'He thought totally educa-tion and to hell with the budget' said one of the executives in cohort one of his predecessor. Continuous, proactive change could create ferment without time to build the necessary organization to support changes. Continuous, proactive change could prevent visions being fully accepted before the next vision is articulated. Continuous proactive change was not what these CEOs were observed doing.

Policy processes and issues

There are no standardized categories in observation research so interna-tional comparisons are not easy. Observation of an Australian equivalent of an English CEO classified only 3 per cent of activities as decision-making. Thirty-three per cent were grouped together as being related to strategy, tactics and planning. The other major part of the subject's work was information processing and management (Macpherson, 1985a, p. 192). Seventy-five per cent of Canadian superintendents' work was classified as managerial, as opposed to educational (Duignan, 1980).

Table 6.1 Stages of policy-making occupying CEOs' encounters as a percentage of the total policy-making time

	1 County Tory margin 1986	2 County hung 1986	3 County Tory 1987	4 County Tory margin 1987	5 City Labour 1987–88	6 County Labour margin 1994	7 County hung 1995	8 Town Labour margin 1995	9 City Labour 1995	All 1986–88	All 1994–95
Consultation (1)	31.70	37.44	37.35	0.00	13.5	42.62	32.8	29.31	16.9	30.47	32.83
Selection (1)	9.46	6.21	12.61	0.00	11.75	0.39	26.32	2.46	4.79	8.62	13.08
Implementation	33.11	33.07	47.41	87.06	46.88	55.70	14.92	63.52	72.68	41.20	40.45
Review	25.73	23.28	2.63	12.94	27.87	1.29	25.96	4.73	5.63	19.71	13.64

(1) With people other than politicians for whom consultation and selection are their whole role.

Table 6.2 Content of encounters with subordinates and politicians as a percentage of total encounter time

	1 County Tory margin 1986	2 County hung 1986	3 County Tory 1987	4 County Tory margin 1987	5 City Labour 1987–88	6 County Labour margin 1994	7 County hung 1995	8 Town Labour margin 1995	9 City Labour 1995	All 1986–88	All 1994–95
Political (1)	31.09	22.40	37.95	30.61	33.54	43.91	74.35	21.15	22.58	30.70	31.65
Managerial – finance (2)	3.08	12.38	3.31	5.44	18.58	31.26	5.95	22.81	13.98	7.32	20.72
Managerial – people (3)	22.89	48.73	27.69	20.27	44.56	6.44	12.26	25.06	13.98	33.10	18.02
Managerial – sites (4)	8.96	0.69	4.25	1.09	1.81	2.30	3.72	0.00	0.00	3.97	0.84
Formal (5)	33.98	15.80	26.80	42.59	1.51	16.09	3.72	29.31	37.63	24.91	25.61
Other (6)	0.00	0.00	0.00	0.00	0.00	0.00	0.00	1.67	11.83	0.00	3.16

(1) Meetings of full council, working groups, committees, sub-committees, briefings, advisory sessions for politicians on tactics
(2) Annual budget, revisions of policy budgets
(3) Salary negotiations, appointments, inductions, appraisals, redundancies, retirements, disciplinaries, training, motivation
(4) Buildings and grounds
(5) School visits, meals during appointment selection procedures, formal openings of buildings, retirement parties, opening speeches at conferences, Christmas lunches
(6) Meetings with press and local radio

Bredeson's (1995) study of US superintendents classified their work according to its distance from direct classroom instruction. The classification most frequently used was that of 'instructional supporters' who saw themselves as providers of finance and of psychological and practical personnel support. The less commonly found categories were those of 'instructional collaborators who rolled up their sleeves and became personally involved in meetings and work groups to plan instruction and implement the curriculum', instructional delegators who viewed their role as 'systems administrators making it possible for others to be good instructional leaders' and 'instructional visioners who allowed dreamers' dreams to come true' (Bredeson, 1995, p. 8). Note that even in the last, apparently transformational, category the CEOs were still supporters of others rather than providers of the vision themselves.

Incremental maintenance

The CEOs in this survey were very practical in their assessments of themselves and their roles. They all had visions of what good education should be and of what was needed to realize these visions but they saw their activities pragmatically. One had a vision 'to keep a few teachers in classrooms with a little bit of chalk'. They echoed a 1950s' CEO who recognized that 'what I do myself is mostly quite unimportant except in so far as it improves the opportunities for the people in the classroom' (Sylvester, 1957, p. 189). This would have been an appropriate statement for one of the second cohort; he retired renowned for his personal, and individualized, support to teachers and principals. Another realistically described the CEO's role as a 'trimmer', adjusting the sails to the prevailing winds. Another expressed the task as 'charting the path, even though we can't make the journey'. It was also seen as the taking of 'very rough decisions' which have to offend as few people as possible.

The CEOs used various formats for the incremental actions needed to maintain strategies in action. At meetings, these CEOs clarified priorities, indicating the seriousness of issues to other players in the policy game, each group of policy players in turn being used to support the CEOs' desired objectives. They provided advice at meetings and used these events to read and understand steps towards the formulation of policy, as did earlier CEOs (Bush and Kogan, 1982, p. 151) and Canadian superintendents who carefully gathered information before risking action (Duignan, 1980, p. 23). The CEOs ensured that information was in the right place at the right time for action, or decision, to result. They sought to recognize where conflict might arise and to defuse it, as did US counterparts (Chance, 1992, p. 81). They worked to get everyone involved in decision-making, a role long held (Browning, 1972, p. 5). They set, followed and monitored short-term goals.

Chief executives have to work through, and for, other people. These CEOs had to steer the implementation of policies demanded by central government and by the local councillors. Between these two there appeared to be little scope for *ab initio* policies, though there were clearly opportunities for selecting priorities and for deciding which items should be pushed forward at particular times and in particular ways according to the CEOs' views of what was politically and practically expedient. Getting policies accepted required the same endorsement by local politicians' votes as is needed to support developments in central government (Fitz and Halpin, 1994, pp. 45–6). Persuading the politicians to accept the executives' advice on policy took considerable time (this is discussed further in Chapter 9). Site visits (see Chapter 7) enabled these CEOs to spot 'points of local professional growth ... of potential and significance' (Browning, 1972, p. 6) for which they then had to seek resources and adjust the system to encourage their development. These CEOs took the initiative in setting up *ad hoc* working groups and then had to follow up the outcomes. They were adept at inserting pressure at points along the routes to final goals in order to ensure progress at a suitable rate. They climbed 'a hillside every now and then to take a look around; to assess accomplishments' (Isenberg, 1994, p. 131) in order to help them rise above the 'nit-picking little incidents' that one CEO described as occurring during his days being observed.

Examples abounded of these CEOs keeping policy lines intact through incremental maintenance. A meeting to negotiate nursery nurses' pay increases had the hidden agenda that enough must be left to initiate a pay rise for school secretaries. These were not the subject of that meeting but their pay rise was a long-term policy objective. A request for a CEO to attend a school principals' meeting without other accompanying subordinates was side-stepped with the plea that the other officers must attend since they had the detailed information lacked by the CEO; in reality, solo attendance left the CEO much more vulnerable to an undesired change of policy on management structuring. Discussions on moving a curriculum support unit, ostensibly about removal dates and practicalities, was central to the policy of continuing a role for the LEA in advisory services to schools.

The minutiae of keeping policies on the move is indicated by the short time given to them as each rose to the surface briefly and then disappeared for that week or longer. Eight minutes sorted the tactics for the next stage of encouraging a charitable body to contribute to a unit for disaffected children. Thirteen minutes, briefly interrupted by a report on overflowing toilets at a school, covered the prioritizing of items following the drafting of a bid for European Union money. Ten minutes were devoted to suggesting tactics one of the political parties might use to ensure the next day's meeting adopted their policies. One minute was a glance at the budget for special needs and a quick check with the responsible subordinate that it was on time. Contemplating this jigsaw of bits of policies, one CEO remarked, 'I can't get my head round how to get it all to fit together – it's quite hard'.

The complexities of leading through incremental maintenance were summed up for me in the recollections of how Stewart Mason (CEO

Leicestershire, 1947–71) persuaded a fairly right-wing local authority to adopt the left-wing idea of comprehensive schooling. 'It's difficult to pinpoint exactly how it was done', he said (Mason, 1981). It relied not only on the big committees but also on attention to the small details of, for example, terminology. Throughout the discussions Mason used the words, 'grammar schools' to describe the new, senior comprehensive schools thus linking them to the cachet of English schools traditionally well regarded. Such terminological exactitude has to be maintained against pressing dead-lines and without 'identifiable yardsticks in the amorphous mass of work', as Canadian superintendents revealed (Duignan, 1980, p. 21). Each step on the policy-making route taken by this Canadian group was tiny and only half of the issues they confronted needed decisions. On those issues they actually made decisions on less than half of the occasions, usually requiring further information before action (Duignan, 1980, p. 18) as did US coun-terparts (Konnert and Augenstein, 1990, p. 55). In England, the need was to keep creeping forward amidst a 'welter of financial expediencies' (Pratt, 1987, p. 19).

Incremental maintenance like this is not the antithesis of vision-driven policy-making, as some believe (Lawrence, 1972). It is at least three-quar-ters of the strategic process which involves giving a sense of direction, explanations for that direction, making people feel engaged in the process, demonstrating that what is done fits with the mores of the times and, lastly, being original (Duke, 1986). This view of CEOs' roles may be more appro-priate than that of a full-time visionary since:

> CEOs are not equipped to be educationalists. They are ill informed of educa-tional ideas and research and not aware of critical and reflective thought in education ... Their inability to be a leading educationalist is hampered by the fire-fighting nature of their job. Issues must be dealt with quickly because of their political implications ... [Their] expertise lies in knowing how to fiddle money ... to move it from one budget area to another ... the job is to try to strike an uneasy balance amongst the various factions.
>
> (Bernbaum, 1987)

This education professor's rather jaundiced view is supported by a novel-ist whose retired CEO hero admits, 'that though he often said that an administrator's task was to make it that much easier for students to learn and teachers to instruct, he'd too often succumbed to the temptation for the neat solution, that saved money, or cut time he and his understrappers might have to spend' (Middleton, 1986, p. 210). The CEO's knowledge of education is that of a generalist rather than that of an expert. This accords with British civil service traditions, 'officials at the top ... are not experts; they are usually general practitioners ...those at the top must deal with a wider range of questions than those lower down' (Wheare, 1955, p. 16). In the USA, such generalism amongst superintendents is celebrated as enabling them to deal with all the basic functions of a district (Glass, 1993, p. 63).

Generalist, incremental maintenance is not, however, a poor substitute for visionary leadership. It is its base and its apex. It actualizes the vision collated by the CEOs from all the groups involved.

Conceptualizing daily leadership

Transformational strategic leadership requiring grand visions and continuous proactive change as a model for chief executives has to be questioned from empirical evidence. The majority of time is not spent on this but rather on incremental maintenance to implement their own and other people's visions, conceptualized as 'coherence management' (Crowson, 1994, pp. 4–5) or 'organisational maintenance' (McCabe, 1992, p. 2). Both these analogies stress the wholeness and purpose of the leading executives' role. I prefer to consider the processes of that role and to suggest the terminology of 'incremental maintenance', lying somewhere between the transactional and transformational models. It is detailed and painstaking work that requires a character who can rise above being detailed and painstaking to perform it. It requires skills to keep the wide picture evident to the CEOs themselves and to all those with whom they work as described in the following three chapters. It needs ability to 'helicopt' above the niceties while recognizing that it is only through these that the organization will move by very small increments to the next policy goal. It needs humility to accept that the goals are the products of other people's thinking, often just collated by the CEO, sometimes absorbing a CEO's own ideas too.

I would suggest conceptualizing this mode as a garage mechanics' supervisor. The supervisor has legal authority but access to very few financial resources personally to back up this power. The supervisor is in a position to influence strongly the views and actions of others but has restricted legal rights over them since the organization and its personnel department have this. The supervisor has no influence at all on the state of the cars as they are delivered and very little on the characters and actions of the cars' owners. The supervisor mechanic requires detailed knowledge of the workings of all the parts of machine and must be able to perform all the repair jobs personally but is not often required to do so. The supervisor must deploy the other mechanics suitably, retain awareness of what the repair shop has to achieve each day, week, month and year. In emergencies, like the Greek choruses, the supervisor must be able to participate in the full action undertaking tasks that other mechanics would do if there were time. The supervisor must liaise with the bosses, acting as a buffer between them and the mechanics. From the detailed knowledge the supervisor has of the workings of the machines and of the people who repair them, the supervisor can make suggestions which amend the businesses' core missions. The supervisor is acquainted with the sales, marketing, finance and human resource offices and keeps in touch with them from time to time to ensure corporate policy is realized. Cars come into the garage to be serviced by the mechanics. The supervisor watches the mechanics throughout the day, checking for difficulties with the machines or the people and moving in to clear problems as necessary. The supervisor gives the cars a final glance on the way out and goes to reassure the owners that all have been correctly repaired. The customers feel better for this brief encounter with the 'front person'.

Supervising garage mechanics is not as glamorous as the old visionary leader concept but isn't it a more realistic description of the principal activities of chief executives in education or in other spheres?

CHAPTER 7

Servicing the days

The ex-public sector careers service peered cautiously into commercial commencement. Previously protected by its local government status as monopoly supplier of occupational guidance, the service had re-formed itself, after central government directives from the late 1980s, into a business capable of tendering for, and winning, contracts. Businesslike, it had now to charge for its services. If consumers bought those services, then it would be a successful business. If not, it would close. The consumers now being asked to buy had previously received the service free. Would they continue to use it? Those staffing these putative businesses had expected their own professional development to remain within the secure jobs, altruistic ideals, professional dominance and non-performance-related environment of the public sector. Would they make the transition successfully to market-oriented, consumer-led, service providers?

During 1986–95 CEOs played a strategic role in transformations like these. The conglomerates they ruled were being made to shed those parts which did not relate directly to the core business of educating students. The shedding had to take place with as few jobs lost as possible. Morale had to be maintained. A new culture had to be taught. All this had to happen in a milieu which, on the whole, was profoundly opposed to both commercialization and the shedding of parts. How well did the CEOs manage the job of helping these services achieve what must have seemed to many to be the equivalent of 'walking the plank'?

These new businesses in local government are the first discussed in this chapter on the CEOs' relationships with those who provided the education service, thus implementing the strategic plans of the leadership. The numbers of staff who had to be influenced by these CEOs into internalizing the strategic plans ranged from just over 2000 in the smallest LEA in the cohorts, to just over 7000 in the largest. (These figures are full-time teaching staff only; there were also between 500 and 2000 part-time teachers plus support staff). While some of this number were walking the plank and becoming the new service providers, the majority remained in the core.

These are the principals and teachers who run each area's schools and colleges. The CEO's relations with these groups are discussed in the second section in this chapter. Servicing the core are the officers, local inspectors and advisers and clerical staff in the central or regional offices of the LEA. This last group is the one with which the CEOs spent the majority of their contact time as Tables 4.8, 4.9, 4.10 and 4.11 revealed in Chapter 4. Relations with this service group provide the last part of this chapter.

The new business service providers

Becoming businesses

In all English local governments 1986–95, parts of their work had to become effectively private, profit-making businesses both in education and in other aspects of local government work. School catering, refuse disposal, school grounds and building maintenance, curriculum advice services and management training – all are examples of these new businesses. All these had to become rigorously costed as separate entities rather than being unpriced services whose operating costs could be supported by other areas of the conglomerate local authority. All these had to be high-quality, competitively priced, market responsive services. I observed meetings of the directing boards and senior staff of two such services, near the beginnings of their new lives, during 1994–95. One was in a secure Labour urban area, the other in a hung county.

At these meetings, the CEOs' role was that of obstetricians. Once the new businesses were born, they would withdraw but the neonates had to be safely launched and breathing unaided before that withdrawal could happen. Both meetings were concerned with issues relating to the establishment of the new companies. There were salaries and terms and conditions of work to be settled, legal identity issues, roles of directors and marketing matters. The meetings of the two new companies had the same feel in both authorities. The majority of participants seemed bemused and uncertain. Only the CEOs appeared serenely in charge and to be fully aware of the prospects, possibilities and pitfalls ahead. Their attitude was bracing. One could almost sense the old-fashioned school principal at assembly with the message, 'Buck up and face up to realities, it's no use keening for the old days'. Out front, as generals, the CEOs rallied their troops, organized deployments and dug for victory. Behind the lines, the generals muttered somewhat despairingly about the prospects for those facing the new army of customers with weapons left over from the last war.

Each of the meetings presented the same characters as bit players around the stardom of the CEO whether formally centre stage or not. A senior officer, in a nervous new suit, was on prompt duty as chief executive of the new service. Still slightly bemused by the change and relieved that the main agenda item for the day was about choosing a logo for the new service and selecting letterheads, the new chief waited on the old for guidance. Those present included other senior officers there to help decide how hard to push the ex-public sector staff into orbit as outgoing entrepreneurs. There were legal officers attempting to hide anxieties about whether the new organizations were in fit shape to cope with the intricacies of personnel legislation. The two or three business people present, hauled out of early retirement to provide business expertise, were still agape at the prospect of trying to sell the unmarketable and were tut-tutting over the vagueness of accounts which could not yet be separated from their LEA parent. Last year these people were selling fleets of airliners to Australia. This week they were contemplating how to persuade schoolchildren to buy advice on how to make a career as airline staff. The business people got to grips with Years 10 and 11 terminology while the professional, ex-local government specialists got to grips with envisaging these as market segments. Educational expertise was drafted in from a local college and retired HMIs added to this. The business men were silver haired in well cut suits. The person asleep in the corner was the long-established county councillor. There was the obligatory elegant lady (grey hair, black dress) and a serious man in jeans who was the only one who appeared not to have combed his hair in line with the new corporate image. There was talk of audit trails, profit-making, customers and management information. Business people were in shock at what a non-profit service body had to achieve with so few resources; service providers were in shock for the same reason but also wide eyed with naïveté.

Both meetings felt guided by the CEOs whose role here seemed much more definitive than that adopted in committees where politicians were the leaders. The party political battles over these services were long since fought, now it was administrative leadership that was needed without further reference back to politicians. The reference back would be to consumers, a much more amorphous group than councillors, a group for whom the CEO did not have to take responsibility, a group who would speak for themselves through market mechanisms directly to the service providers, a distant group for whom the CEO no longer needed to speak. These CEOs were shedding one layer of accountability and with that came a respite from responsibility.

Leading the services

The responsibility for these services was a minor part of CEOs' accountabilities. During the first cohort observations, 1986–88, these businesses would have been considered as part of the core since they were the support staff to the main work of education. Contact between CEOs of this period and these support staff or their managers was, however, minimal. It was so small as to be not worth measuring as a separate category. The contacts consisted of a CEO chatting to catering staff on a school visit or formally at meetings to negotiate salaries with unions (see Chapter 8). These contacts demonstrated the CEO's attention to detail. The support staff encountered were greeted by name and one was asked about his health, having recently been ill. First names were used although there was a certain diffidence in the contacts.

Indirect contact with support staff arose when issues relating to their services were discussed though these did not give rise to physical meetings with the staff concerned. For example, during 1986–88 CEOs were much occupied with the topic of providing supervisors for children during their lunch-breaks since teachers would no longer perform that duty without pay and regarded the rates of pay for lunch-time supervision as derisory. The pay was much less per hour than a teacher would usually command, but one of the politicians felt it should be less since he thought that supervision did not involve teaching.

The 1986–88 cohort were involved in the early stages of developing support staff as service providers who would be required to tender for local government work. The outcomes of this were inherited by their 1994–95 followers who had reached the stages of launching the businesses as described at the beginning of this section. At the strategic policy level, the 1986–88 early stages found CEOs both persuading politicians to make the issue of privatization and compulsory tendering a priority and implementing details of the strategies once agreed. One CEO was frustrated by his council's continued deferring of decisions on this issue. Another was involved with drawing up precise job descriptions of each type of worker within the services concerned. The minute complexities and personal susceptibilities which had to be managed included coping with four people who objected to what appeared to be alterations to their job descriptions, problems with officers who were involved in the compulsory tendering for contracts but felt their work was insufficiently compensated, a supervisor upset because he had lost a small honorarium awarded for his covering during the absence of his predecessor, and people wanting extra clerical assistance to organize the additional work occasioned by preparing to become businesses. In this LEA, the school catering staff had readily accepted their translation to a catering company; the cleaning staff were fighting their translation to being in a competitive business. The CEO was not sympathetic towards the recalcitrant cleaners. There were penetrating questions to the organizing officers and demands for precise job grading, costings and relationships to be sorted between the new services and the local authority's personnel department. The CEO was aware that time was passing quickly and services unwilling to change would not be in a position to bid against private competition. Without bidding, there was no chance of saving jobs.

In these discussions, it was clear that the CEOs were pushing the service providers into thinking strategically and into seeing the long-term implications, not always with success. This continued with the 1994–95 cohort when, for example, a CEO tried to raise the interest of a service meeting to future plans from detailed personnel issues: 'I don't want to spend hours revising these unless there are major holes' was the CEO's firm statement. Within this long-term approach, the CEOs were also responsible for finding outside funding from private or public sources such as the Manpower Services Commission and other government agencies. A 1995 CEO admitted hating this aspect of the job and not being very good at it.

Services in corporate policy

Linking the services into corporate policy was an important role for CEOs. They were the spokespersons for these services when the politicians were deciding how to distribute funds amongst them. One 1990s' local authority, for example, had continued corporateness into tactics as well as strategy by centralizing all services' provision. The promotion of the head of the centralized services to a new job led to redistribution back to individual parent departments and a confidential meeting for the CEO concerning the services reincorporating into the education department. This resulted in the CEO being deputed to obtain users' views on the services concerned and hence a discussion later the same day on how best to collect views.

Events in a 1987 LEA demonstrated the same strategic role. The CEO made clear to the leader of the local youth service that the policy of concentrating its efforts on disaffected youths, to the virtual exclusion of assisting the development of top quality team games and sports competitions for young people, was not endearing the service to the politicians who controlled the money. The youth service leader responded with a request that the whole service be reviewed, a response quashed by the CEO who pointed out that money had already been spent on such a review and no more could be made available. The CEO made it clear that his role was to defend the service to the politicians but that in order to do this successfully, he needed some good reports of the service to convey to them. The officer continued with complaints that the youth service was struggling with increased costs since it had to pay schools for use of their premises (previously free). The CEO explained his responsibility to balance the budget for each section of education provision and that he had responsibilities to obtain the best deals for each section.

CEOs also saw their responsibilities to obtain the best business advice for their services. Hence 1994 found one CEO producing contacts to advise on running the motor car unit linked to the crime prevention service and checking that the probation service users were paying for it.

By the time of the 1994–95 cohort, the privatization of LEA services had extended to include all services. Schools had themselves become autonomous businesses who could choose what services they wished to buy from the local authority. In one LEA each school had a service-level agreement. It specified what services each school would receive in return for what levels of payment. The establishment of these agreements had been a major issue. It was referred to as 'having sold the family silver' and tensions had arisen as it had been realized that the employees and politicians no longer determined what the services provided – the customers did.

The core providers: principals, teachers

Principals

'Superintendent behaviours and activities can facilitate the role of the principal' concluded a USA study (Griffin and Chance, 1994, p. 81). The amount of time spent by the English equivalents of these superintendents with principals was not great (see Tables 4.8, 4.9, 4.10 and 4.11 in Chapter 4) if they were to play a facilitator role, but this low contact time accords with some Canadian research in which superintendents in the larger districts did not suggest principals as having a major impact on their work (Allison, 1991a, p. 34). Other Canadian evidence showed that CEOs spent more time in meetings with school personnel than with any other group (Hickcox, 1992, p. 12) including the politicians on the school boards. English CEOs during 1986–88 spent 12.28 per cent of their time with school personnel and 11.03 per cent with politicians. By 1994–95, time with school staff had considerably reduced to 7.61 per cent although time with politicians remained roughly the same at 11.23 per cent.

Employing principals

A major influence over school principals held by the 1986–88 CEOs, but not by their 1994–95 counterparts, was the power of selection and appointment. For the first cohort, their powers were shared with governors and councillors but the CEOs' influence was generally dominant. The importance of holding the power of selection was stressed by earlier CEOs (Bush and Kogan, 1982, p. 105). Stewart Mason, for example, felt that 'if you secure a winner, he passes on the same confidence and trust to his staff and you could, in a way, forget about that school' (Mason, 1981). A 1987 CEO echoed this on the retirement of one school principal which produced the reaction: 'That's good. Now we can get someone in there who understands what we're at'. Principals could only be replaced when they chose to leave their posts. If they did not, removing a principal from post was (and is) difficult. 'Education in the dark ages, at that school' commented one CEO but there was nothing that could be done to replace the principal. The CEO's effect could only occur at initial selection as was demonstrated at a 1987 principals' selection committee.

At the starting gate of this committee meeting were three councillors (one from each party), three governors from the school concerned, the CEO, the chief adviser (for curriculum matters) and a subordinate officer as secretary.

The governors led the race initially, having prepared their own short list from the long list of candidates. Their short list had been drawn up after consultations with the school's staff thus giving them the necessary support to get over the first hurdle. The second was not so easy. Galloping up ready for a quick pass was the CEO's team who had not short-listed any of the governors' choices but had selected alternatives. Councillors stepped in ready to declare a false start by demanding to know why the governors' choices had not made the grade. Deeply concerned, the CEO cleared the next hurdle by instructing an officer to go and duplicate further copies of the governors' choices and to reinstate them in the list. While the stable lad was away, the riders jogged along companionably with the CEO carefully explaining the process of interviewing since the governors would have had much less experience of this than had the LEA jockeys.

Once the duplicated documents reappeared, the CEO's team began to pull away from the field. First, of course, the governor and councillor riders were easily distracted into giving their views first so their strength began to falter. Carefully responding to each challenge, the CEO team took on the qualifications hurdle. Only those professionally qualified, like themselves, could comment on the records of those competing in the principalship stakes. This applicant went to a better college than another; that applicant had a better mix of experience; 'I've met him – he's good but unimaginative'; 'He's from a lively school', 'You may remember we interviewed him once before'. The distance between the CEO's team and the rest of the field had widened considerably at this point in the race. The governors' choices were fast fading; the governors were unable to negotiate the hurdles. Magnanimously, the CEO's team turned back to help them over, neatly emphasizing the unbridgeable differences between lay people's emotions and professional knowledge. 'The LEA can't give you guidance on this one – it's how you *feel* about the application … he may not be the right man for the job – but that would be your decision'. The governors attempted a last spurt to catch up – 'We like this one's letter, it's warm' they said. 'We have no feeling for the one the director put first – could you give us more supportive information?' Of course, the CEO did. The CEO's team was home and dry and so were their original selections.

Such is an obviously cynical record of the proceedings. Being a professional teacher myself, I was delighted that professional views dominated. Being a professional teacher of school principals, I was delighted that qualifications mattered. Being a trainer of school governors, and a governor myself, I was uneasy about the simplicity of overriding governors' views since they were directly concerned with the school. On the other hand, using the proof of a 'warm' letter as the basis for a principal's appointment did not seem adequate.

By 1994–95, governors could be less easily manipulated since many had received training in personnel appointments themselves and the CEO could, by law, offer only advice. Each school's governors were the ones who selected those for school principalships. There was much less competition for principals' posts during this later period than there had been in 1986–88. This declining interest was a topic of debate amongst education officers who shared discussions with a CEO on how to encourage more people to apply for principalships. The choices for governors should also be simplified after 1996–97. Candidates for principalships will have to have nationally recognized qualifications from institutions licensed by a central government agency. The personal advice of a CEO will be superseded by a nationalized standard.

There were no opportunities during these observations to assess the extent to which a CEO's advice would be heeded in the 1990s. There was one brief exchange concerning the appointment of a deputy school principal. The CEO said an external candidate should be selected; the subordinate officers with whom the issue was being discussed felt this was not necessary as the school 'was not in need of a shake-up'. I did not discover whose views prevailed.

Once selected, principals became the employees of the LEA in 1986–88. By 1994–95, their employers were *de facto* the governors of each school. Some 1986–88 scenarios were, therefore, unlikely for the 1994–95 cohort. A school principal came to inform the CEO of his secondment to a principals' professional association in 1987. The CEO was concerned about the effect on the school of this extended absence and contacted the chairperson of the Education Committee for discussions. There was no mention of discussing it with the school's governors. By 1994–95, the governors would take the decision on a principal's secondment.

Being the employer entailed CEOs ensuring common interpretations of conditions of service. In issuing written documents about these to school principals, CEOs were very aware of the susceptibilities with which they were dealing. Drafting a letter for dispatch to principals, a CEO was concerned that the letter looked too bald, as if the LEA were dictating to principals. 'I'm not anxious to rock the boat with principals' stated the CEO.

CEOs performed the functions of any good employer with concerns for their employees' health. Several times, in each observation period, there were enquiries about progress of principals such as one not coping with stress and consequently giving a school's staff a hard time. Prevention was also regarded as important as cure. A CEO visited a principal who had steered two schools through amalgamation in very difficult circumstances. The CEO advised the principal to consider taking some holiday. CEOs in supportive mode for the human resources they led also took shape as advisers in times of difficulty. A principal rang in one morning to 'cry on the CEO's shoulder' about poor examination results which were attracting criticism to his school. There was nothing the CEO could do other than offer a little encouragement: 'Well, it happens to all schools sometimes … we all have those difficult groups of parents.'

Principals in policy-making

Having personal contact with school principals was regarded as crucial by past and present CEOs (Bush *et al.*, 1989, p. 151; Gedling, 1986, p. 71; Goodwin, 1995b, p. 9; Mason, 1981) and this began with induction meetings for new appointees, the CEOs taking responsibility for ensuring that such sessions were arranged. Other meetings were to seek views in the early stages of policy formation, to offer principals updating training, to build confidence and trust, to demonstrate support for principals and to respond to queries regarding interpretations of central and local governments' policies.

'We want to identify your views so we can put them to committee' was a standard opener from a CEO for such meetings. Such statements linked the CEO and the principals, underlined the corporate whole and demonstrated the role of the CEO as conduit to the local politicians. The tone of such meetings notably stressed the autonomy of schools even before this was legally enshrined, with CEOs insisting on their deference to principals' views and on principals taking their own decisions. One CEO neatly enquired of the principals if they wanted to take their own decisions or preferred officers to do it for them. The answer, predictably, selected the first choice but there was satisfaction that the choice had been offered. The mode of these large meetings varied from a ten-minute leader speech from the CEO followed by one and a half hours of rapid questioning from principals to a one and a half hour speech from the CEO followed by ten minutes of sluggish questioning from principals. Most of the CEOs had subordinate officers with them on these occasions and it was usual for these to be called on by the CEO to answer some of the questions.

The need to link principals into the corporate whole, which an earlier generation would call, 'a family feeling' (Mason, 1981) but which a 1994 CEO referred to as 'bonding', surfaced regularly. Over all the years 1986–95, the bonding was regularly reinforced with CEOs' praises of principals at formal meetings with them, such as 'I reiterate that we owe an enormous amount to our teachers but you also need congratulations for getting so much off the ground'. The 'family' was also united against a hostile world: 'Our own view of what we want here differs from that of central government and we will continue to follow that line until such time as it becomes unlawful,' firmly stated one CEO in the unusual family role of a parent inciting rebellion. Sometimes, the 'family' had rows which came to a CEO to sort out as, for example, when two principals were exchanging angry memos with each other. The CEO told them to clear their differences by meeting personally.

Maintaining the family feeling had become very important by 1994–95. By then, full autonomy had been granted to all schools and there was the possibility of schools leaving the LEAs while those remaining were in competition with each other for pupils once parental choice was allowed by central government. Autonomy also meant that school principals could feel isolated from a support group. One CEO in the 1994–95 cohort organized a lunch meeting to bring together principals from the same geographical area. The CEO several times referred to this isolation during the remainder of the 1994–95 observation period.

The importance of this possibility of schools 'opting out' was marked by a change in meeting patterns between the first and second periods. In 1986–88 meetings were much as they had been for the last 20 years. Principals served, first, as co-opted members of the political Education Committee. The extent of their influence here could vary considerably. If it were a hung authority, then co-opted members could sway the vote. If it were an LEA with a secure Conservative majority, co-opted education professionals could be regarded as the opposition with little effect on votes or debates. If it were a secure Labour authority, principals' views tended to become submerged in those of the majority party. Secondly, there were union meetings (discussed in Chapter 8). Thirdly, there were usually principals' formal consultative groups meeting two or three times yearly in their phases of primary, secondary and special education (Bush *et al.*, 1989, p. 134; Jones, 1988, p. 179: Peschek and Brand, 1966, p. 94). By the time of the second cohort, principals were additionally incorporated into officers' decision-making meetings, were more likely to participate in selecting officers and advisers than previously, were offered more frequent meetings with officers and were co-opted on to council working parties. Such a change in status was symbolized by the CEO who handed over to principals and school governors the writing of the CEO's column in the weekly journal *Education* (Goodwin, 1995b). Principals did not always seem comfortable with the new relationships. They were moving from partnerships from which there could be no divorce into a situation in which they had to be wooed afresh by the suitor of local government. Neither the principals nor the CEOs could be expected to be sure how to respond to the changed circumstances.

The style of meetings with principals varied. Those with the inevitably large numbers of primary school principals tended to be confrontational. A CEO and a subordinate officer sat in a line facing lines of principals. Even where the meetings involved smaller numbers of primary school principals, the tone continued to be more formal than in meetings with secondary school principals. The exchanges were more stylized and there were fewer exchanges of opinion than with secondary groups. Fewer primary principals spoke than did their apparently more assertive secondary colleagues. Topics worked up through the minor to the major. First, encouragement from the CEO for principals to make more use of the LEA's teachers' centres – countered by a primary principal who could not get cover staff to provide teaching while staff went training. A rapid discussion of the rights and wrongs of school tuck shops followed – should schools encourage healthy eating or lose pupils to nearby sweetshops? School uniform taxed their minds next – could schools insist on this or not? Praise from the CEO for schools mounting an exhibition, announcements of a corporate Christmas card and the speed of head office mailings to schools completed the foothills of the meeting.

Climbing the first ranges brought the CEO to budget crevasses. Principals habitually complain of insufficient money so the CEO moved to deflect this by passing blame elsewhere and by reminding them how well off they were.

> We're one of the best resourced LEAs and it gets increasingly difficult to justify requests to Councillors for more ... we came out of the budget process better than other departments ... we had to accept some cuts ... Councillors want savings ... but we're saving £1.87 million with good management ... we lobbied strongly for your views favouring retaining school pianists but something had to go.

There was no time to discuss this before the next item on departmental restructuring. This had been organized to improve communications with schools. It was all a matter of report including the item asking for principals' opinions on whether or not primary principals should join the local principals' association (currently secondary only) or should have their own association or a residential conference. A few minutes was spent on how to organize and pay for lunch-time supervision – 'We don't need to rehearse the agonies on this, do we?' asked the CEO rhetorically before passing on to the next item. The CEO did not escape debate on this one as arguments about whether or not a supervisor would be entitled to a free school dinner passed back and forth. A dinner represents a tiny sum to one school and a large gain in staff morale. To the LEAs, free school meals multiplied by 500 every day represent a not inconsiderable cost. 'We mustn't fall out over this,' stated the CEO, firmly closing the debate, 'we should have mutual confidence in each other – we're doing our best'. Finally, centre stage was relinquished to the chief adviser to talk about the increased importance accorded to primary schools in the new management restructuring. In the best traditions of meetings, the heat had been generated over the small, personal issues of piano-playing part-time staff and free school meals. Restructuring departments and budget allocations were strategic issues not for discussion by the field workers.

Secondary school principals received more personal treatment on the model of Stewart Mason's encounters with his schools' principals, 1947–71. 'We never had a circle of more than twenty-four' (Mason, 1981). Indeed circular formats were in vogue for both these cohorts, usually without the intervention of a table, but none had the 'rather charming entertainments' Mason recollected as being provided by each host school.

Such small meetings with principals usually involved considerable exchange of views though the CEO was dominant as the one with access to the political information. Principals were dominant as the ones with practical information. Both sides walked carefully on each other's territory as the following exchange demonstrates.

CEO: Broadly, you have to be sure that you can manage your schools despite the industrial relations problems ... I've outlined what seems to be a reasonable position but I don't want to stand in the way of individual principals meeting their circumstances ... how you explain that to your staff will be up to your ingenuity ... I'd be glad of your comments on how it's going in practice ... I take every opportunity to meet politicians, civil servants and HMIs to tell them there must be cross-curricular initiatives.

Principal: We'd be happier if we could approach the situation knowing that our LEA, which in essence means you [the CEO] had shown a policy line ... presumably, work is in hand behind the scene on this?'

In most of the meetings attended, there was something of a 'them and us' feeling apparent from the tones of the CEO and officers and of the principals. This worker/manager dichotomy occasionally surfaced overtly. One CEO, on reporting a principals' meeting to a subordinate officer, said. 'We couldn't give in to them'. Another carefully avoided lunching with a group of school principals at a teachers' centre, preferring to remain with the officers. Reflecting on competition developing amongst schools, one CEO remarked that, 'the principals need their heads banging together' for not supporting each other. Another CEO had to choose between attending a planned meeting with school principals and another engagement. The alternative was selected, not without angst: 'I don't mind not going and not getting beaten up but I'm conscious that my absence might be noted'. There were occasional notes of despair: 'I'm asking heads to consult their staff on this but I don't suppose many will'; 'We have to stick with existing principals' consultative mechanisms however unsatisfactory' (this latter in response to a suggestion to bypass these in favour of a 'trusted group of heads, confidentially'). Developments during 1986–95 had led CEOs to concentrate on the managerial aspects of their roles recognized by one principal at the end of one meeting, who remarked, 'Where is the education in all this? It's terribly sad' and this reinforced the 'them and us' separation.

Generally, however, the CEOs were seemingly relaxed and friendly, greeted principals by their first names and stressed that they were open to ideas. Inclusive language was used with heavy emphasis on 'we' especially when either side was making criticisms of the other. 'We have been moderately irresponsible in not responding to consultative documents on the National Curriculum' asserted one 1987 CEO. 'If we don't make our views known to councillors at this stage, we won't get what we want ... Do we want to make representations to the Treasurer to allow schools to enter pupils for different examination boards which will cost more than just all using the same board?'

The nature of meetings and, possibly, the expectations of the listeners, did not sustain relaxation and inclusion, and the 'them and us' feeling remained. All of the meetings inevitably involved the CEOs providing a large amount of information didactically. Principals wanted to know the latest news, what was going on behind the scenes and how this was interpreted by the CEOs. In such circumstances, many of the meetings entailed speeches from the CEO. Many of the meetings had to be repeated so that CEOs could meet all the principals in their areas. Repetition bred formality. For the principals, the CEO was their employer and the route to promotion and other opportunities. A certain deference was bound to result.

Beyond these reasons for distance, however, one sensed that CEOs at meetings with principals were out of their usual milieu and, therefore, somewhat uncomfortable.

Teachers' employment

There were the same changes in the legal employment status of teachers between 1986 and 1995 as there had been in the positions of school principals. These changes could have decreased directly and indirectly the influence of the CEOs. Though still legally employed by LEAs, their *de facto* employers became the governors of each school who gained full responsibility for hiring and firing their staff. Teachers' salaries were set nationally in negotiations between central and local governments but during this period, local government's position in bargaining was ended. There were rumbles of schools being allowed to set their own salaries. There were the beginnings of a performance-related pay system for teachers. The local authorities had some discretion to set the conditions in which merit awards would be paid but the determination of merit had to be by the individual school. By 1995, teachers had ceased to view local authorities as the major source of their post-qualification training. What little money was still available for training was devolved to schools to make their own choices amongst LEA or other providers, for all of which schools had to pay (only one LEA, Dudley in the West Midlands, continued to provide free training).

CEOs still retained an employer's responsibilities so they saw it as important that teachers were kept informed of pay and conditions of service issues and changes. Hence one CEO was found chasing the personnel department to check that an informative newsletter on these matters had been issued. Responsibility for teachers was also interpreted by CEOs as requiring them to speak on behalf of teachers in outsider forums. CEOs defended teachers against an unsympathetic world. Such a role was adopted by a CEO attending a Confederation of British Industry meeting in 1987 and again at a meeting of the councillors who were chairpersons of sub-committees.

Teachers in policy-making

Teachers, as ever, had to be treated with respect by a CEO but it was unlikely they could be treated with the 'firmness' recommended by a 1950s' CEO (Binns, 1957, p. 141). Consultations with teachers were expected from the 1960s onwards and their powerful influence was welcomed (Browning, 1972, p. 8; Bush and Kogan, 1982, pp. 89, 99, 105) although one 1994–95

CEO noted that such meetings were often only attended by 'five men and a dog'. Perhaps it had been recognized that meetings were not the best way to achieve objectives. One CEO remarked that 'the teachers' lobby on covering [for absent colleagues] is so well organized that the slightest risk will set off a spate of letters'. Hence, although these CEOs rarely met teachers (see Tables 4.8, 4.9, 4.10 and 4.11, Chapter 4), they were frequently approached about them by officers, by letters and by phone calls.

Meetings for overt conveyance of information during these observations were, however, well attended and CEOs in both cohorts addressed large meetings which included teachers. The CEOs' function at large meetings was largely ceremonial, marked by their role as opening speakers during the first 15 minutes followed by an early departure. The information usually seemed well known already, or provided on paper, but the leaders' presence was important to the maintenance of the corporateness of the service. It was also important that the CEO obtained opinions from teaching staff since it was the CEO's job to defend their points of view to councillors. These opinions were not gathered at meetings, however, but from the subordinate officers whose role was to be link person with groups of schools. There were several such prearranged encounters to ensure that CEOs had precise information on practice to back up a general case.

Teachers' lack of personal involvement with policy-making was noted in a jokey exchange between a 1987 CEO and a subordinate officer discussing school holiday dates. There had to be consultation with teachers concerning these and the CEO thought this would be one of the few positive involvements of teachers in policy-making. It was not clear, however, how such involvement would be arranged. The meetings with such packed agendas did not allow for much participation although all CEOs would have agreed with the one who said to principals, 'I'm ready to listen and respond … what I'm really looking for is ideas from you'. When the ideas could be expressed was uncertain.

Teachers' protector

CEOs protected teachers against deprecations by local politicians. They ensured that a good case was put for teachers' views at committee and council meetings. CEOs ensured that councillors received news about the education being provided: pupils winning competitions were mentioned or given time at committee meetings to display their achievements. Principals came in to give talks to working groups of councillors and officers. There were myriad, tiny, scarcely noticeable actions by CEOs protecting teachers. Councillors, for example, who thought teachers should help move furniture from one school amalgamating with another were quickly dissuaded from this idea by the CEO. Councillors who queried high expenditure on a multi-sensory experience for multiply deprived children were shown a video of the event which stilled criticism. Teachers' concerns about their transport to training sessions were made a priority. CEOs also knew they had to adjust to the round of the year: 'Teachers are following an exacting calling and one that entails a lot of nervous wear and tear. Towards the end of a long term some teachers are a bit "on edge" (Binns, 1957, p. 141).

School visits: the theory

Contacts between principals, teachers and CEOs arose mainly at large, formal meetings, not an ideal venue for exchanging views. School visits gave opportunities for CEOs to talk with individual principals and to meet teachers, support staff and students. School visits were regarded with universal importance. Such visits were not intended to meet a particular agenda but more to encourage support for central visions, to demonstrate that the leaders were in touch with providers' views and to enable these CEOs to feel, and to demonstrate, that their job was about improving education for pupils.

All the CEOs observed took the trouble to emphazise to me how important were school visits. All of them remarked that, on first taking office, they had planned a regular routine to ensure that each school was visited by the CEO and that site visits were a feature of each week's work. One had the ordered plan of visiting first those schools likely to be a concern of councillors. Next there would be a rolling programme to visit all schools. Eventually, a subject-based route would be followed until the nirvana of being able to 'drop in when I'm passing was reached ... my officers could do it for me but I like to get the feel myself'. Other English CEOs, and their equivalents in Canada, Australia and the USA, likewise attached major importance to school visits and realized that professionals expected them to make many such visits (Gedling, 1986, p. 71; Griffin and Chance, 1994, p. 76; Hickcox, 1992, p. 11; Macpherson, 1985a, p. 187).

Attempts were made to schedule regular visits. As a CEO explained:

> In my first year I spent a lot of time chasing round schools in order to get to know the teachers: soon there was a reputation established that 'here was an education officer who spent his time in schools'. The reputation survived and grew during two terms when I failed to visit any schools. Then a rigorous day a week was set aside and held sacrosanct for school visits. The reputation lived on. Now I spend a continuous three–week period a year in schools.
>
> (Brighouse, 1983, p. 103).

Around the same time, amongst a group of 22 Canadian superintendents, five:

> had attempted to deliberately integrate school visits into their regular work activities. One ... declared that he visited one school each week, another that he visited three schools a month. ... Another ... tried for a half-a-day each week in schools. [Some] complained that they had difficulty finding the time to get out to the schools but in one very dispersed area, the superintendent had visited every classroom.
>
> (Allison,1991b, p. 34).

One USA superintendent is described as embarking on 'a highly visible tour of every school in the district during her first few months as superintendent' (Roberts, 1985, p. 1038).

The importance of the school visit in history seems variable. Brockington (Director of Education, Leicester, 1903–47) himself undertook 412 school visits in one year 'by the use of a motor car ... without unduly interfering with interior office work' (Seaborne, 1968, p. 204). These visits included all 266 elementary schools, some of them twice, and were additional to visits made to governors' and managers' meetings. How long each visit lasted is not recorded. Brockington's contemporary, Henry Morris, the renowned Cambridgeshire CEO, did very few visits and nor did his officers (Mason, 1981). A 1956 CEO maintained that CEOs had 'at best irregular and superficial contact' with schools (Fisher, 1957, p. 252). Commenting on the pre-1972 period, Claire Pratt (CEO, Hillingdon) said 'I went round the schools a great deal more than some CEOs because I felt this to be so important. It is part of my way of personal contact' (Bush and Kogan, 1982, p. 99). Another 1972 colleague (Taylor, CEO, Leeds) remarked that: 'Whenever I was free, I used to go into schools' (Bush and Kogan, 1982, p. 112). One wonders how often he was free. It is also worth noting that he did not think it important enough to make appointments to visit. One CEO noted a change after 1972 when it became impossible to maintain such personal contacts as school visits (Bush and Kogan, 1982, p. 24).

School visits: the practice

Despite all the talk of importance attached to school visiting, only four such visits were made during the 36 days' observations. If something in the diary had to be cancelled to allow for other events, it appeared to be generally the school visits. Always such cancellations were made with regret and indications that something enormously important had superseded the planned visit. None of the CEOs appeared to have a schedule of open visits to schools to fulfil the objectives outlined at the beginning of this section. Only one went on such a visit during the periods of the observations. Other visits were made but they had specific agendas. Canadian superintendents were found to visit schools rarely (Duignan, 1980) and wished they could do more such visits (Hickcox, 1992, p. 11). USA superintendents did not visit 'to the extent that teachers and principals might anticipate' (Griffin and Chance, 1994, p. 76), saying that their days would be very long if they spent more time in schools than they did already.

The CEOs' reasons for visiting schools included attending a breakfast to launch a school's bids for industrial funding during the 1994–95 cohort (see Chapter 3) and taking councillors to visit schools to impress on them the need for building-repair funds during the 1986–88 cohort. The principals and the councillors were encouraged to talk to each other. The CEO talked to teachers, pupils and support staff. He joined in the water play with children, watched a dispiriting science lesson and deflected councillors' suggestions of laying plastic grass and building centralized toilet blocks. The one 'open ended' visit during the observations occurred in 1987. A school particularly wanted to lobby the CEO to increase its funding for science education and the visit was arranged with that primarily in mind. The CEO added a call on the disaffected pupils' unit, a tour of most of the rest of the school and lunch shared with pupils. Superficially, the visit gave the CEO an opportunity to spread the corporate message to a fairly recently appointed principal, provide an apologia for the lack of science resources since needs here had to be balanced against all those of the rest of the area and to boost morale by offering praise to the principal and staff. Covertly, the CEO wanted to assess prospects for the post of deputy principal which was shortly to be advertised. The visit was comprehensive and pacey. Talk was with the principal and a senior member of staff. The visit stayed focused on the central issues.

It would be easy to criticize these CEOs for making few site visits to make contact with their customers, i.e. the core professionals. Do CEOs in other public or private services regularly visit their outlets and arrange to meet frequently, formally or informally, those who might be termed, the line managers? LEAs are large organizations with substantial numbers of schools; the smallest of the LEAs in this study maintained just over 100 schools and the largest had just over 500, with additional study and teachers' centres, and some centralized curriculum provision services. It is, perhaps, no accident, that the CEO amongst these cohorts best remembered for his approachability was in the smallest organization in which no school was more than 15 minutes from the central office. It has also to be remembered that CEOs attended many school functions, often in personal time, and obviously there were visits to schools for more official reasons that often included informal chats with school staff. All these CEOs had delegated subordinate officers as links with the schools so that there were ways of finding out what schools wanted. None the less, they all stressed the importance of personal site contact – yet they all seemed to have decided that other work mattered more.

The core servicers: deputies and officers

An officer class

The in-house subordinates of CEOs in English local government are titled, 'officers', an interesting terminological contrast with those doing the same work in central government whose nomenclature is 'civil servants', or with those undertaking similar tasks in businesses who might be termed, managers or office staff. I prefer the neutral Americanese, staffers, for this group but officers is what they are called and this term will be used here. The word seems to imply an expectation of military discipline and hierarchy with clear line management but, since all are officers, there is also the expectation that they are capable of operating with creative autonomy within a generally agreed mission. The largest part of the CEOs' encounter time was spent with fellow officers (39.33 per cent in 1986–88; 42.39 per cent in 1994–95) and these are discussed here in the groupings of deputies, senior teams and other ranks.

Deputies

The 1986–88 cohort spent 10.5 per cent of their encounter time with deputies; for the 1994–95 cohort, this was reduced to 5.07 per cent. This is explained by the reduction in the number of deputies. One or two deputies had been common (Griffith, 1966). Three of the 1986–88 cohort had one each and two had three each. Those with more than one deputy had functional delegation. Those with only one had more multi-purpose delegation. By 1994–95, financial stringencies had led to deputy posts not being replaced as the holders retired. Two of the second cohort had no deputies (one of these had previously had three) and the other three had one each. One CEO retained a deputy but the deputy was located in another building at considerable distance physically from the CEO's office.

The decrease in deputy support between the first and second cohorts obviously created increased workloads but also the loss of companionship (deputies popped in for brief informal sessions more frequently than any other group) and of someone at senior level with whom to have tactical discussions which occupied much of the time with deputies. 'You can't present it to committee like that, you'd be massacred' was one CEO's advice to a deputy. 'When shall we set the date for the union meetings?', 'What should be included in that letter to teachers?' 'Are we all agreed that this is our common line on this issue?' 'What statements should we make publicly – a lot of professionals are going to feel let down by this'. Deputies were also the people with whom CEOs reflected on implications of changes in central government policies.

Regular CEO/deputy interactions were exchanges of information about events each had attended separately or about progress on policy initiatives for which each was responsible. Deputies also shared the work at political committees in which some CEOs alternated the leadership on items with their deputies. Meetings with deputies were informal and wide-ranging. A 1987 example had no agenda and its 30 minutes wandered across

- union meetings on budgets
- a dispute at a school which might get out of hand
- the need for more educational psychologists
- charges for exercise books and pencils
- gathering views on the 1987 Education Bill on its passage through Parliament

- debates about whether deputy principals should be allowed to apply for principalships in their own schools
- speculation on how politicians would react to the list of schools needing increased maintenance budgets
- naming of small schools for closure and more speculation on politicians' reactions to this most emotive of issues
- appointments of LEA representatives as school governors
- a decision not to establish a post of an arts development officer
- discussion on a new examination board
- whether an officer could have secondment
- who would accept an invitation to lunch
- who would lead on multicultural education
- which senior officers would be available during the schools' half-term holidays.

None of this was world-shattering. One assumes the week might have managed without it but the system moved on more easily because of it. Miles of paper were potentially saved. The corporate whole was better served and linked. The CEO knew there were supporters and sharers. The deputies were gaining insights into top levels of policy-making that were important for those going on to CEO posts. Discussions with deputies were the second stage of a CEO's strategic thinking, as it was with deputies that ideas would be tested in their early stages. A deputy was defined by one CEO as providing a complementary role – 'the CEO is concerned with broad strategy, the deputy with detailed implementation ... we share between us the monthly meetings that we hold with each member of the senior team'. Setting these advantages against needs to save money, political and public feelings that LEAs are over-bureaucratized, the fact that no one would mount lobbies to save deputies and that CEOs feel responsible for maintaining the core providers in classrooms, the loss of deputy posts seems inevitable. 'Councillors have the idea that you can solve budget problems by chopping off a few managers', commented one CEO.

Chopping off the deputies was proposed by both the Maud (1967) and Bains (1972) Committees on local government restructuring but Jennings (1977) considered that local government reorganization in 1974, which created larger authorities, revived the need for a deputy role. The coming year, 1996–97, will see some LEAs returned to their pre-1974 size and with that, presumably, will come reinforcement for executing the deputy role. Its history does not appear to have been very long, as Stewart Mason, for example, who became Leicestershire's CEO in 1947, had to insist on having one appointed because of the workload. He appointed from outside the LEA because his existing staff 'were hard working and very good chaps but they weren't people of vision' (Mason, 1981). In this interpretation, the deputy paralleled the strategic role of the CEO. During both periods of these observations, this role was also shared with a whole team of senior officers.

Senior management teams

'White, male ... patriarchal ... [and] charismatic' (Heller and Edwards, 1992, pp. 12–13) is the persistent image of effective leadership (Al-Khalifa, 1989). Delegated authority, empowered staff and team working are the late twentieth-century additions which appear to conflict with it. The conundrum is that it has to be the strong leader who gives away power and organizes teams (Bennett, 1994, p. 42; Kirby and Colbert, 1994, p.48; Wallace and Hall, 1994, p. 184). The need to delegate arose from practical difficulties in ensuring an adequate span of control in large organizations and in meeting demands articulated in the wider political environment for greater participation in decision-making (Hoyle, 1986). These acquired almost messianic force as 'Belbinized' teams (Belbin, 1981) in the 1980s. This had also been anticipated earlier in local government with the reforms of the 1970s. These not only expected corporateness within local authorities as wholes (see Chapter 5), but also within each department of local authorities. The CEO's responsibility was defined as 'to keep the staff operating as a powerful team' (Browning, 1972, p. 5).

All the CEOs in both cohorts had senior management teams. Their meetings were much as those imagined by the novelist Stanley Middleton as having been managed by his fictional retired CEO. These were monthly strategy meetings in which he 'suggested new approaches, criticized current proposals, showed how much money could be saved, roughed up the government ... he had energy and grasp' (Middleton, 1986, p. 105). The real-life Gedling (CEO, Dorset) reported a monthly meeting of seven of the senior education officers, for a day with agenda and papers 'widely circulated throughout the department and on each occasion we invite two colleagues ... papers for each item are carefully prepared, the minutes of other groups are received ... the morning is spent on ... specific ... immediate matters, the afternoon devoted to a wide-ranging and forward-looking review of a part of the service' (Gedling, 1986, p. 71). Senior team meetings do not seem to have changed in function since Jennings (1977, p. 119) wrote that CEOs did not use these meetings to resolve problems but as a 'gathering point for opinions, for questions, for the issuing of further orders'. Canadian superintendents were reported as having similar meetings. Working with senior officers 'is ... an important medium though which the CEOs draft the scripts, rehearse key parts and ensure the readiness of essential props in preparation for meetings with the ... board' (Allison, 1991a, pp. 32-3).

A 1994 meeting summarized the genre. The team arrived in informal mode but chatting stilled as they lined up around the table. The CEO took the position of power at table head but the discussion travelled equally around the room with apparently little need to move the agenda items formally. Discussions started at various points around the table. Not all of them involved the CEO nor were all remarks directed through the CEO.

Personnel reports covered applications for principalships, restructuring of departmental responsibilities, a new officer's appointment, contracts for the privatized cleaning service, induction on health and safety issues and updating of the handbook on teachers' pay and conditions. School matters centred around meetings to be arranged for CEOs to address governors. The major strategic issues concerned social deprivation and tackling equal opportunity needs, the likelihood of schools opting out of local maintained status and the current central government initiated review of the structure of local government. After these CEO-led items, other members of the team introduced their concerns and queries; small schools wanted more 'user-friendly' finance systems; the inspection service reported success in its bids for contracts to inspect schools; the police had requested information about statemented[1] pupils as part of research into analysing links between offences committed and pupils' academic records; there were proposals for an HIV/Aids discussion; councillors were implying that officers were not giving them full information on some budget issues in order to ensure that officers' views dominated those of councillors. Like all such meetings, it dithered frequently from the major to the minor but the meeting lingered only on the strategic items. In another authority, the meeting concerned itself only with one major, strategic item.

Assessing the effectiveness of corporate management teams was not possible from short observations. Given, however, the large number of contacts between CEOs and individual officers in ordering the activities of LEAs, one wonders how much change there has been from the 1960s and 1970s. Despite the importance attached to collegiality even then (Browning, 1972, p. 9), 'in conducting relations with senior staff, CEOs could operate entirely one-to-one, maintaining separation amongst the service branches' (Birley, 1970, p. 85). Team operation could blur responsibilities and cause resentment though with care, 'it is an effective and natural way of conducting affairs'.

Officers

How CEOs ordered their relations with their subordinate officers other than in the senior team meetings was significant, especially as they were the people with whom they spent the majority of their encounter time (28.83 per cent, 1986–88: 37.32 per cent, 1994–95). This time was used in much more frequent and much shorter interactions than with other groups and hence there are difficulties in categorizing the myriads of brief exchanges which took place in and out of offices, in car parks, corridors and in the few minutes before and after major meetings. Local authorities have been described as 'personnel bureaucracies' (Allinson, 1984, pp. 24–5). As such, there is a high concentration of authority (thus the centrality of the position of CEO), standardization of procedures and control of the work flow and low structuring of activities which collectively provide opportunities for the exercise of initiative, but an initiative that needs monitoring since the CEO is responsible for it.

Tactical plays with officers

Many of the meetings with officers were similar to the warming-up and warming-down exercises which began and ended the CEOs' days (see Chapter 3). Informal discussions on tactics with officers preceded formal meetings with other players in the game. Informal discussions with officers followed the formal meetings in order to plan action on the outcomes. At the warming-up stage, questions were posed such as: 'How can we present the options so that everyone feels they have achieved something?' (preliminary to a meeting about the opening of a new school in 1986). Officers were asked to redraft documents so that they were clearer for political consumption. CEOs teased out the essentials of long reports to be summarized in speeches to the politicians. The niceties of voluntary association politics and of how an officer should cope with these were outlined. Agendas were carved up amongst the officers so that each would speak on particular items. The CEO was helped with speech-writing for an event presenting prizes at a college. Warming-down sessions included checking what had to be put into effect immediately before formal minutes were typed, interpretations of speeches at meetings, and chat about what political attitudes had been revealed and how these would affect future developments. CEOs summarized decisions and indicated levels of importance to be attached to decisions and how quickly they should be tackled as a consequence.

Canadian superintendents' meetings with officers were largely focused on the 'internal operations of the system' (Allison, 1991a, p. 33), by which was meant issues such as implementing a school computer system or negotiating with teachers. The distribution of English CEOs' time with officers can be judged from Table 6.2 in Chapter 6. The three managerial items listed were largely the outcomes of the time spent with officers.

The CEOs' personnel management functions

The importance of this aspect of the CEOs' work is indicated in Table 6.2 (Chapter 6). The 1986–88 cohort spent 33.10 per cent of their encounter time on people management, just slightly more than the time they spent with politicians. By 1994–95, the people management time had decreased to 18.02 per cent, apparently having been replaced by more time spent on financial management.

Following a CEO through one day gave some indication of the formal personnel matters which arose. Four minutes early in the day dispatched letters about salary payments for an officer and one about a salary increment for a teacher. Both matters were brought to the CEO's attention by a subordinate officer without prior warning, yet the CEO was clearly knowledgeable about the individuals concerned (total staff was approximately 5,000 teachers, 250 officers). The CEO had an important role in protecting the size of the service and justifying the continued employment of staff. Hence there was preparation of materials and tactics with an officer so that the CEO could present a well-supported case at a committee meeting later that day. The CEO's function in that committee was to expound on notions which might have seemed complicated to the non-educational expert politicians such as 'full time equivalents' and the significance of variances in these especially when obfuscated by the necessary statistical data revealing, for example, that there was a 92.5 manpower implication or that the totals had been offset by demographically calculated reductions. The CEO at the committee which considered a report containing this terminology congratulated those councillors who understood the report. The CEO's role as staff protector was also evident at discussions with the senior management team concerning answers to be made to politicians' queries about how schools were staffed. The politicians were very interested in using pupil–teacher ratios as a staffing measure. The CEO saw his role as making politicians aware of how crude a measure this was.

The senior team that day also reviewed overall staffing levels in the service, again as preparation for later presentation to politicians. The CEO also had a brief chat about a new principalship appointment. Staff training was a further responsibility within the CEO's ambit. On this day, it came up as decisions to be taken on whether staff should be recommended to attend courses on negotiating skills or education law. There was planning for a departmental seminar on quality and another on education's place in the authority's medium-term plan. At the end of the day, the CEO had to consider an application for a year's secondment.

All these formal items took up 25 minutes of that particular CEO's day. In addition, there were many fleeting interactions which constituted good, informal personnel management. Staff were made to feel important, staff were made aware that the CEO was around – the CEO had to maintain a friendly working atmosphere. Casual remarks to staff about their holidays, their health, their appearance, visiting staff in their offices rather than sending for them, calling staff by their first names – all these made staff feel good. The CEOs were adept at delivering praise and support, 'You must have put hours of work into that – it's really good'; 'It's a good thing you're on top of this issue so well'. Several spent time touring the offices expressly to give thanks for good work (one added to the verbal thanks with champagne). Most remarked that they thought that such touring was vital but mainly built it into other required movement around the building (such as travelling to committee meetings). Officers were made to feel that the CEO had personal knowledge of them. A list of 57 staff for redeployment or premature retirement was presented to one CEO. The CEO seemed aware of the personal circumstances and professional roles of each of them.

In addition to delivering praise to the officers concerned, the CEOs had a role praising officers to others involved in the education service, as when school principals were told that 'pressure from officers will ensure you get what you want from councillors'. The chief executive was phoned after a council meeting to defend education officers who had been criticized. 'Our AEOs (assistant education officers) have done more than those in other departments' stated a firm CEO.

On formal personnel issues, the CEO was the last court of appeal for queries. Could a member of staff be re-employed as a part-timer once having accepted premature retirement compensation? (No.) Are relocation packages applicable to trainees? (Maybe.) Is it to be a half- or a full-time appointment for a post leading governor training? (Full.) How many staff would be financially supported to attend a conference? Which of the candidates interviewed should be appointed?

Delegation to officers

Superintendents in the USA were found to delegate, assigning specific responsibilities for a school effectiveness programme to officers who also took on the political role of liaising with the district advisory committees on effectiveness (Griffin and Chance, 1994, p. 79). Similar patterns of delegation were instituted by the CEOs in this study. Usually the formal patterns of delegation were combinations of geographical and functional responsibilities and were usually assigned with the agreement of the senior management teams. Alterations of job responsibilities and regradings of posts then had to be reported to the political committee responsible for personnel by the CEO.

Observation revealed little about the reality of individualized delegation. Colleagues of the CEOs gave their perceptions. Of one CEO, it was said that 'he only appears to delegate to other officers. He could equally well answer the questions asked in committee himself – he gets himself into a state before committees'. To me as the observer, this CEO seemed very content to leave much to other officers to decide. A second seemed much more involved but not in the interventionist sense. There was more of a spirit of intense interest in all that was being done. A colleague later described this CEO as 'centralizing'. Observed delegations were fleeting and often entailed asking officers to seek information the CEOs needed as background for committee presentations, or drafting letters that would later be issued in the name of the CEO. Delegation also gave CEOs the chance to allocate degrees of importance to events. Meeting a parents' lobby against closure of a small school was passed to the officer with responsibility for that geographical area. Meeting a lobby for the revival of football in schools was retained by the CEO.

Once there is delegation, there must be some monitoring. For senior staff this occurred mainly informally since there were many contacts daily to enable the CEO to be informed of progress. In addition, some CEOs arranged monthly review sessions with staff and these were shared with the deputy. For junior officers, there would be checks through the CEO reading documents which would go out under the CEO's name. 'This letter is "oldspeak". It must be rewritten' demanded a CEO throwing the offending document back *via* the writer's line manager with the advice to help the subordinate learn new words. On another occasion, there was, 'Has that letter gone out yet – it's important we make a rapid response – and you must go to the school personally – and arrange for a psychologist to go and talk to them – the LEA will pay'. All this was the CEO's instructions to an officer responsible for a school needing help following the deaths of children on a school outing. An angry CEO confronted another officer with 'Why isn't this ready? We're in desperate trouble. Get it round to the deputy's house this evening and I'll pick it up on my way to the meeting'.

Officers were aware of the need to delegate upwards anything that might have political repercussions. A letter was brought in from the school allocations department. It contained complaints from the deputy leader of one of the political parties. The CEO took over the matter from the officer. Queries popped up about to whom should a free LEA video about Industry Year be sent. The items promoted to the first division of the CEO were invariably those likely to have political or public relations implications or on which there was no case law to follow.

Making policy was sometimes a shared delegation. Departmental meetings have been described as bringing 'the department more closely together and achieving a greater coherence of policy' (Gedling, 1986, p. 71). One such meeting occurred during the observations so they were not a common occurrence but their role in strategic planning was important. The day began with strategy relating to only one area of the LEA's work and this was lead by the relevant specialists, not the CEO. It was, however, at the CEO's instigation that the meeting was held: 'There are some big problems here that I'd like us to get some answers to ... I'm very committed to changes ... our record is a disgrace compared with other LEAs'. The CEO's role was to feed in such comparative information to encourage action. Once decisions were agreed, the CEO's task was then to find the money to expedite them and to get councillors' agreement.

A monarchical concept

CEOs' decisions to have much less contact with principals and teachers than with officers may be significant in that principals and teachers have tended to see the CEO in a monarchical role. In opting out of this role, CEOs may have lost their subjects. Once the subjects are emancipated (given freedom to manage their own schools), the monarchy needs to be prominent to hold the schools together. Being prominent entails being seen, in order to meet the wish-fulfilment needs many have for authority figures.

'In my early days as head,' wrote one principal, 'the first time I rang the CEO personally, he actually came directly on to the line and I thought, "It's

God himself"' (Dudley, 1996, p. 10). The same CEO was described on his retirement as having 'reigned supreme'. The monarchical mode was marked in other ways too. One visiting principal remarked on leaving the CEO's office that 'I always feel better for seeing X' and this was despite the fact that the CEO concerned had been unable to accede to the school principal's requests. It was interesting to note that the principal walked out of the CEO's office backwards, head slightly inclined. School visits had a feel of a medieval monarchical progress. Touring a refurbished primary school and its new nursery, for example, a fluttering of assorted teachers accompanied the CEO's inspection procession all pointing out different features to the CEO and his officers, the assumption being that even one close to the CEO might be usefully approached to transmit views to the person at the top. The visit culminated in a feast lovingly prepared as a 'special' by the dinner ladies.

Meetings with large groups of principals inevitably concluded with a queue of supplicants requiring a CEO's personal responses to their individual enquiries. Usually, these were very trivial issues which appeared to give the questioners the chance to remind the monarch of their existence more than to seek information, to request the CEO's blessing for something already decided or to issue personal invitations to visit a school. The importance of the visual blessing was also underlined at a large meeting with primary school principals, one of whom remarked how important it was as 'They're the only way I get to see you, Director'. The other way was to invite the CEO to school concerts or exhibitions but with between 100 and 500 of these each year, it would be impossible to attend them all. Those that attracted the CEO's attendance considered themselves favoured indeed. Similar anticipations attached to US superintendents who had to attend 'more ball games, concerts and community events than one thought existed' (Konnert and Augenstein, 1990, p. 219), and they were expected to take their partners too.

The monarchical mode was one of those which found expression in the CEO's relations with their subordinate officers. While none of the CEOs observed could be described, as was one of their predecessors, as having 'surrounded himself with cyphers' (Jones, 1988, p. 180) there was generally a sense of being at a medieval court in which followers visited the CEO to obtain approval, present their achievements in a good light, subvert future criticisms, pass information (especially concerning praise for the CEO's accomplishments) and plot action. Medievalism was most evident in the case of the CEO whose office was at the extreme edge of the building at the end of a long, wide corridor. Office doors on either side of the corridor were ajar as the CEO passed and officers leapt out to speak with the CEO briefly almost as if seeking the cure for the King's Evil.[2] Medievalism was least evident in the case of the two women CEOs, one of whom continued to use the more domestic surroundings of the small office she had used while a deputy CEO. Medievalism was generally visually supported by the size and furnishings of CEOs' offices (see Chapter 2). The term 'medievalist' used here is not intended to imply criticism; it is rather a naturally arising format of leadership as other studies show (Gronn, 1996, pp. 14–15), though the specific terminology has not been used.

How do all the changes in service provision affect the CEO's monarchical role? Can the leading manager be a strategist when all the units over which to strategize are each sovereign and required to make their own plans? Can the leading manager be a services' tactician when each service must operate autonomously and balance their own accounts? Can the CEO be seen as the spokesperson for the consumers who can now make their views effective as customers? Answers to these questions might, at first sight, seem likely to be negative. The monarchical role has tended to leave CEOs isolated amidst their small courts of officers.

Positive rethinking might leave the monarchy intact. In 1996, Tony Blair, leader of the national Labour party, described Britain as becoming a stake-holder democracy. The stakeholders are the customers, but recently enfranchised and in need of education for their new role, education which it might be the responsibility of a leading educationalist to organize. The stakeholders could well include the CEOs themselves, relearning the skills of affecting central policy from a lobbyist viewpoint. Amongst the newly enfranchised stakeholders of late twentieth-century democracy, CEOs would be the most politically experienced and hence might become significant in local circles. Managing stakeholders has long been a role for CEOs who can put those abilities to good use in the new state format. The restructuring of the education services could move the role forward from the Middle Ages to the Lord Protectorship of Oliver Cromwell's seventeenth-century English republic or to a modern analogy with the managing director of a franchised business. Someone still has to hold together the franchisees and to be the front person for accountability to stakeholders.

This could be the CEO. The next chapter investigates the relationships with stakeholders to see what are the auguries for this Lord Protector role.

Notes

1 Pupils with extensive special needs arising from, for example, physical or mental impairments, have to have a statement made of their needs and their entitlement to special assistance. Less than two per cent have such statements.

2 Ceremonial touching to cure illnesses was initiated by French medieval kings and imported to England in the sixteenth century by Henry VIII.

CHAPTER 8

Stakeholders in the days

Compacts,[1] contacts, revitalizing inner cities, new factories, new training, enterprise, NVQs, GNVQs,[2] single regeneration budgets from the European Union, information technology capabilities, less academic emphasis, mobile workforces, multi-skilling – these were the topics of conversation which intercalated the courses of a dinner for an area's leaders of economic and social life attended by a 1995 CEO. Several such moments occured for the 1994–95 group. Not quite so many for their 1986–88 counterparts but it was during this first period that the industry–education links began and which had extended by 1994–95. Industry and Education Year marked the start for the 1986–88 cohort. It was one of those items in the 'it seems like a good idea' category. By 1994–95, it had become an accepted part of the CEOs' theatre of operations. This included, stage left, other stakeholders with the business leaders, notably parents and governors who were only standing offstage in 1986–88. Centrally, but moving stage right, were the politicians (see Chapter Nine) and the unions. Still outside were the pupils, and hanging around the set at odd angles were the academics, religions' representatives and the media. In the centre were the CEOs, 'visible honest brokers' as defined by one of the group observed.

Tables 4.10 and 4.11 mark the changes in contacts with these stakeholder groups between 1986 and 1995. The most obvious change was in CEOs' contacts with their internal stakeholders, i.e. the officers (Chapter 7). Contacts with them rose significantly whilst interactions with elected politicians and with principals and teachers declined. Less obviously, there were slight increases in contacts with most other external stakeholders (except school governors where there was a small decline) and a growth in the variety of stakeholders. The unions remained in their established, formal consultation mechanisms but these had a feel of being 'yesterday's solutions'. The newer entrants to the stakeholders' groups were still milling about as not-quite-legitimated pressure groups with a recognition but an unclear role and without established routes within which to play this role. A simplistic interpretation would be that the old pathways of power through influencing principals, teachers and elected politicians were no longer so important, and these had been replaced by an introverted approach in which CEOs looked to their own officers as their prime constituencies. Will this inward-looking period be a short phase as CEOs pick up the other routes to power offered by alternative stakeholders? Indications may be sought from the qualitative data in this chapter describing CEOs' inter-actions with parents, governors, the media, unions, pupils, businesses and other pressure groups.

Parents

A local party leader in one of the 1995 LEAs in which observations took place said, 'Parents as a lobby are always suspect because they're thinking only of the current – just how effective can they be on governing bodies?' The CEO countered this with evidence that parents are often the most committed governors and stated that parents must be encouraged to be involved and informed. One CEO wanted to see a parents' representative body in the area, separate from the local governors' association. Such sepa-ration of stakeholder groups could increase the power of those in the centre, such as a CEO, who would be the link amongst them all.

CEOs in these observations welcomed the idea of parental involvement as a generalized concept and worked to encourage teaching professionals to do the same. In one LEA, it appeared that the 'welcome to parents' policy was an initiative of the CEO but by 1987, he could still only hope that 'there is a fair amount of commitment amongst primary schools now for our atti-tudes. If we get it right at primary, we've a secure base'. Such a view was echoed by a 1988 CEO who thought that parents had considerable influ-ence. 'What we believe to be professionally best ... may not be what the community thinks is best. If the arguments are good they would probably win and rightly so' (Bush *et al.*, 1989, p. 117).

On specific issues relating to parent involvement, CEOs could be less sanguine, in particular where proposed school closures could attract oppo-sition from parent lobbies and in matters relating to parents' rights to choose their children's schools. Prior to 1980, parents had to send their chil-dren to the schools in their zones as determined by the LEA. Appeals against zoning were possible but it was an arduous route and few parents changed their children's schools. Between 1986 and 1995, zoning was relaxed and parents gained the right by law to express a preference for the school they wished their children to attend. LEAs were then left with the problems of planning for unpredictable demands, having to make decisions on what free transport would be provided, being unable to meet all parents' preferences for places at the most favoured schools, and deciding the fate of unpopular schools which too few parents wanted for their children.

Consequently, numbers admitted to popular schools were a cause of interest to parents. 'My phone will be leaping off the hook later today,' predicted a 1995 CEO when admissions figures looked likely to cause reactions. A 1987 CEO had more control; an amalgamated school that was low on numbers had its roll increased by the LEA's refusal to fund children's travel to schools outside its zone. In selecting which schools had to close,[3] CEOs included the absence of parent lobbyists as a determining factor.

Direct contacts with parents were few for either cohort. A couple were encountered during a school visit and the CEO went to talk to them specifically. The rest of the contacts were at large formal, meetings. Such a style has been criticized for deterring parent involvement. Marsden's study of working class access to education found parents 'baffled at the ... bureaucracy ... they had imagined a personal chat with the CEO' (quoted in Birley, 1970, p. 107). A 1960s' CEO, however, thought that parents were clear about what they wanted and were more articulate 'as a result of our having educated them better' (Bush and Kogan, 1982, p. 102). Such strong articulation of parents' demands was suggested as of prime importance in the development of bilingual schools in Wales (Humphreys, 1989, p. 43). Formal meetings with parents duirng these observations concerned, for example, community consultations on the opening date for a new school. Such formal meetings had been the system in the past too when, for example, Stewart Mason, Leicestershire's CEO, had instituted public meetings to explain the LEA's comprehensive school plans to parents in the 1960s (Jones, 1988, p. 178).

CEOs were not prepared for this public role. 'He's weakest in public meetings, especially with parents' commented a councillor of one CEO observed in 1986. This was to be expected. CEOs did not train for this type of persuasion exercise nor did they experience it very much in their progress to the top, as exemplified by Middleton's fictional retired CEO who 'had been faceless ... he had kept out of the public eye while he was at work' (Middleton, 1986, p. 210). The 1986–88 role was to inform parents (usually through written publications) not to persuade them. By 1994–95, CEO meetings with parents had become almost the equivalent of hustings in which CEOs touted for parental 'votes' for locally maintained schools.

Parents were talked about by CEOs and their subordinate officers, rather than talked with. Parents' letters were passed on to CEOs from councillors. Parents' views were guessed at and the guesses used to justify CEOs' resistance to ideas proposed by councillors and teachers. Parents wrote to complain to CEOs about reductions in staffing at their children's schools. Very occasionally a CEO talked to parents by phone or had phone messages relayed by subordinate officers. Usually, these concerned individual children with specific learning difficulties. CEOs were rapidly helpful in such cases, possibly mindful of the prospects of media interest in children with special needs. Parents emerged as school governors. Parents were criticized in CEOs' discussions for not attending the annual parents' meetings at their schools.[4] Parents were seen as a group to whom the education service had to be marketed. Parents' rights were recognized if not overwhelmingly and lovingly supported since CEOs had to support the rights of everyone, including those of the pupils who usually have no voice.

CEO–parent links were tenuous and in the very early stages of gestation even by 1994–95. Parents had not acquired the position of legitimated stakeholders. There were no parents' consultative committees as there were for teachers' unions and, in a few cases, for governors. There were no co-opted places on the Education Committee for parents. Enfranchised parents were very new. Their pressure groups were not well established nor knowledgeable in the ways of micro- or macro-politics. No one had assessed their power and in 1994–95, CEOs needed the force of the old power élites, i.e. the teachers' unions and councillors, rather than parents. One of the 1986–88 cohort recognized this conundrum at a meeting of governors and councillors about opening a new school; the CEO suggested that as they had all been guessing what parents might or might not like, then there should be a meeting with parents to find out. Councillors opposed the idea. The public, consultative meetings I observed symbolized the coming of the parents' new power élite to replace councillors. While it remains uncertain how far this new élite will develop, CEOs stay with the old.

Governors

During the years since 1986, LEAs began to realize that governors could be valuable allies. They were in schools, like the Trojan horse, sent in there by central government presumably expecting governors to support their views. Governors, however, quickly become co-opted into being school supporters (Bacon, 1978, p. 182; Thody, 1992). From this position, LEAs could rescue them by offering training and by encouraging the formation of local governors' councils. Local authorities also appointed some of the governors. Thus the inhabitants of the Trojan horse could change sides before the war began. These warriors were, however, volatile. Their track record as non-stipendiary mercenaries was not well enough known for CEOs to be sure how to marshal them most effectively.

Governors have a secure power base in schools, mandates from outside the LEA and legal authority to manage schools. Potentially they offer alliances for CEOs, although this was not recognized at the beginning of the 1980s when CEOs appeared reluctant to cede power to governing bodies and defined them as unimportant and incapable of understanding education (Bush and Kogan, 1982, p. 142). Governors' methods of appointment put them in opposition to elected councillors. Most of the army of governors[5] are on short service commissions[6] which inhibit outsiders gaining their loyalty. Some are elected and others co-opted from sources external to the LEA. Governors' legal roles relieve CEOs of both administration and direction of schools. Governors need educational expertise which CEOs and their officers can provide but which councillors cannot. Governors need someone external to their schools who can assist them in retaining some independence. What did the observations show about CEOs' recognition of governors as potential allies?

For the 1986–88 cohort, the governors' roles were in their infancy. This was the period in which CEOs had discussions about appointing governor training co-ordinators. These were to organize the education of these new stakeholders almost in a re-enactment of that late nineteenth-century demand to educate our masters when the suffrage was extended to working men.[7] There were the first consultative meetings with governors and promises to establish regular sessions similarly. Those first meetings gave governors the CEOs' interpretations of what the 1988 Education Reform Act might entail. One such meeting set a tone of interaction. Governors were divided into discussion groups and the CEO circulated to gather views. Pulling these together at the end of the meeting, the CEO asked governors not to resign in view of the potential workload. Another such meeting was being organized during a 1987 observation. 'The CEO must address it' said the officer concerned, 'the governors will come if it's the director leading it, but not for me'.

By the time of the 1994–95 observations, there had been a subtle shift in the tone of CEOs' connections with governors. The time spent with governors decreased slightly, and they were more often a topic of conversation in cohort two than in cohort one. The powers of governors in self-managing schools were well established and recognized by 1994–95. At a party briefing by a CEO, one of the 1995 councillors pointed out that governors are 'now really clued up – just as knowledgeable as school principals now that governors have to carry the can'. At a meeting with councillors, many of whom were also governors, there were questions about how many teachers were to be made redundant. It was made clear that this was a governors' decision alone.

Officers and councillors were, however, sceptical that governors were capable of this level of decision-making. In one LEA, the local inspectors presented a report indicating that they perceived school principal appointments made by governing bodies to be erratic and idiosyncratic, and to show preference for internal, instead of external, candidates. One councillor said he wouldn't like too many meetings with governors, because they were just not clear, a view supported by an officer who, on presenting budgets to governors found them so overwhelmed that they forgot what they wanted to say. The CEO reminded both officers and councillors that 'the governors are frightened of you – we need to groom some of them'.

Grooming included CEOs demarcating where their remit ended and that of governors began. In 1995, when governors threatened to resign *en masse* nationally, a CEO made clear to the local party leader that the local education authority could not issue advice to governors on this matter – it was a case for governors to decide what they wanted to do. The CEO could issue data which could inform governors' decisions but could not take the decisions for governors. In the case of the threatened resignations for example, a CEO first took soundings to see what other LEAs were doing. Then a note was issued to all governors to alert them that there was no such thing as mass resignation (it could only be by individual school), that if they resigned the LEA was required by law to seek replacements for them and, if none could be found, the LEA would have to govern the schools themselves and would suspend the schools' powers to manage their own finances.

In other areas of responsibilities, CEOs indicated the limit of their authority over governors even though some councillors assumed CEOs could issue instructions to governors. Governors also intimated that they looked to the leadership of the LEA, as when they wanted a CEO to orchestrate a campaign against cuts imposed by central government. The CEO made clear that leading such campaigns was not a role for the LEA; governors had to lead it themselves. The campaign did not materialize. In one LEA, the party leader proposed finding extra funding to reduce class sizes in certain schools. The CEO asked the leader to make quite clear to schools that the differential funding being proposed was not on the advice of the CEO. 'There will be governors' objections if some schools get the extra and others don't ... the formula for funding has been welcomed by schools as equitable ... this proposal will change that', one CEO stated firmly. That same CEO had that week had representations from school principals wanting explanations why some schools received funding for nursery education and others did not – they complained of their governors wanting explanations for the inequities.

CEOs were between governors and councillors. When governors were discussed during these observations, the CEOs' intentions were to persuade councillors of the importance of keeping contact with governors. Hence a 1995 CEO tried to encourage councillors to organize a meeting for school principals, chairs of governing bodies and councillors. Behind the scenes, CEOs were searching for ways of finding more active and effective involvement for governors. 'We need to kill off vague partnership groups and find something specific' was a chance CEO thought. In one LEA the 'something specific' became area meetings for school principals and their chairs of governing bodies. The topic was the major system restructuring proposed in the Local Government Review of 1995 which resulted in some areas having their schools transferred to new authorities.

Governors' regional representative associations were new entrants to the stakeholder scene by 1994–95. Two of the areas in which I observed had these associations. They were clearly part of the consultative mechanisms, being present at meetings to discuss appointees to fill vacancies on governing bodies and to discuss the LEA's future budget. These two meetings were symbolic of the growing legitimation of governors in policy-making. The budget projections were bleak and governors were asked what they could do to help. Schools were retaining some funding to carry forward to their next financial year, hence central government was claiming that there was unspent money that should be used for education; but the LEAs did not have control of this money – the governors did. Other items at the meeting related to the governors' role as teachers' employer in their own schools: redeployment, holiday pay, sickness and maternity leave. The seating at the meeting emphasized that governors were still outside the main stream of strategists. Councillors and officers sat together facing the governors' representatives. The CEO orchestrated responses from councillors and officers. The sophistication of governor associations showed in their segmentation. One area had sub-groups for governors of nursery schools and for Black governors though the CEO would have preferred to see one united group. Governors were also honoured in their absence; a CEO reminded the responsible officer to consult the local association when preparing recruitment literature for potential governors.

An unresolved issue was the dismissal of governors. There is no provision in the legislation for removing governors who are either performing their governorship duties unsatisfactorily or who are unsuitable for other reasons. A CEO reported to the senior management team the case of a governor who, in his main work, had been accused of sexual harassment. If the case were proved, such a person might be considered unsuitable for governorship but there was nothing the LEA (or the school) could do.

Media

'We must always remember that we have a big and watchful public, sometimes suspicious, and seldom sympathetic.' Such was the conclusion of a local government author almost 60 years ago (Hill, 1938, p. 123). Local government had, he thought, an adverse press and was much misrepresented. The officers' role was to correct misapprehensions so public opinion moved in favour of local government. This was a continuing role since 'all departments are carried on as it were behind a shop window' (Fisher, 1956, p. 251). All this advice remained apposite for late twentieth-century CEOs.

The CEOs had obvious media awareness although direct contact was very rare. This was noted as unusual by one 1995 CEO. He remarked that it was strange that the four days' observations contained no phone calls from press or radio; 'it must be the only four days in the year when I've heard nothing'. The importance of hearing from, and responding to, media requests grew between 1986 and 1995 since, towards the end of this period, examination results for all schools had to be published in national league tables. CEOs during 1986–88 needed only to worry about league tables published for consumption amongst fellow professionals. CEOs in 1994–95 had every national newspaper and the broadcast media producing league tables for public consumption. The 1986–88 leagues were, however, significant: 'We've got to consider how we'll look in our pupil–teacher ratios' briskly reminded one CEO. The teachers' dispute over pay and conditions prompted the same type of reaction: 'How will the public react when they see what hours teachers are expected to work?' mused a CEO.

CEOs kept an eye on the press cuttings they were sent to see if any responses were needed. One 1994–95 LEA was accused in the *Times Educational Supplement (TES)*[8] of not spending all that it should of its government grant. The deputy CEO drafted a letter to the newspaper to discredit this story. The letter was brought to the CEO for approval. Discussions about shedding staff were felt to need careful handling with local newspapers since it was 'the sort of stuff picked up by the *TES*'. National TV news alleged that the 'education chiefs' of one of the LEAs in which I was observing at the time, were spending 'only £x on administration and were removing 11,000 school places', all of which was a misinterpretation of a press release, according to the CEO. In 1986–88 one CEO was arguing with the *Sun* newspaper[9] about its disproportionate treatment of a story alleging sex parties held by a teacher. The CEO's arguments drew a dismissive letter from the editor about which the CEO complained to the Press Council.

Keeping the press briefed was another responsibility for CEOs in both cohorts. A 1987 first edition of a new religious education syllabus was delayed until the press release could be organized since religious education could be controversial. The CEO was not happy about issuing a press release, feeling it could unnecessarily stir up confrontations, but it was wanted by the chairman of the working party who had produced the syllabus, 'so if he really wants it, he should have his moment of glory,' sighed the CEO. To requests from the local press for information, a 1995 CEO made an appointment to see reporters later that week but stalled their request to interview other staff. An officer asked for a CEO briefing, 'so I don't look a prat with the local press'. Another officer was summoned to a briefing as the local press was rumoured to be attending a public meeting on a school closure, 'an event likely to blow'. A major local press conference was attended by one 1995 CEO but the talking was done by the political leader with the CEO in the background. In return for information and briefings, the press kept their side of the bargain; a local reporter rang to request permission to interview the principal of a local school where there had been problems. 'We've trained them to ask for permission' noted the CEO approvingly and then phoned the principal of the school to warn him and to state that the CEO did not mind if the principal talked to the press. Such was the protection of the CEO in 1987. By 1994–95, CEOs were not in a position to offer that type of preliminary screening.

Unions

Teachers' and principals' unions had several formal, and well-established routes to influence during both 1986–88 and 1994–95. In all these CEOs' LEAs there were teachers' consultative committees which met regularly with the senior officers during both cohorts. The committees had representatives of all six teachers' and school principals' unions. Governors were not represented on these committees, even during the 1994–95 observations although governors were, by these dates, the teachers' quasi-employers. From these formal meetings CEOs carried unions' views to councillors, and to these meetings the CEOs reported councillors' views. 'Councillors are not happy about your unions' inabilities to control your members – they don't like your attitudes and antics'; 'Unions want to feel they've been realistically consulted on that policy … they don't like to feel left out'. The CEOs' role seemed not dissimilar to a solicitor attempting to act for both parties in a divorce and with about as much chance of keeping everyone happy.

The meetings followed standard formats, during both periods of observations, with almost predictable agendas and almost predictably standardized union representation. At least two of the union representatives were 'the men with insider knowledge', usually the ones who also held the places for co-opted teacher representatives at council meetings. They had served long, knew everyone and everything, addressed the CEO comfortably by first name and appeared informally co-opted into the LEA establishment. They usually wore suits. The same types were recorded in the 1960s when the co-opted representatives were four school principals with much personal authority, and a general secretary of the local union branch who made regular personal visits to the CEO (Peschek and Brand, 1966, p. 43). The late twentieth century added the 'once I was an angry young man' group. These sported casual, and unfashionable, sweaters which proclaimed the unlikelihood of their progressing further in their teaching careers. Representative female principals wore suits and were often the unofficial group leaders. Female other ranks either wore soft frocks with gold buttons (and were slim, bubbly and blonde) or wore serious pleated skirts and dark cardigans. One person would sport some indicator of being a real teacher by wearing a lab coat or carrying a bulging bag of marking. The teachers leaned forward, arms on the table. The principals leant backwards, hands across their tummies. All the delegates were apparently closely *au fait* with the agenda items and detailed questions were the norm.

In contrast to other stakeholder meetings, teacher consultative committee meetings could be jargonized as both parties were at home with the educational in-language. This formed a bonding mechanism that appeared to break the employer–employee relationship, although education itself rarely surfaced at these formal meetings which were concerned with pay and conditions for teaching staff. Many CEOs had themselves been teachers, thus facilitating bonding with teacher unions and the legitimating of the CEO by professional colleagues, as had been found in the 1960s (Peschek and Brand, 1966). The importance of this became evident in the many informal conversations between CEOs and union leaders, in which both sides were working to avoid teacher industrial action. Such conversations were private and revealed a degree of disenchantment with the rank and file teachers by both CEOs and union leaders. 'Please regard this conversation as not having taken place' asked one union leader of a CEO after a phone call exchanging mutual disenchantments. Other CEOs shared the sentiments: the unions 'fill me occasionally with despair when they look for conflict not consensus ... will they continue to strut on the teachers' behalf convincing nobody but themselves ... They reflect the growing conflict of management/employee relationships' (Brighouse, 1983, p. 100-1).

The importance of the educationalists' bonding was obvious when there were CEO meetings with school support staff unions, such as nursery nurses, with whom they did not share the same closeness of language and experience. Nursery nurses received little sympathy from one CEO who stated privately 'their job's a doddle' and from another who found it relatively easy to outmanoeuvre the union representative negotiating a pay rise for nursery nurses. The occasion of those negotiations was the only time when I observed a very angry CEO. The anger seemed, however, to be part of the tactics since it caused the union negotiator to lose control and hence the battle too.

The agendas for the formal, regular consultative meetings in both periods of the observations covered issues such as the interpretation of merit pay rules, the consultations over what constituted the teachers' working hours, appraisal, cover for teachers invigilating examinations, sick leave procedures and pay dates. Involvement in policies, such as special needs, was discussed. There was a range of types of meetings in addition to the regular ones including informal *ad hoc* sessions and working groups, as there was in the 1960s and 1970s (Bush and Kogan, 1982, p. 144).

At all of these meetings, the CEOs defended councillors' views to the unions but also indicated areas which, once union agreement had been reached, the CEO would take to councillors to be 'rubber stamped'. This indicated a degree of acceptance of the unions in policy-making that did not emerge with any other groups. Evidence from earlier periods on union acceptance is varied so it is difficult to know how general this union involvement was at the beginning of the observations. In some areas, CEOs saw it as necessity to consult the unions and obtain their support for changes (Bush and Kogan,1982, p. 90; Peschek and Brand, 1966, p. 28). In others, 'the lack of influence is due to the fact that the CEO has taken a very strong grip on educational development' (Peschek and Brand, 1966, p. 100).

The style of the CEOs' meetings with unions during both cohorts' observation was rather cheery. There was a sense that everyone was taking part in a play. Each had a role. The roles were known. There was a tautness while everyone recited the lines the playwright had written but once those lines had been said, everyone could relax and ad lib. When the talk toughened, there was still a restraint which avoided anything boiling over into confrontation. There was bargaining, consensus, working to achieve compromise. There were the standard negotiating ploys of isolating the troublesome and of indicating solidarity with the less problematical. Everyone patiently understood everyone else's point of view even if no one could do anything about differences. There was encouragement for all to participate. There were opportunities for the assertive to shine. They were all part of the establishment.

Smaller meetings were for personnel matters related to individuals. A 1995 member of staff was on sick leave due to stress. The union had to protect the worker's interests but seemed more on the side of the CEO. The CEO clearly knew the details of the case and had several options ready to offer the union so that it did not seem that the CEO was dictating an outcome. The union representatives thanked the CEO profusely for being willing to spend so much time on the case (one hour).

Very much smaller meetings were for jointly agreeing tactics with teacher unions; the importance of joint professional bonding became apparent at such sessions. Two co-opted union representatives on an Education Committee had discussions with a CEO prior to the full committee meeting in a 1987 LEA. The preparatory session was obviously a regular event. 'The co-optees aren't important to the outcomes of votes in this LEA,' the CEO explained privately, 'but it helps to keep good relations'. This meeting discussed how the union representatives could help rephrase a letter to schools. They shared views with the CEO on how a meeting had progressed the previous week when conditions of service were considered. 'If we can keep the hardline backwoodsmen under control, we can be flexible on both sides' commented one union representative approvingly. The CEO concurred and stated that he would indicate to councillors that if they didn't push teachers too hard, then teachers could be malleable. Discussions continued, with the CEO and the union representatives agreeing what not to highlight from the committee papers. Having agreed to the CEO's tactical requests, the union representatives then tried tentative decision-making on issues not for committee discussion that day. They wanted to assess the CEO's views on paying for staff to cover classes of teachers attending training courses. The CEO's response was not quite what they apparently wanted but the CEO reminded them that 'publicly, teacher unions may not be ready to admit that there is agreement on this privately'.

Behind the formalities, the attitudes to unions seemed much the same as those of the public face at meetings with the unions. CEOs were overtly close to the unions because of shared professionalism. On the whole, though, the CEOs leaned towards supporting school principals more than teachers. Additional meetings were, for example, arranged with teacher unions during disputes over conditions of service, 1986–88, because 'principals will need our support over this – we must keep talking to the unions'. One such so-called 'consultative' meeting with the unions was a lengthy (over two hours) session as unions and CEOs mutually reached conclusions on interpretations of conditions of service. The CEO encouraged involvement and listened courteously. What the unions did not know was that the letter to be sent to schools as an outcome of these negotiations had already been written and duplicated ready for dispatch as soon as the meeting ended. The unions left the meeting under the impression that the CEO had still to conduct further internal deliberations and then spend time drafting the letter. 'They'll be hopping mad when the letter reaches schools so soon', commented the CEO.

Business leaders

Consorting with business leaders is not new for CEOs. There are 1960s' records of meetings with the local Trades Council for one CEO and this functioned as a consumers' pressure group which, interestingly, concentrated on 'day-to-day administration in the schools rather than ... questions of educational policy' (Peschek and Brand, 1966, p. 37). Such specific interest was noted in Leicestershire in the 1960s when the Leicester brick lobby was well represented amongst councillors with the consequence that Leicestershire red brick was used for a new school building against the advice of the architects and the CEO (Jones, 1988, p. 144).

In these observations 20 years later, cohort one consorted with business leaders at the formal opening of a management centre, at a regional Confederation of British Industry meeting to launch the competency standards for managers, at a large gathering to initiate a compact between schools and businesses and at a committee planning industry year events. These were all formal and all directly related to education. Cohort two devoted more time to managing the business community. There were events similar to those of 1986–88 (such as raising sponsorship for a technology school) but there were two developments. First, education was, at least superficially, participating in corporate initiatives to decide the future of the authorities as a whole. Whole-town regeneration, and making bids for funds for this from the European Union, required the participation of CEOs in committees and dinners shared with business leaders. Secondly, there were business people incorporated as advisers into the new privatized services of the LEAs (see Chapter 7).

Cohort one talked about business people; cohort two talked with them directly. While business notions still sat somewhat uncomfortably amidst CEOs' responsibilities, there was apparent ease in the relationships between CEOs and business leaders – an ease that was less easy to see in relation with any of the other groups. Despite the formal nature of the contacts observed, it seemed that the CEOs and the business leaders occupied the same status ground unlike any of the other groups. One sensed an almost grudging respect from both parties. Like was, on the whole, talking to like. This was not in the language codes of the contacts CEOs had with their officers, but it had its own codes. As for relations with the other new stakeholder groups, the contacts were still vestigial but this group appeared to have been accepted to some extent within the micro-politics of local government as well as its formal macro-politics.

Pupils

There were no pupil consultative groups in any of the areas in which I observed, nor, as far as I know, in any others. The direct users of education services have no direct contacts with decision-makers, Most are too young to vote and only in very rare circumstances will they be school governors.[10] CEOs' contacts occurred *en masse* at special school events, such as concerts and reading exhibitions and *en passant* during school visits. CEOs did stop to chat to pupils on these occasions. One took every opportunity to talk to the pupils. Those working on computers were asked to explain what they were doing. Another group were asked about the dinosaur displays. Others were joined at water play and helped on to the climbing frame. Pupils came to show the CEO their work which was duly admired. Secondary school pupils were quizzed on why they were doing nothing at the end of one lesson and asked if they had enjoyed a lesson we had seen earlier. A councillor reported that this CEO would 'normally pop off and talk to children on a school visit – he doesn't miss much and is very genuinely concerned'.

Other pressure groups

Both legitimated and non-legitimated groups emerged for these CEOs, though for neither cohort were contacts extensive. A formal, regular consultative meeting was held concerning anti-racist issues in one 1988 observation. A formal lobby was received for a one-off meeting from the Schools' Football Association seeking greater support for football in schools. Irregular lobbies were formed for specific protection rackets during the 1994–95 observations, lining up to prevent cuts in specific services or to prevent closures of particular schools. This accords with observations of a 1988 CEO who reported a change from general stakeholder groups fighting school closures to individualized groups fighting for particular schools (Bush *et al.*, 1989, p. 115).

The regular consultative meeting with the race relations lobbyists was a cause for concern for one CEO. He doubted if it were useful even as an information exchange and was frustrated at the slow pace of change. One of the other participants felt it was extremely important. It was the chance to ensure that the CEO saw the reports: 'for me, the most useful feature is access to the CEO. His presence shows he's taking personal and professional interest – it signals its importance'. Note the similarity here to the monarchical role suggested in the previous chapter. The topics that arose during the anti-racism committee meeting included Indian students who lost entitlement to grants for higher education by taking extended holidays in India on family business, and schools being encouraged to adopt anti-racist policies by being required to establish a committee to deal with this. The CEO opposed this latter on the grounds that 'schools must fulfil their statutory responsibilities but not necessarily all in the same way'. The best way was to require schools to report to their governing bodies, thus indirectly achieving local authority aims. The Black Workers in Education group reported on the needs of new entrants to the profession in order to avoid their feeling isolated. The CEO suggested supports for this. There was a warning that Muslim parents were considering using the provisions of the 1988 Education Reform Act to create Muslim schools. The CEO suggested meeting with those Muslim parents.

Suggesting such meetings with additional pressure groups in order to hear all views and to try to be responsive to several stakeholders was a role suggested for CEOs in previous studies (Griffith, 1966, p. 123). There were concerns that the largest and most articulate groups would most influence policy (Bush and Kogan, 1982, p. 48-9) and that these were middle class dominated, hence the need for the pressure group arena to be opened up. The Muslim representation mentioned in the previous paragraph was of particular significance. Religions are legitimated with representatives co-opted onto the Education Committees of LEAs but it is the Christian denominations which hold these positions, so leaving more recently imported faiths as non-legitimated groups. The Jewish community in the 1960s acquired a 'certain prominence that must be almost unique' in West Ham (Peschek and Brand, 1966, p. 38). During these observations, the Jewish community surfaced briefly for a discussion on a Jewish school opting into local maintained status. Elsewhere the CEO's contacts included a date with the Anglican diocesan education board as part of a regular series of meetings and discussions with officers on the date for release of a new religious education syllabus but, otherwise, religious matters did not impinge on CEOs' activities.

Stakeholder democracy?

Not yet arrived, would be my general conclusion on this. If it is to arrive, it is the CEOs who can make it happen. Observations showed the CEOs to be aware of, and to make use of, views from various stakeholder groups, but how did they gain this awareness?

Only the teachers' and principals' unions were fully legitimated with regular, representative, channels of communication, supporting earlier findings that CEOs appeared to select particular groups on which they conferred legitimacy (Bush et al., 1989). The type and scarcity of CEO contacts with stakeholders did not change significantly between 1986 and 1995 and remained largely unchanged from the conclusions of the Bush et al. (1989) study of CEOs which reported that 39 per cent of their sample had only formal contacts with stakeholders and that only four of their 67 respondents had regular meetings with them. I sometimes felt that there had been little change from the 1970s when a CEO could state that, 'I don't think that public opinion significantly affects the work and policy of a good local education authority' (Cook, CEO Devon, in Bush and Kogan, 1982,

p. 89). This was despite an increase in the numbers of stakeholder groups which had been developing since the 1970s.

For the CEOs in these observations, it appeared chance whether stakeholders became involved. It was almost chance whether CEOs met groups or not and, when they did, time with them was limited and not most suitable for conveying views. Could CEOs claim to be any more in touch with the views of parents, governors or others than could councillors? If not, should CEOs consider structuring relationships with the stakeholders so that it can be shown that other groups are fully consulted?

The coming of the stakeholder in the lives of CEOs is a recognized phenomenon in the USA: 'Community mores, values, needs and educational expectations are of utmost importance to the superintendent ... it exerts the greatest immediate pressure and influence' (Konnert and Augenstein, 1990, p. 13). North Americans are possibly less deferential than are the British (to risk racial stereotypes) and hence do not view the superintendents as quite such educational experts as British CEOs are perceived to be. US citizens have their own ideas about education and pressurize superintendents to put these into effect. Superintendents, however, recognize the parochial nature of community concerns and see it as their job to adapt community wishes to those of national goals (Griffin and Chance, 1994, p. 81), an objective which would not be foreign to English CEOs.

There is general agreement on the rights of stakeholders to be involved. This involvement requires the CEOs, like US superintendents, to provide 'information ... regarding academic achievement, [to seek] the involvement of parents and advisory groups in district programs, [to foster] a relationship with union leaders built on trust, [to ensure] that district instructional goals are communicated to everyone' (Griffin and Chance, 1994, p. 78). This definition puts the onus on CEOs for action and little emphasizes the possibility of a two-way relationship. This was also apparent in the lack of agreement about how far these stakeholders affected policy-making (Bush *et al.*, 1989, pp. 79–80) and about how far they should be allowed to affect it (Griffith, 1966; Hornsby, 1984, p. 116) in view of their undemocratic and partial views (Mann, 1988, p. 25).

On their own, stakeholder groups lack unity, knowledge and the political skills to act effectively. For CEOs, it could be in their interests to organize groups so that they gain these attributes, a task that requires a 'high level of interpersonal skills' (Hackett, 1994, p. 6). An example of the skills needed to mobilize external stakeholders came from the USA in 1996. In California, in one weekend, 20 per cent of its schools were connected cost free to the information super-highway 'in a rare demonstration of community spirit' (Parkes, 1996, p. 3). Sixteen thousand volunteers were directed by experts from 1000 sponsoring companies, led by KQED public television station and the chief scientist at Sun Microsystems, to link five classrooms and the libraries of each of the schools to the Internet. Is not this the type of organization for which CEOs are ideally situated? In this example, there was no mention of the role of the school board superintendents, so perhaps they have as little contact with their external stakeholders in practice as do English CEOs.

Canadian superintendents likewise seemed to have as few interactions with external stakeholders as do their English counterparts. Only four of Allison's 22 Canadian superintendents referred to parents and when they did so it was to associate them with problems (Allison, 1991b, p. 36). Hickcox (1992, p. 11) recorded surprise at finding that for the group of Canadian superintendents whom he studied in 1991, the least time was spent on community meetings 'given the prevailing view that the political aspect of the role at the board and community level are paramount'. Duignan's study of Canadian superintendents in 1980 found that only 0.4 per cent of superintendents' time was spent with pupils.

It could be in the CEOs' interests to spend more time with new stake-holders, to create new allies from amongst these and to legitimate their roles in the micro-politics of LEAs. It is not in councillors' interests since they must retain a general electoral mandate as their strength against central government; consultation outside of government remains as unpopular with elected members as it was in the 1970s (David, 1977, p. 170). CEOs could, and can, claim professional expertise as their mandate but it is no longer politically correct to do so unless there is willingness to put that expertise at the service of the new stakeholder groups. Does this sound altruistic? It is meant to, since CEOs have in the past held the altru-istic high ground as guardians of education. Their guidance on the meaning of 'education' has come almost entirely from within their own profession and from local politicians. It could be time to change that.

Notes

1   Contracts made between local industries and schools that pupils who attend regularly and fulfil certain scholarly requirements will be offered work experience, guaranteed interviews for jobs, possibly training and selection for permanent posts.
2   National Vocational Qualifications. These are the national standards set for each vocation. General NVQs are those being set in schools to provide transferable skills as preparation for later vocational training.
3   Throughout all of 1986–95, there were too many school places for the number of pupils available and the cost of maintaining small schools was disproportionate to their size as the full curriculum had to be provided whatever the size of school. LEAs, therefore, had to select schools for closure. This was always unpopular with teachers, parents and council-lors so it was neccessary to select the schools which were least likely to attract opposition lobbyists.
4   Each school's governing body is legally required to hold a meeting annually for all parents of children at that school. At this meeting,

governors report on how they have managed the school during the previous year. Parents can question the governors and move resolutions if meetings are quorate. They rarely are, as very few parents attend.

5 Each school has between nine and 20 governors depending on size. Hence, with 24,000 schools in England and Wales, there is indeed an army to govern them.

6 Four years is the usual term of office.

7 'I believe it will be absolutely necessary that you should prevail upon our future masters to learn their letters' (Robert Lowe, introducing the Reform Bill, 15 July 1867, in House of Commons).

8 The major weekly newspaper for teachers.

9 A tabloid paper with a large, popular circulation.

10 Pupils were excluded from school governance in the legislation of the 1980s although some areas had pupil governors before this. It is possible for a local political party to select a pupil as an LEA representative and this has happened in one LEA in 1996. Students do serve as elected representatives on the governing bodies of colleges of further education and universities.

CHAPTER 9

Political days

It seemed, from my observations, that there was little overt difference between what appertained during 1986–95 and what happened pre-1986, and that there was little distinction amongst the political parties, at least in their attitudes to central government, as has been noted by other commentators (Edwards, 1991, p. 37).   Two examples illustrate these points.

Example One: Pre-war to pre-millennium

The development of local authorities being elected on party political lines was making the officers' work more difficult as were increasing demands from central government... within his own Council Chamber, 'tomfool' resolutions may be passed against the [CEO's] advice'.
1938 – Hill, L. *The Local Government Officer*, pp. 30, 139

Part way through [the committee meeting] there is a little scurry. One of the opposition has unsportingly asked a question ... to which the sub-committee Chairman does not know the answer. In response to an agonised signal ... [there is] a hasty scribbled enquiry to the Education Officer ... A puzzled visitor notes of committee meetings that nothing seems to be happening.
1956 – Cole, M. *Servant of the County*, pp. 20, 21

It is a seemingly unending task ... like the labour of Sisyphus. Whenever we rolled the stone [of the policy] near the summit of acceptance ... some pressure group or political whim ... would push it back to base again.
1990 – Commentary on the problems of getting council support for the introduction of comprehensive schooling: 'Birmingham's Mr Standfast', *Education*, 16 February, p. 161.

Example Two: Local government and central government. Which party has a majority?
Context: a chat in the CEO's office

Chair of Education Committee: Our view is that our party has to go ahead on this today but we'll ask you for a formal report for the next meeting.
CEO: But will your group hold together on this? If you go ahead and lose, what then?
Chair: It will – we've got [xxx] going around portraying himself as the schools' saviour in the press. We have to close uneconomic small schools – this latest circular from central government doesn't impress me – it's just election propaganda. By the way, we'd like you to come to the lunch meeting of the party group – we're deciding the way forward [on school re-structuring] … it might get a little politicized.
CEO: I haven't been known to walk out yet.
Chair: The leader's under some pressure – apparently the [local school] bandwagon turned up at his house at the weekend to protest. I heard about the change in central government policy in the hot dog queue at the fête. There'll be an open meeting about the [local school] of course. Councillor [xxx] will speak. You'd better write a speech for her.

Local: Conservative.   Central: Conservative.   Year: 1987

Context: a briefing from CEO and chair for local Members of Parliament.

CEO: (gives out notes) These are summaries of the committee's position. Do you want to start? (query to chair)
Chair: This is our position after meetings with governors. Central government's given us so little time for consultation …
CEO: We're concerned about the curriculum issues and the encouragement to schools to opt out of LEA control.
Chair: The major concern of officers and politicians is preserving the tertiary sector and the core curriculum.
CEO: HMI have stressed how well we've achieved locally. This central government initiative could destroy that. Our curriculum is what pupils want and need.
MP: We've come for a briefing, not a debate.

Local: Labour.   Central: Conservative.   Year: 1987

Despite this, there does seem to be acceptance of the view that local government politics and their implications for CEOs have altered drastically, whereas observations indicate that the changes have perhaps been more subtle and the CEOs' role may not have altered significantly from that described in the Chapter 10 on the history of CEOs. This replicates the findings of a 1977 study. 'Political changes do not have a dramatic impact, such as modifying the administrative style of the education officers ... They do affect the overall value framework, scope and speed of a solution to be adopted' (David, 1977, p. 209). The administrative style is susceptible to revelation from observation. The other items would be less visible in a short period.

The visible items selected for this chapter focus around the balance of power between appointed CEOs and elected politicians. Factors predisposing to the dominance of CEOs are described first, followed by discussion on the relatively recently acquired political role of CEOs. Factors supporting councillors' dominance are examined next. The chapter concludes with consideration of the ways that officers and politicians are linked through the relationship between CEOs and the chairs of Education Committees.

The dominant CEOs

Leadership tactics

'Will there be political view on this?' muttered one of the 1994–95 CEOs to himself, following a pressure group request to use school playing fields. 'Yes, there will – if we take it to councillors, but not if we don't', he answered himself before writing the letter to agree the group's request. 'Will there be a political view on this?' muttered one of the 1986–88 CEOs, reading a letter suggesting that the LEA might join a national education pressure group. 'Yes there will – if we take it to councillors, but not if we don't,' he noted to himself before listing the subscription as one to be paid without further discussion.

Such thoughts lie at the heart of the CEOs' potentially dominant position in the making of policy. The CEO is the gatekeeper to most of that which goes before councillors for decision. Others have access to politicians, notably constituents, but their interests are likely to be partial and short term. Establishing major thrusts of policy has to come from elsewhere. CEOs are well placed to lead in this.

- CEOs can develop a climate giving councillors access to educational ideas.
- CEOs can organize meeting agendas and papers that direct councillors to a solution desired by the CEO and can deliver these with appropriate tactics.
- CEOs' educational expertise usually exceeds that of councillors.

- CEOs have greater political and administrative knowledge than councillors.
- The new stakeholders of governors and school principals conflict with the power of the councillors.
- CEOs could be the gatekeepers to special treatment for councillors' constituency matters.
- CEOs last longer than the next election – they are better placed than councillors to determine long-term strategy.

Each of the above points is elaborated below.

First, CEOs can develop a climate giving councillors access to educational ideas. For example Gedling (CEO Dorset) (1986, p. 71), arranged for a series of presentations to sub-committees on educational issues and informal seminars as social occasions enabling councillors to mix with officers, principals and curriculum advisers. One of the 1986–88 cohort organized a day of school visits for the chair and the leader in order to show them the value and low costs of remodelling schools. Another made a speech to Education Committee about the National Curriculum though he despairingly remarked that he would be branded a Marxist for doing so and the councillors would not understand the jargon.

Secondly, CEOs can organize meeting agendas and papers that direct councillors to solutions desired by the CEO and can deliver these with appropriate tactics. Doctoring agendas is nothing new. A 1956 councillor reported that 'officers carefully arrange the agenda to secure that one or two contentious proposals, to which they attach no particular importance, appear first on the paper, draw all the fire and exhaust the committee' (Cole, 1956, p. 160). More recently, Liverpool LEA had to cut £2.8 million from its £116 million budget. The CEO presented advice to the Education Committee in a report which outlined two choices of action. The first was marginally cutting all services by the same percentage. The second was a radical proposal to cut severely the marginal services. 'It has been suggested that he was not serious about the more radical suggestion ... it seems hard to believe that officers would seriously propose such drastic surgery and seems much more likely that the director was indeed seeking to present an "impossible" scenario' (Boaden, 1986, pp. 29-30).

The importance of the format of officers' advice was underlined by a 1994 CEO. There had been suggestions that officers and councillors had conflicting views over budget proposals and councillors were having a 'think in' to specify their ideas. The CEO discussed with the senior management team how officers might put their proposals in a more 'politician-friendly' way. 'Documents can be indigestible to councillors', he commented and suggested modelling ideas instead.

Presenting such documents would not be the beginning of a CEO's attempts to influence the policy process. 'You have to know what to give them to get the discussion going the way you want it to go' stated Wood-Allum (CEO, Leicestershire) at a lecture in 1985. To do that requires the slow introduction of ideas to councillors, careful lobbying of senior councillors and the chairs of committees, planted questions in committee with the CEO becoming a politician himself (Hornsby, 1984, p. 110). It also requires manipulation of documents for committees. One CEO asked his deputy if he wanted to speak about a proposed curriculum initiative to be presented to committee later that day. The deputy declined the offer, remarking that he was sure the Conservatives wouldn't want a major debate on the issue. The committee later that day passed a very substantial curriculum document 'on the nod'. Speeches from officers might have stirred up the matter and created delay. Teacher representatives, meeting with the CEO before the committee session, noted an item they thought important was on page 22 of this large document and they wanted it given earlier prominence for discussion. The CEO advised against it and told the teachers that 'at least it's on the public record'. Being 'on the record' was a useful safeguard; a councillor asked a CEO if he was just allowing overspend on an item and turning a blind eye to it. ' Not exactly,' responded the CEO, 'it's all been reported to committee'.

As gatekeepers, CEOs decided what items to put forward for councillors to discuss. In the frequent meetings with officers, a regular topic for decision was whether or not an item was a 'matter for the members'. Decisions often hinged on whether there would be public interest which might come to councillors' notice by other means, thus bringing questions to officers. School meals, for example, got an automatic transfer to division one of committee consideration because it was guaranteed to have parents becoming annoyed. Once privatization of the service was on the agenda, there was major councillor attention such that an authority's chief executive rang the CEO to warn him to be ready for a 'cafuffle' (commotion) at committee. Avoiding political 'cafuffles' was the CEOs' aim. Tactics to achieve this included, for example, collecting comparative data from high-spending other LEAs when a CEO desired to show councillors how cost-effective was their own authority, or selecting LEAs spending the same when the objective was to demonstrate that their own authority was acting according to the norm. 'We'll sort out the money', asserted one 1995 CEO, 'the councillors will just have to agree'.

The third reason why CEOs may dominate councillors is the CEOs' educational expertise (Ozga, 1986, p. 44). One of the CEOs observed noted that 'politicians are now generally less well educated than teachers or officers – unlike in earlier periods – this has muddied the relationship'. Several times during these observations the lack of educational expertise was acknowledged by councillors themselves; in two different LEAs suggestions were made to their CEOs for policy developments with which the CEO clearly was not very impressed. In each situation, the councillors backed off muttering, 'Of course, I don't know anything about education. I don't want to interfere with what you're doing'. Another councillor apologized for 'asking silly questions' and one stoutly affirmed that, 'I never go against the advice of professional officers'.

The challenge is for the CEO to champion those parts of the education service which party politics do not want to reach. Hence a CEO might aim to put all primary schools into good buildings which 'will hardly gain any advertising kudos whereas councillors would want to build schools in a publicised new area ... [where you can get] newspapers to publish photos of blind children plying all manner of crafts' (Cole, 1956, pp. 16–17). Alastair Murray, the fictional retired CEO in Middleton's novel, was described as having been 'to great lengths to educate [his] political masters and ... didn't mind making himself unpopular' (Middleton, 1986, p. 26). He was said to be full of ideas. He was 'on the watch to kill catchpenny schemes or blast election winning slogans' (Middleton, 1986, p. 105).

Education is the largest service of the local authorities and, therefore, the most difficult for part-time councillors to grasp in its entirety compared with the CEO at the hub of the information spokes. A CEO should always be able to claim greater knowledge than councillors. One CEO reminded councillors that the policy convolutions in which they found themselves were of their own making since they had voted earlier for issues against which he had advised them. They could hardly expect him, therefore, to sort it out for them. Clearly, CEOs had a role to fulfil of providing councillors with information, helping them to understand the sometimes esoteric nature of both central and local government documents, and of reducing information to manageable size. Three hundred and sixty pages of documents faced a sub-committee, for example. They were talked through a government circular, an area's school provision, a parents' handbook on special needs and strategy for 16–19 age group provision. The bulk of this session was what teachers would recognize as 'question and answer' technique skilfully using Platonic style dialogue to reach the desired conclusions from councillors.

Fourthly, CEOs' political and administrative knowledge can help them dominate councillors. A helpful summary of CEOs' roles arising from this was provided by John Patten when Secretary of State for Education in 1986. CEOs should '1. warn the politicians of the dangers of inaction; 2. give advice, much of it unwelcome; 3. pilot [the] Authority's decision through the intricacies of the dual system, and the morass of local controversy; 4. advise [the] Authority on the gentle art of persuading the Secretary of State' (*Education*, 1986b, p. 103). The Widdicombe Committee which reported just as this research began in 1986 gave CEOs the pre-eminent administrative role. CEOs were responsible for 'day-to-day management matters ... The committee found that although there were many authorities where things were carried on as they always had been, there [was] a ... group where conventions had broken down and where there was considerable uncertainty about the roles of councillors and of officers' (Strength, 1986, p. 6).

CEOs acquire political knowledge from councillors and from their own longevity. The committees are useful sounding-boards for CEOs who need to discover how the public feel about the service. Councillors' questions, especially those which betrayed a lack of education expertise, could tell CEOs what the users of a service might be thinking and highlight areas where consumers might need explanations. In return, CEOs displayed their political understanding by advising councillors how the public might view their actions. In one LEA where many of the councillors were newly elected, the CEO, with eight years' experience, had a role in socializing them into an understanding of what they ought to be doing. A party briefing in 1995 included advice to councillors from the CEO on how to respond to parental restlessness concerning opposition to rationalizing school sites. 'We won't give way', inclusively opined the CEO, 'the important thing is to avoid reopening the arguments concerning the merged schools at the public meeting'. He then directed the councillors' attention to issues relating to a new highway and wildlife which might distract parents.

Access to administrative, legal and financial knowledge in excess of that of councillors, greatly benefited a 1987 CEO who was opposed to a policy much desired by the majority party (though not by its chair, who was united in opposition with the CEO but who could not reveal this unity to the party). 'This is a bloody awful idea which has to be stopped,' firmly asserted the CEO, 'but we have to stop it without allegations of officer bias. We have to appear to be ultra-reasonable'. CEO consultations with finance and legal officers discovered irrefutable arguments about, for example, possible legal action against the LEA if the maligned policy went ahead. With these, and financial contra-indications, the CEO could safely brief the chair to ensure the policy was killed in the inner caucus of the party before it saw the light in public committee. In this the chair happily colluded, sharing the ways in which the party would be forced to give in. 'I want to put the fear of God into them about their election prospects and make them see it's horrendously complicated and time consuming', stated the chair. In return for this collaboration, the CEO gifted the chair another issue brought forward, 'so your party can be seen to be taking the initiative'.

Fifthly, the new stakeholders of governors and school principals conflict with the position of the councillors and can thus, indirectly, reinforce CEO dominance. Some of the Education Committees in the 1991 NFER survey interpreted the new roles of governors and principals as a passive one, resenting the transference to governing bodies (Brown and Baker, 1991, p. 31). CEOs can have better contacts with these new political groups than can councillors, as discussed in Chapter 8, and can thus reinforce their position of power as possessors of knowledge to which councillors do not have access.

Sixthly, CEOs' dominance could be reinforced because they could be the gatekeepers to special treatment for councillors' constituency matters. This applied more strongly for the 1986–88 cohort than for the 1994–95 group since, by the latter date, most finance was held by each individual school and these could take their own decisions on how best to use it. Hence, a 1987 CEO's early morning warming-up exercises included a telephone fencing match with a councillor desirous of having a giant chessboard in a school playground in his constituency and attractively landscaped grounds as recompense for mining subsidence. Another 1987 colleague was pressurized to accept a councillor's constituent's child at a local special school. A third was approached with a councillor's request somewhat apologetically offered with the words, 'I know I shouldn't ask you for personal favours but I don't often do it'. A CEO able to accede to such requests might then build up support to be called on from the councillors concerned at a later date.

Seventhly, CEOs usually last longer than do many councillors. CEOs are not dependent on votes to survive and are thus better placed than councillors to dominate the determination of long-term strategy.

> You have to try and create time … to have a strategic look at what is going to happen over the next ten to fifteen years … to try and encourage the committee to have some sort of medium term plan … It is not just planning for this year, not just planning until the next local authority election. It is planning something that will mean that … the education service will be in the right shape … to withstand the stormy seas of the next ten years.
>
> (Atkinson, CEO Northamptonshire, 1987)

Finally, CEOs' dominance appears to be reinforced by their attitudes to councillors. Some comments recorded during the observations indicated that CEOs were less than enchanted with politicians: 'Councillors don't listen'; 'They're a pain in the neck'; 'There's a lot to be said for sending an officer with the councillors on a public trip like this'; 'The Liberals don't know what they're doing'; 'Preserve us from politicians'; 'Politicians have mono-minds'; 'Unscrupulous lot these politicians'; 'They really are luddites'; 'If they won't give us a focus, we'll have to do it ourselves'; 'I'll attempt to direct their discussion towards being an educational one but it'd be doubtful whether I shall succeed'. These were a few of the random, off camera comments from CEOs after meetings with councillors. Fortunately, for good relations between councillors and officers, there were relatively few such candid moments. The more usual attitude was a balance of the style encapsulated in a 1987 CEO's view that, 'It's very valuable working with councillors but when they do go astray and you can't be there to stop them, it's hard work'. Others expressed positive support privately, for a 'really good chair' in one LEA and in another for one who was a 'really skilled politician – he's no teacake'. The Labour party in a hung authority were described by the CEO as the 'brightest and most questioning' councillors. The last comment related to the party group with whom the CEO appeared to be most in sympathy politically. This party political sympathy amongst CEOs became a matter of debate particularly during the years 1986–95.

The political CEOs

The CEO as political adviser

However subtle or extensive have been the changes in the strength of party politicization in English local government, they have created a new role for CEOs, that of political adviser to politicians.

CEOs added to their educational expertise with a command of political tactics. The party leaders consulted CEOs on how to manage their parties in order to achieve the desired outcomes. CEOs would advise on how best to tailor recommendations within party political boundaries, a role early noted by Jennings (1977, 68, pp. 154). CEOs reminded party politicians of the political pitfalls of adopting a certain line and would add party political dimensions to suggestions in order to make them palatable. Like Canadian superintendents, they had an important role in socializing politicians into the system (Allison, 1991a, p. 30). In the process, CEOs have themselves become politicized (Cooke, 1986, p. 31), a role much argued about when it gradually emerged during the 1970s. By 1985, it was accepted that CEOs would be politicians, 'The thing will not go away' (Sloman, 1985, p. 38). By the time of the observations for this study, politicization was an accepted fact of life, to be manoeuvred not moaned about. One of the CEOs in the first cohort expressed it succinctly as providing the politicians with ammunition with which to persuade their parties to the point of view which he, and they, wanted to push.

'Don't run that for debate in committee unless you're sure you can hold your party together on the issue' advised one 1987 CEO in a cosy discussion with the chair of the Education Committee. 'Don't reopen that issue in Education Committee' warned a 1995 CEO at a party briefing 'but you should get this one on the agenda quickly'. 'I suppose he wants me to tell him how to vote' commented a CEO on being told that a councillor wanted the CEO to ring him urgently. Indeed he did, together with advice on 'how to stiffen up the whole party group'. 'What's best for managing my right wingers?' enquired a 1987 party leader of a CEO, 'that's the part of my job that's tricky'. 'I'm very nervous about getting the budget through' confessed a 1987 party leader to the CEO. 'Don't be,' he responded and then proceeded to work through all the possible tactics with the leader.

CEOs in these observations also advised councillors on when to run for public consultations and how much time was needed for this and what might be the party political hindrances to action. In hung LEAs where the CEOs had to brief several parties, the CEO transferred information about each party's views to the other. In a 1995 example, this was overt with a statement that 'this is party X's view on this'. In a 1987 example, it was covert; the CEOs' advice on tactics to each party took into account the advice the CEO had given on tactics to each of their rivals.

The party political CEOs

In becoming politicized, one new element did emerge during the late 1980s and early 1990s – the party-politicized CEO. Prior to this time, the accepted theory was that CEOs were neutral and would serve any party political leaders in the same way that civil servants are deemed to be neutral in British central government. During the years of these observations, the neutrality became less acceptable to politicians who wanted someone of their own party to serve them in order to ensure loyalty. 'There have been issues in the air about our loyalty' commented one 1994–95 CEO, 'after eight years of party X, we now have party Y'. 'I had to mind my Ps and Qs about grant-maintained schools when the Conservatives were in power' commented another.[1] 'How do we remain true to ourselves when we disagree with local political views?' was the beginning of a casual discussion amongst officers in 1995. 'We can't disagree in public, nor defend ourselves' continued the discussion group.

Meanwhile, CEOs themselves were finding that they might not want to serve in LEAs with a different political tendency to their own. It was suggested, for example, that Tim Brighouse left his post as CEO for Oxfordshire because he did not feel in sympathy with a local incoming Conservative party. He considered however that he 'may have reached that point of being out-manoeuvrable ... in an environment which he enjoys because it is so intensely political ... If professionally you are going to give leadership, you are going to offend politicians of whatever party' (O'Connor, 1988, p. 23).

Avoiding offence might be achieved by working for LEAs whose politics matched one's own. Bill Walton (CEO for Sheffield, a secure Labour Council), for example, spent almost all his career in northern Labour controlled authorities. He was a miner's son and the first from his council estate to go to university, the consequences of which would be to assume a left-wing bias in his political views. In contrast, James Pailing was forced out of his Newham CEO post in 1985. It was a hard left authority and the assumption seemed to be that his politics did not match those of the councillors. There was dispute about this, though. 'There is not really much party politics in all this ... it is likely that Mr Pailing has the same middle-of-the-road attachment to the ... education service as most CEOs. Other far left LEAs do manage to get on with similar CEOs' (Sloman, 1985, p.38).

Appointments in line with the professed party lines of LEAs continued in the late 1980s when CEOs selected for the new London LEAs appeared to be mainly in line with the professed political complexion of many of the areas they served. Concerns about this matching led the Secretary of State for Education to take powers to veto senior education authority appointments in London, a power he temporarily acquired to allay Conservative fears that Labour-led LEAs would appoint CEOs for their political correctness rather than their management skills. (The power of central veto over CEO appointments was abolished in 1972 for other areas of the country.) Labour-held Derbyshire LEA was criticized in 1990 for making a political appointment as their CEO; Geoff Lennox had been a Labour councillor and chair of the Education Committee in Derbyshire while working as an assistant education officer in neighbouring Nottinghamshire. His appointment made him, at 33, the youngest CEO since the war (but only by three years – Naismith was appointed at 36 to head Richmond LEA) and gave him a salary increase of £23,000 per annum (*TES*, 1990, p. 1). Michael Stoten (CEO Brent) clearly shared the views of local Labour politicians on racism (Parshotam, 1987; Stoten, 1987). His appointment followed an advert for a CEO who showed 'real sensitivity towards the needs of the ethnic communities in the borough, an ability to manage in a highly politicised environment ... commitment to anti-racist and anti-sexist policies' (*Education*, 1986a, p. 570) His predecessor, Adrian Parsons, had resigned in his mid-40s. He had had to cope with sudden changes of political control and a hung council (but so do many CEOs) and his retiring chairman described him as having been politically neutral (*Education*, 1986a). Stoten later translated happily to Kensington and Chelsea, a borough of a very different political complexion to Brent.

Bush *et al.* (1989, p. 44) reported the growth of CEOs having to follow what was laid down in local party manifestos and the extent to which local politicians felt that CEOs should follow their party line. John Mann, CEO Harrow, 1983–88, said 'I may have been the wrong horse for the course in Harrow. Councillors ... demand immediate answers and quick results to everyday questions and problems ... [whereas] the CEO ... [is] the architect of long-term projects and improvements' (*TES*, 1989b, p. 10). Clashes with political leaders were also claimed as the reason for the departures of Derek Esp (CEO Lincolnshire, 1988) and Peter Edwards (CEO Berkshire, 1988), their positions becoming 'dogged by political interference ... as Tory councillors tried to come to terms with their party's highly controversial education proposals' (*Education*, 1988a, p. 200). In contrast, CEOs who have settled happily with their political leaders report, e.g. 'the commitment of members here continues to surprise and encourage me, and frankly, I could not have thought three years ago that such a level of intrusion would be not just tolerable, but positively advantageous' (Hendy, 1987b, p. 227). He also admitted that, though for some of his fellow CEOs the level of political interference seemed intolerable, the numbers do not seem great. 'Of course a few have been pushed and a handful have fallen out with their political masters but there is no hard evidence of councillors putting more pressure on officers than they have previously done' (*TES*, 1989b, p. 10).

CEOs' party politicization would not be overt but there were clues occasionally during the observations. One CEO ensured that the local majority party were able to demonstrate that they were rapidly achieving the promises of their manifesto. Of course, any CEO might do this, even as a neutral, but this CEO had commented approvingly of the party concerned and talked of making trade-offs with them to ensure the required priorities.

CEOs in hung authorities

'Politicians in hung authorities make daft decisions to show who's in power,' remarked one of the 1987 CEOs. In a hung local authority, no one party has an overall majority. Usually, the two parties will have equal numbers of elected councillors and the balance will be held by independents or a third political party. This appears to make strategic planning harder for CEOs. There are three party briefings to give, three parties to be persuaded, three different approaches to be devised and a less certain outcome at committee or council meetings than when in a local authority with a dominant party where the decision is often known in advance of committee sessions.

It can be difficult to obtain a clear policy line to follow from the hung politicians who are also very anxious to avoid contentious policies which might upset the voters (Ozga, 1986, p. 43). Alternatively, as in one of the LEAs observed, hung politicians will 'play to the gallery' as one CEO described it. The Labour party in this LEA pushed through a decision to have a common date of school entry for five-year-old children across the whole of the local authority area and for the establishment of nursery education in the deprived areas. There was no money to achieve either of these. 'They did it to show their power over the Conservatives and because they were pandering to the parental lobby,' commented the CEO. At budget time, when the financial implications of policy decisions have to be accepted, a minority party might change allegiance during the debates and hence cause collapse of the budget and of policies planned. This happened in one of the LEAs observed where the Liberal minority refused the budget and this resulted in a change of power. In another LEA there was an annual ritual of each party presenting its budget, each being voted out and then a period of horse trading amongst the parties to reach the agreed version. Long-term strategic vision is lacking in hung authorities although the interest in medium-term planning is likely to be greater than in authorities with solid majorities (LGTB, 1985, p. 21).

Lack of a clear policy line from hung politicians can provide CEOs with opportunities to fill the policy-making gap, though they have to be strong to do this (Boaden, 1986, p. 33). Policies in hung councils are often debated in terms of their educational content rather than their relationship to a party line (Ozga, 1986, p. 43). In the hung local authorities observed, less effort was needed by the party leaders to keep their parties united than in LEAs with a dominant party. The Education Committee chair in one of the hung authorities said that the party would stick to decisions and the CEO would know from party briefings which way the vote would go. In authorities with a large majority, there seemed, paradoxically, more discussion between party leaders and CEOs on how to manage the party. Parties with solid majorities were likely to split into factions. The leader of a solid Conservative majority confirmed this: 'With the Tory group, I have difficulties keeping them united. It contains some idiots who don't read beyond the first five lines of documents'.

In the hung and almost hung authorities I observed, the CEO's ability to give each party political advice on how to manage their caucus and the whole party seemed to offer the CEOs opportunities for power as did policy documentation. Policy documents submitted to committees in hung authorities often did not carry recommendations but offered options in order to appeal to different groupings. Into these options, CEOs had more scope for interjections acceptable to themselves than when only one recommendation had to be offered. This was not confined to hung authorities; increasingly, it was happening in non-hung authorities too.

The dominant politicians

Defining the relationship between CEOs and councillors remains elusive. It is more than that of a managing director with the non-executive directors of a company board but less than the managing director's relationship to fellow directors or managers. It is much more than the connections between a public service and its consumer representative panel. It has some similarities with a Minister's relations with Parliament and with a school principal's relations with a school's board of governors. In all of these parallel relationships, the patterns vary in different contexts and with different personalities. Thus it is with CEOs and the local party politicians with whom they work, though less so from observations than others have claimed from alternative research methods (Edwards, 1991, p. 36). None of the CEOs in these observations matched the obeisance to their political leaders which that of a fictional counterpart achieved: 'If his political masters had asked him to draw up a scheme to garrotte all teachers over the age of fifty ... [he] would have produced it and it would have been efficient' (Middleton, 1986, p. 127). Nonetheless there were factors which predisposed councillors to dominate CEOs.

- Councillors have greater political sensitivities than CEOs.
- Parties insist on councillors' adherence to party policy thus leaving less scope for policies varied by CEOs.
- Transference of day-to-day administration to schools has led to political committees concentrating on strategy.
- Although CEOs are the gatekeepers over what goes to politicians for decision, external events beyond their control can alert councillors to items that they must discuss.

- As a last resort, it is the politicians who have the legal power to decide.

First, councillors' political abilities have to be acknowledged, so much so that one commentator has noted that councillors emerged as political advisers to CEOs given the greater politicization of the CEOs' roles (Edwards, 1991, p. 37). CEOs were noted, for example, asking councillors for political guidance on such matters as how best to reassure parents on progress on a new school. Deficiency of CEO political skills was suggested for the demise of several female CEOs who lacked 'wheeler-dealing' abilities in authorities in which councillors saw it as their role to make policy (Hackett, 1994, p. 6). Councillors' political abilities are underpinned by required connections to constituents who provide individualized information which CEOs may be less likely to acquire. Hence councillors would contact CEOs about particular problem families in their areas, or specific schools needing relandscaped gardens or crossing patrols.

Secondly, the whole period of this study was that of disciplined parties. Majority party groups were well established. The caucus was the heart of decision-making. The whole council and committees had lost their centrality in setting strategy as policies were decided in advance of the formal, public meetings. I recollect one of the Conservative party councillors during a cohort one observation in 1986, lamenting the efficiency of the local Labour party in caucusing and being sad that the Conservatives had to follow the same route. The increase in caucusing was referred to by a Conservative politician in one of the hung authorities studied. Even with working parties, she noted that the Labour party had parallel working parties before the joint one met, 'All this must make the CEO go nearly round the bend' she said but 'over the years, he has mellowed. He used to get really het up when politicians didn't seem to understand what he meant'. The CEO concerned, when asked about his views on relations with politicians said that he saw himself as the continuity man through political changes but 'politicians are more demanding – they want you all the time'.

Thirdly, the transference of power for the day-to-day administration of the education service to governors and school principals led to rationalizing and restructuring of LEA committees. Their roles moved to those of setting strategy and monitoring it (Brown and Baker, 1991, p. 31). In addition, councillors were organizing working groups within their parties on specific issues, so greatly enhancing their specialist knowledge. These changes could dilute the CEOs' dominance in this field. The committees had less to do and met less frequently so that when they did, they could concentrate on major items. This blurred the boundaries between officers and councillors according to CEO Brighouse (*TES*, 1989b, p. 10). In order to transcend this councillor movement into long-term strategic areas, CEOs needed alliances, as recognized by the 1987 CEO who pleaded with principals for partnership in order to present a strong, conjoint case to councillors. Chapters 7 and 8 showed that these strong conjunctions had not developed greatly by 1995.

Fourthly, although CEOs are the gatekeepers over what goes to politicians for decision, external events beyond their control can alert councillors to items that they must discuss. During the 1986–88 observations, there was a circular issued by central government concerning the closure of small schools. In response to this, the CEO asked officers to prepare copies and extracts from other related documents for a sub-committee meeting of councillors. It would not have been possible for a CEO to omit consideration of such an item – it was in the public domain and some councillors would be aware of it.

Finally, as a last resort, it is the politicians who have the power to decide. Neither CEOs, nor their senior officers, can control what happens in political committees. They can be present at these meetings but cannot vote, nor is it their role to argue for policies at this stage. Hence, they can be powerless to affect final outcomes. 'It's been a bad day for officers', commented one CEO as an item failed to get through the committee stage. 'You'll have to wait', another CEO advised a subordinate officer, 'the chair will only say at this point that they're interested but won't go further'.

> You have to have a siege mentality ... you ask, what is the will of the committee ... I have to try and put it into effect in a way that least harms the service ... I have to present the issues and indicate to committee the outcomes of their commitment to certain policies.
>
> (Atkinson, CEO Northamptonshire, 1987)

'In my view, the councillors' proposals are quite illegitimate,' stated another 1987 CEO, but there was nothing he could do to alter them.

Examples of councillors dominating CEOs include 1988 Berkshire where the Conservative councillors, who were in the majority, decided to dispense with their LEA's racial equality policy. This had been devised by a working party chaired by the CEO six years previously. The policy was regarded as pioneering and had been praised in the Swann Report (1985). In 1987, the Conservative group drafted a new policy on multiculturalism, reflecting a very different approach. The CEO opposed the changes and retired shortly afterwards (though he stated that his retirement was not connected with the policy change) (*TES*, 1988a, p. 1). Race issues caused political problems for another CEO when Brent Council announced in 1988 that it was to investigate a black councillor's allegation that the CEO was a racist. The allegation arose from the CEO's refusal to short-list a principalship applicant favoured by a local councillor. The councillor stated, 'It is the councillors and not you who decide on the educational policies of this borough and if you wish to express your disquiet you should do so by resigning' (*TES*, 1988b, p. 3). The *TES* leader writer noted that the CEO had done his

> 'professional duty according to his lights ... he had to give his political masters advice which some of them would resent bitterly. That he did so without flinching must have won him general respect. If the local authority ... decide to reject

[his advice] they have the legal right to do so ... The issue is not one of racism
... but of professional experience.

(*TES*, 1988b, p. 2).

In cases of disputes such as these, CEOs can only give advice to the councillors as has been true since 1870 (Thody, 1976). They cannot dictate. In
the 1987–88 Kirklees case in which parents refused to send their children
to the school selected for them by the authority, the CEO apparently recommended that the children should be allowed to attend the school of their
parents' choice because they had been given conflicting information on
school capacity. The Councillors chose to ignore this advice which was later
presented as evidence in the High Court case brought by the parents
against the LEA (Fisher and Spencer, 1988, p. 1).

In day-to-day relations, the politicians can also dominate because of their
control of the committee agendas. Brighouse reports a CEO who said a
paper of his had been altered even before it went to committee and that
some CEOs are pressurized not to give advice that would 'challenge the
status quo' (Brighouse, 1983, p. 101). This was similar to a CEO told by his
Chief Executive to be more supportive of the politicians' policies (Bush *et
al.*, 1989, p. 137). Sometimes officers, in my observations, suggested policy
items which would be removed from agendas by the councillors, leaving the
CEO to develop a more subtle style of leadership.

The CEO and the chair

Mulling over the options in a relaxed, comfortable manner, sharing personality assassinations of mutual acquaintances, passing information to each
other on events each had attended separately, smiling over successful
tactics, ruefully commiserating when tactics failed, opening post side by side
and routeing items to each other – these were the stuff of CEO–chair relationships in both cohorts and in LEAs of different political persuasions. In
two of the Labour-held authorities, the chairs had their own offices. In one
case, this was next door to the CEO and both wandered into each other's
offices with barely a knock. In another Labour authority, the chair's office
was in another building and there seemed relatively little traffic between the
two offices. In the hung authorities, meeting with party leaders varied from
formal set pieces in committee rooms when the CEO briefed each party in
turn to similar party specific meetings held in the CEO's office in a more
informal manner. In the Conservative LEA, the chair came to the CEO's
office by invitation but the atmosphere was always informal with a very close
working relationship.

The work of the LEA is facilitated when relations between chair and CEO
are close. One of the 1994–95 CEOs noted approvingly that the new chair
of the Education Committee was committed and participative so that there
was 'dialogue with our new political mates ... he keeps the wheels moving.'

Such a good relationship helps the CEO find out what policies are developing in the party hierarchy and helps the chair begin the process of making acceptable to members what the CEO wants. Before committee meetings, there will be agenda briefings and usually a weekly briefing meeting too. These briefings point to issues likely to cause controversy, discuss how party members may vote to alert the CEO, give the chair time to adjust to officers' views and how these might be fitted in with political views. The chairs are the mediators between officers and members. The chairs keep their parties in line.

The significance of this was made evident when a chair, in something of a flurry, contacted a CEO to tell him that while she was temporarily absent from a sub-committee meeting, the other councillors had decided to move a particular item for further consideration at another committee, so disturbing the plans they had made.

Despite these examples of closeness, there is some dispute over the continued importance of the CEO–chair relationship. One of those intervieweds in the Kogan 1988 survey considered the chair's role to be a weak one (Boulter, CEO Cumbria, in Bush *et al.*, 1989, pp. 107–8). This contrasts with Lenney's views that the relationship remained central and that the chair had moved into areas which were legitimately those of the CEO (pp. 128–9). The standard view is that good relations with the chairs of education committees have long been regarded as vital to the successful functioning of the LEA and its achievement of strategic developments (Bush *et al.*, 1989, p. 51; Griffith, 1966, p. 118).

International comparisons make the same point. Hickcox's (1992, p. 14) study of Canadian superintendents found that discussions with their Board chairs 'seemed to cover a wide range of topics, far beyond particular agenda items for the next meeting. Several of these Canadian CEOs tried to emphasize looking ahead, seeing what was down the road, working out an educational philosophy. Talk was also political, as to what was happening at the board level'. Allison's report on his 1985–86 study of Canadian superintendents said their meetings with the chairs were important to discuss

> the general state of affairs and the business of the next board meeting. Often … meetings … revolve around the agenda for the next board meeting with both content and procedure … reviewed, and potential problems and possible solutions are discussed. Semi-formal review meetings of this kind may occur weekly, but in some instances … much more regularly.
>
> (Allison, 1991b, p. 30).

Beginning to emerge as a newly important relationship for CEOs is that with the leader of the council – the principal party politician for the whole local authority (Bush *et al.*, 1989, p. 51). This personage did not surface in the 1986–88 cohort observations but played a more significant role for a 1995 CEO. This CEO reported to a meeting of school principals that 'the leader has made it clear that he'll be working to find savings from education'.

Forces combine: an Education Committee meeting

The differential power of CEOs and councillors, the CEOs' positions as political advisers, the preplanned tactics with chairs and stakeholders, the caucus agreements, the party briefings – they all reached their apogee at committee meetings. Education Committee meetings and sub-committees followed similar patterns in the different LEAs and remained the same across the two cohorts. An outline of one will give the flavour of what happened at the end of the political processes discussed above.

The ambience was described in Chapter 4. The rooms came in two styles: the late nineteenth-century solidity of civic pride realized in dark wood, mullioned windows and heavy doors or the late twentieth-century simplicity of light wood sweeps, chrome, and industrial carpeting of those authorities which needed large, new buildings to accord with their post-1974 status.

The agendas rolled along. Sixty pages of agenda items. Detailed maps and tables. Minutes of last meeting. Apologies.

> *Item One* Extraordinary – CEO announced the death of a student.
>
> *Item Two* Request for information. CEO replied to say he was obtaining this from the DES.
>
> *Item Three* School closures and it was the co-opted priest who had the floor. He was headed off by the party education leader together with an attempt to call a vote on the issue. The CEO would prepare a report on the matter, was the leader's soothing response, relaying what had been agreed privately with the CEO. Slight rumblings amongst the majority party were placated with promises of future working parties. The councillor for the area in which the school was threatened with closure was on his feet with a speech to placate the parents' lobby. During this, the party education leader wandered the table for *sotto voce* consultations, first with CEO and deputy, then with councillors dispersed around the table and then back with the CEO again.
>
> *Item Four* A new date to be fixed for the next meeting of the Education Committee because of conflicts between local councillors' political responsibilities in an impending national election. The new date had already been settled between leading politician and the CEO. Twenty protracted minutes of debate failed to get agreement and the axis powers of CEO and party leader were defeated on this oh-so-vital issue!
>
> *Item Five* The budget. Councillors had already worked through 71 minutes and it was not far from a lunch-break. Perfect timing to ensure not too much debate. The CEO was asked to speak on this item. Fulsome stroking of councillors followed for their work on the group producing the budget review. Fulsome

support of staff and reminders to councillors of the horrendous workload of officers came next. Eight minutes of oiling the financial wheels ensued and it was all passed. The preliminary committee had done its work well including that little end note guaranteed to confuse: 'Items are in priority order for this year *only*. Items do not necessarily have the same priority for increases in the following year; nor do they necessarily rank in priority for that year above items listed below which have been excluded for this year but will remain under consideration for next year.'

Items Six, Seven and Eight Reports on 16–19 education, an HMI report on a local school and a special education item – all through without discussion. Consultations off-stage again between CEO and party education leader.

Item Nine School meals. The last issue before the lunch-break and the one most likely to raise ire. Feeding children is always emotive. Feeding them through a privatized catering service was a political hot potato. Breathless hush time as the pre-agreed tactics unfolded. Would they work in avoiding a division? The CEO spoke. 'Councillors may wish to reopen this issue' (always offer the option, of course) 'but I was convinced that the working party had done a thorough investigation.' Mumbles of support. Four minutes and it was all over.

Item Ten A CEO check to see that all councillors were aware of a written submission from the county engineer reassuring them that drivers of school transport were investigated for their backgrounds and their vehicles checked for safety. Without this reminder, it was feasible that no-one would have read the letter, printed in ten-point faded font tight packed onto one A4 sheet.

Lunch CEO, party education leader and insider councillors departed for private lunch to move the real intricacies of policy-making.

Item Eleven Occupied the post-prandial nod slot. This was the CEO's own written report which exceeded in length all the other papers collectively. Almost two hours for 24 items. The CEO highlighted the issues on which he wanted the councillors to reflect and on which there were likely to be major areas of difficulties. Consultations with the teacher unions were not one of these. The CEO knew it was necessary to tread carefully and not open up this issue to debate. One councillor proclaimed that his patience with the teachers' demands was very thin, but the party line held. The disgruntlement did not spread to general discussion. The CEO used exactly the form of words agreed that morning prior to the committee with the teachers' representatives who sat, nodding supportively, amongst the committee members. A simple decision on allowing flexible interpretations of when a teacher must start the school day was taken with a very casual vote. Then the councillors were led into the immense complexities of training days, holidays and occasional days with a recommendation for option seven from a complex list of suggestions. It passed without comment. No decisions were to be taken until the issues became clearer.

With an hour left, the meeting dozed through the CEO's continuing report. Sometimes the CEO handed leadership on items to the deputy while himself going to chat to other officers. Councillors rose and fell on matters relating to the sale of school land in their constituencies and on worries that a multicultural initiative might lead to the paths of extremism. The CEO wandered to chat to officers during these items. Finally, councillors' attention was drawn to a selection of good news matters reporting students' and schools' achievements.

And at the end of it all? 'If I were a councillor, I'd give in to whatever because I'd find it hard to follow' commented the CEO privately before joining the party education leader for post-meeting tactical discussions.

A future for politics?

CEOs were neither the leaders nor the servants of politicians. Overtly, CEOs deferred to the politicians, spent much time advising them on political tactics and continually reflected on how their policy ideas had to be presented to politicians. In authorities with majority parties, relationships could be informal and generally very friendly. In hung authorities, they tended to be more formal. Politicians and CEOs were united in attitudes of opposition to central government. Covertly, the CEOs' deference was less marked. Away from politicians, CEOs often had to be the defenders of what they privately thought were indefensible, party political, policies.

CEOs had to be buffers between politicians and other stakeholders (Bush *et al.*, 1989, p. 134) as were their Canadian counterparts (Allison, 1991b, p. 29). This is an important role temporarily as the new stakeholders learn to fit into the LEA political frames. One 1994–95 CEO noted a school principals' meeting to which the chair of the Education Committee had not been invited: 'if the chair wants to go,' remarked the CEO, 'then the sensitivity is that the person organizing the meeting has to be approached to suggest that the chair be invited'. The same CEO arranged for the new stakeholders to deal directly with councillors; principals were asked to make presentations at a councillors' working party to demonstrate the effect of budget cuts. Eventually, schools and councillors may contact each other directly but, for the moment, it is CEOs who must build the road to facilitate the contacts and who must remind schools and councillors that they have to travel along it.

Observations indicated that there was some differentiation in the levels of policy-making by CEOs and councillors respectively. Politicians set the frameworks for the strategic decisions, albeit with the advice of professionals on what was feasible. Politicians also decided quite small things too, almost at the level of worrying about the price of chalk. In the mid-ground, CEOs seemed dominant. They selected the policies that would actually be in force within the foreseeable future. A further distinction lay in the CEOs' and politicians' relationships to the corporate whole. CEOs did not readily link in to corporateness, as discussed in Chapter 5. Party discipline kept the councillors much more closely tied to the policies for whole authorities.

By the time of the second observations, there seemed a distinct change in tone, atmosphere and attitude, though not of behaviour. The local political controls through councillors seemed almost an irrelevance, CEOs continued to be punctilious in deferring and referring to politicians, there was still awareness that policies had to be 'sold' to councillors but the councillors seemed remote from the real action in a way that had not been so apparent during the first period of observations. Councillors represented the sound and fury but the storm was elsewhere. This was summed up in a remark from a lower tier officer in 1995 who said, 'We're different because we have elected members, but we don't use them well. We must also remember that democracy is empowered citizens as well as elected Councillors'. He could also have added that democracy also meant empowered officers and a central government duly elected with a manifesto to implement. Councillors no longer seemed to have a monopoly of political status and influence on policy.

In the extended political scenario of stakeholders, central government and local government, CEOs seemed in limbo, waiting to see which way the fox would run before organizing the hunt. In 1994–95, they were more like the hunt followers, watching and waiting for others to lead the hunt. Once the quarry is exhausted, perhaps they will move in for the kill? That possible future is examined in the final chapter of this book and as a harbinger for that, the last words in Chapter 12 should be from a politician. One of the councillors encountered in this study remarked of the CEO: 'When we're all being exasperating and he must feel like knocking us all on the head, he retreats into a patient smile as if reflecting that there will be another tomorrow.'

Notes

1. The possibility of schools opting out of locally maintained into grant-maintained status was a policy introduced by a Conservative central government. Local Conservative parties felt constrained to support the national line but some were equivocal since opting out undermined their own position. It made for confusions in setting local policies and for CEOs whose sympathies would generally have been to retain schools within LEA control.

CHAPTER 10

Past days

Opening a copy of Moulton's 1919 concordance to *The Powers and Duties of Education Authorities,* I discovered that the flyleaf contained a handwritten mark redolent of original ownership, 'The Director'. The legalistic book, with its brown leatherette cover and gold lettering, emitted an aura of once having been perused by one 'attired in the official dress of pin-striped trousers, black coat and newspaper' described in Hill's (1938, p. 134) *oeuvre* on *The Local Government Officer.* Has the image changed from this 1930s, description? In 1989, the professional organization to which these chief educational executives belong (the Society of Education Officers) was 'old-fashioned, reactionary, grey, male and middle-aged ... a superior gentlemen's club', (Hugill, 1989). A gentleman's club it remains (8 per cent of 1996 CEOs were women) and a director's club too since the title returned to fashion from the 1980s.

This chapter investigates pre-1980s' interpretations of CEOs' roles. This historical summary includes examples of particular individuals whose records dominated conclusions on the roles of the chief executives for education. Their dominance led to assumptions being made that there was a 'golden age' for CEOs as strategic leaders which is now, regretfully, past. Revisiting the evidence indicates, however, that the 'golden age' may have been a myth. This finding is important to strategic leadership studies generally. Myths such as these have contributed to the 1980s' belief that a strategic leader had to be a visionary charismatic. Deconstructing this myth can support other 1990s' reinterpretations of leadership.

The terms adopted elsewhere in this book, of strategic leaders, senior managers or chief executives, would have been foreign to understandings of the role of a leader of the education provision of a local authority prior to the 1970s. For this reason, the nomenclatures adopted in earlier times have been retained in this chapter. The chapter describes English and Welsh experiences with brief references to Australian and North American history, and discusses the changing role of the administrators who led public educational provision at local levels from the late nineteenth to the late twentieth century when this study began.

Changes in the title over the years mark different attitudes to the role. In the 1990s Northamptonshire, for example, has a 'Director of Education and Libraries'; Cheshire gained a 'Group Director of Education Services', and elsewhere there was a 'Director of Education and Community Services', 'Director of Education and Leisure', a 'Director of Education and Culture' and two new terminological entrants as 'Executive Director'. The term, 'Director', was little used during the 1960s, 1970s and 1980s when 'County', or 'Chief Education Officer' was the most usual nomenclature, a choice attributed by Bush and Kogan (1982, p. 24) to the corporate managerialism that emerged during this period. Where 'County' was preferred to 'Chief', this was deemed to indicate that the LEA envisaged the CEO as a political adviser (Birley, 1970, p. 154; Heller and Edwards,1992, p. 205) as it was in those few authorities which used the title, 'Secretary' (Shropshire, North Riding, Cornwall; Fryer, 1988b). Despite such a rationale, the choice of title seems largely arbitrary with 'Director', the most popular nomenclature in 1996 and often used colloquially even when other descriptors are applied formally.[1] While the choice of terminology throughout the century may not be significant, the roles adopted illustrate the differing interpretations of strategic leadership which have been envisaged.

Emerging roles
Pre-1900

A novelist's view leads us into this period.

> *Miss Garrison [Board School headmistress]*
> 'The majority of the Members [of the school board[2]] are men of education. But we all know from experience how little they influence school affairs. Some amount of trouble is required to get well up in School Board matters and it is seldom taken. The Board official, in most cases, is the Board; and naturally so. His position requires knowledge of the details of the business and he acquires the power and influence that knowledge in every relation of affairs brings.'
> *Harry Claxton [assistant master]*
> 'And his personality is everywhere felt. His likes and dislikes are elements to be reckoned with. His master-ship is the bane of the profession.'
> *Miss Garrison*
> 'In truth, the Board official with the knowledge of affairs at his fingers'-ends, is often a buffer against the meddlesome Inspector.'
>
> (Rule, 1894, pp. 114–15)

Rule's view of CEOs' nineteenth-century forebears is somewhat at odds with the more general view that school board clerks were merely administrators appointed to relieve voluntary committees of the work of organizing schools and to account for the increasing amount of public funds devoted to education. This view parallels the emergence of the US superintendency (Wilson, 1960) and of directors of education in Australia. Appointments there 'intended ... to free education departments from the vagaries of political whim and the conservatism of administration by seniority ... and to place educational administration in the hands of experts' (Ling, 1986, p. 87). The USA district superintendency emerged earlier than the English and Welsh CEOs, and became more influential and prestigious much sooner with a much more formative role in the development of an area's education than seems to have been the case in England. In Canada, inspectors and district superintendents appointed by governments of each province from the early 1800s, performed matching roles. By 1900, US 'city superintendents were in the position of chief executives' (Allison, 1991a, p. 218) although this was not true of the many small town superintendents whose numbers dominated the system then as they do now.

In England, evidence is inconclusive that the school board clerks might have dominated elected members because of the members' lesser interest, knowledge and education. However, persons of the stature of T.H. Huxley served as elected members on the London School Board, for example (Maclure, 1970) and in Leicester, a Midlands provincial city, of the 53 elected members who served on six of the school boards, 13 were clergymen, ten were manufacturers, seven were professionals, three were 'gentlemen', three were 'ladies', five were shopkeepers, three were managers and nine were artisans (Thody, 1968, p. 162). One would have thought that these might easily have been dominated by professional officers.

1902–44

All-purpose local authorities subsumed specialist school boards in 1902. Each local authority had an education committee of elected councillors and this had responsibility for the local authority's educational tasks, as Lawrence (1972, p. 45) has indicated:

> The minutes of the early [education committee] meetings may make strange reading to modern eyes, for in those days the professional element provided by the education officer and his staff was not developed. Often a local solicitor served as a part-time secretary of the education committee, but before long the need for qualified staff was recognised and 'Director of Education' was sought.

The increasing number of schools and of central education regulations, required local inspection, school visiting, interpretation of the statutes and guidance to the newly emergent profession of teachers and school principals. Consequently, the secretary's role began to develop proactively.

This proactive role emerged while central government established itself as leader of education policy, moving from the assistance role of the nineteenth century to a supervisory one. It took time for central government to assert itself. By the time it did, the local education service had attracted educationalists; local senior officers became the 'natural enemy of HMI and the natural defender of the schools', with the general pattern becoming established for the localities to 'do more and go faster' than the centre (Maclure, 1970, p. 8). The emergent CEOs had the headmasterly characteristics of paternalism, authoritarianism and messianism. 'When they spoke, it was the "Word"' (Browning, 1972, p. 7).

Such local officer proactivity did not emerge fully fledged nor in every LEA immediately. Directors had to find roles in between implementing the wishes of local politicians and those of central politicians and administrators. Locally, the CEO's expected role was 'not ... the determination of policy; [he is] limited to advice and explanation, not criticism' (Hill, 1938, p. 20). Centrally, there was a powerful Board of Education, established in 1902, with wide requirements. Not only did the Board direct statute-making but it could also decide on questions arising under statute. It had to give approval to LEA actions in most cases and had to approve LEA by-laws. It could withhold grants for failure to meet statutory demands and acted as prosecuting counsel, judge and jury in cases of dispute between central and local authorities (Thody, 1976, 1988). LEAs in those early days, still concerned themselves with issues that appeared far removed from strategic planning. 'A gas bracket at Caerleon Endowed Schools needed mending ... Much earnest negotiation resulted in the [LEA] providing new mantles and the [school] managers paying for a new spring for the ball and socket pendant' (Morgan, 1986, 21–2). Education Committee members took the lead role even in day-to-day matters such as the selection and appointment of school principals (ibid., p. 93). In 1924, Monmouthshire Education Sub-Committee, with the intention of setting up a county library service, 'asked T.G. James (director) to compile a list of books and authorised him to employ a typist. By 1934 ... the bookstock [was] 40,000. The sub-committee still kept a close watch on the selection of books' (ibid., pp. 117–18).

The position of director was not readily apparent. Moulton's (1919) book on the powers and duties of LEAs, for example, makes no mention at all of directors or other officers although it does discuss councillors. In Morgan's review of Monmouthshire Education Authority's history from 1899 to 1944, there are only the briefest mentions of a director or directors.[3] A 1938 book on the local government officer made only one reference to the 'head of the education department' and that was in relation to the need for a degree and teaching experience as qualifications for the office (Hill, 1938, p. 79). The same author advised that the role of all chief officers (who would include a CEO) was that of writing reports, of advising the committee and of administering the department (ibid., p. 20). A director of education for Monmouthshire existed from 1924 but he was not recognized as the chief education official until 1936 (Morgan, 1986, p. 79).

Morgan considers that the origin of the 'concept of one director of education with comprehensive responsibilities' was the 1921 Education Act (ibid.,

p. 107). Although this contained no direct reference to any administrative post, Morgan's view could have arisen from the Act's requirement that Authorities had to provide 'progressive development and comprehensive organisation of education' (Education Act 1921, cl. 11). This view of an assumed directorship role was echoed by Eric Briault (CEO for the Inner London Education Authority, 1971-7) in relation to a later period. He stated that 'The responsibility for matters of curriculum and conduct of the service has been given by statute to the l.e.a. whose role in this respect must be exercised directly and indirectly through the CEO' (Lello, 1979, p. 57). Commentary on Australia indicates similar developments: 'The tidiness of the twentieth-century bureaucratic mind demanded a philosophical framework into which untidy educational developments could be slotted and this the Directors ... did with alacrity' (Ling, 1986, p. 87).

Some English directors likewise responded with alacrity to the possibilities of leadership arising between 1902 and 1944. This was the period when the noted Morris, Brockington and Graham emerged whose reputations were to help establish a myth of the golden age of CEOs (discussed below). Their stature, however, should not dominate our understanding of the period; the roles of CEOs varied greatly amongst LEAs.

1944–86

A centralized context

By 1944, there were approximately 300 CEOs in England and Wales. The legislation of that year, however, made the appointment of a director a statutory requirement while cutting the numbers of LEA (and hence of CEOs) to about half that number. While this reduced the career prospects of potential directors, the larger responsibilities probably increased their power. The 1944 Education Act required LEAs to submit plans for the educational development of their areas and from this arose CEOs' roles in leading that planning. As the Act stated: 'A primary function of each local education authority is to consider the needs of its area and to put forward proposals to the Department for the building of new schools to meet these needs' (Griffith, 1966, p. 115), the needs being the 'overall policy and future development' (Peschek and Brand, 1966, p. 96). Clearly a strategic role was envisaged.

Further reduction in the numbers of CEOs, but also a potential extension of their spheres of influence, occurred in 1974 when local government reform again reduced the numbers of LEAs. They became larger, more efficient and equipped with more technical and professional staff, all necessary concomitants of power (Boyle and Crosland, 1971, p. 171). The period 1972–86 thus appears to have offered much less central dictation and more opportunities for strategic leadership than did the periods before or since. Nonetheless, Stewart Mason (who retired as director of education for

Leicestershire in 1971) stated: 'My heart really bleeds for my successor in having to contend with all the obstacles which he now has to face' (Mason, 1981). This expectation seems supported by David (1977, p. 88) who found that, despite the increased size of LEA, CEOs seemed reluctant to be proactive. LEAs continued to face a central authority which had major 'overlord' powers to direct local initiatives through national planning, quangos and statutory enlargement (Griffith, 1966, pp. 50, 506). Central governments can, and could, stop grants, disallow capital expenditure and prevent local authorities raising funds. The centre lacked the power to direct the form of secondary education but this 'anomaly' (ibid., p. 51) was removed from 1966 onward.[4] Since 1986, the curriculum too has moved from LEA control, first to school governors (1986 Education Act) and then to central government (1988 Education Act).

Lack of uniformity

CEOs' development of their roles has not been uniform despite the common context of centralized government. The 'role played by the chief education officer, is not of universal application' was Griffith's (1966, p. 128) conclusion. The David (1977, p. 43) study found 'no clear consensus ... about the role of the chief education officer', a conclusion demonstrated by the CEOs interviewed in the Kogan trilogy of studies which spanned the 1970s and 1980s (Bush and Kogan, 1982; Bush et al.,1989; Kogan and van der Eyken, 1973).

Griffith indicated that the immediate post-war period had special characteristics. A CEO

> had a very great incentive, in the post war period when the demands for better education have been so strong, to embark on extensive schemes ... He [sic] does not wish his tenure of office as chief ... to be remembered as a period when little progress was made, when problems remained unsolved, and when the standard of education failed to improve.
>
> (Griffith, 1966, p. 118)

Despite this, both the Griffith (1966) and David (1977) studies stressed the variation amongst LEA attitudes. CEOs influenced these attitudes whether they were policy leaders or interest brokers, since they had 'considerable discretion' (David, 1977, p. 40). Exercising that discretion was considered important to national development in so far as individual LEAs' experiments could be tests for policies to be nationally encouraged (Boyle and Crosland, 1971, p. 127).

Such lack of uniformity contrasts with the simplicity of a definition offered by a 1950s' CEO. The CEO's duty is to 'advise his employers, fearlessly and competently ... and having given his advice he should carry out the instructions of his employers cheerfully and efficiently whether or not his advice has been taken' (Binns, 1957, p. 140). The dual characteristics of hero-innovator and humble clerk encapsulated in that quotation emerged in different terminology in David's 1977 study of CEOs. She sought to delineate CEOs as either conciliators or educators although stressing that these two styles could and did overlap and co-exist. Both roles received her criticism. Conciliators' sensitivity to others' views meant that the CEOs' 'educational objectives [were] never clearly articulated ... lost in a sea of opinion' (David, 1977, p. 87). Educator CEOs wanted 'to be innovative ... [but] they did not readily perceive the opportunities available' (p. 88).

Managerialism

Although David delineated CEOs as either educators or conciliators in their roles as strategists, the 1944 Education Act stressed their essentially managerial role of adjudication amongst the demands of central government, the local authority, the school, teachers and parents (ibid., p. 17). The development of managerialism brought the CEOs' administrative roles to the fore, 'segregating certain elements in the decisions of the members of the organisation and establishing regular procedures to select and determine these elements and to communicate them to the members concerned' (Simon, 1947, p. 8). This managerialism entailed education becoming part of the corporate entity of the local authority and, therefore, subject to the centralizing forces of local authority resource management. This managerialism enabled CEOs to introduce ranges of management techniques to monitor education department outcomes. This managerialism brought in professionals other than educationalists to LEAs. This managerialism reportedly depressed CEOs. They found

> their transition into mere service department heads, with less direct influence than technocrats ... a shocking and dispiriting experience. Personnel controllers, internal auditors, critical path analysts, heads of research ... were now able to obstruct, delay and sabotage the work of education departments which they viewed as professionally arrogant'.
>
> (Heller and Edwards, 1992, p. 15).

Relations with local politicians

Managerialism largely concerned the day-to-day operation of the service as an effective support for strategy. The strategies themselves continued to be set under the leadership of locally elected politicians who comprised the Education Committee. The CEOs' conduct of relations between politicians and officers was, however, controversial (David, 1977, p. 43). Their prime role was giving policy advice (Peschek and Brand, 1966, p. 32) which required CEOs to 'collect, analyse and sieve ideas' prior to presentation to committee (Bush and Kogan, 1982, p. 87, reporting a 1972 CEO). This left a CEO with potentially considerable discretion on what ideas to collect and sieve but some LEAs restricted this role by instructing their CEOs in considerable detail (Griffith, 1966, p. 128). The purpose of this restriction was to ensure 'that the policies approved and the decisions taken by the education committee are put into practice, and at the right time' (Browning, 1972, p. 5), a definition echoed later, for example, 'to interpret the needs of the service to the education committee and to carry out the committee's policy, shaped to meet those needs, effectively and economically' (Hall, 1984, p. 83); 'The director advises the LEA on all matters relating to education policy, carries out the decision of the LEA, and makes decisions that lie within the broad terms of that policy' (Ozga, 1986, p. 42).

Dominance of CEOs

The CEOs' policy advisory role permitted scope for the CEO whose professional advice 'will … have played an important part in shaping the policies or in arriving at the decisions' (Browning, 1972, p. 5). In 1950s Reading, for example, CEO Taylor was unquestionably dominant since 'there were few things on which the Education Committee did not take his advice … No question came up without leadership from Taylor. No building programme would be proposed but by Taylor' (Peschek and Brand, 1966, p. 95). It was clearly the officers who led policy (pp. 17, 67–8).

CEO dominance would be assisted first by the simple fact that CEOs often outlived politicians and, secondly, by the tactics CEOs could employ. Binns, writing of when he was CEO for Ealing, recalled that 'I knew if I gave them half a chance the dominant group would have had my blood. That group passed away, however' (Binns, 1957, p. 140). He also revealed his tactics to control the politicians. He gave advice but not in such a form that the politicians realized that was what he was doing. Likewise, he did not confront them over disagreements but led them to reach the right conclusions under the impression they had thought it all through for themselves and he let them take credit for the ideas. The CEO must be both 'humble and authoritative'. Mason, CEO Leicestershire, 1947–71, behaved likewise. The councillors 'usually took my advice … I served them up memoranda they could understand and which were written so they did not get confused over what was being proposed' (Mason, 1981). None the less, Mason did not underestimate the politicians. He always supported his professional advice with detailed evidence, 'used meeting techniques well … and always gave forcibly presented arguments' (Jones, 1988, p. 185). If such tactics failed, CEOs had the option of circumventing councillors and liaising directly with central government. CEOs in Griffith's (1966, p. 128) study of school building for example, informed the Minister 'of proposals which … are not to be encouraged' even though their councillors had proposed them.

CEOs may not have had a very high opinion of councillors. One of their own, Councillor Cole, described her 1950s' political colleagues on the London County Council as varying from, 'an intelligent layman asking sensible questions … to a jungle animal indulging in periodic and inexplicable forays' (Cole, 1956, p. 115). She was not over-complimentary about her companions, regarding some as being 'unpractical and importunate', over demanding of senior officers and foolishly whimsical (ibid., pp. 116, 158, 159). Such disenchantment with politicians emerged in Middleton's novel about a retired CEO who reflected on councillors so ignorant that they

> wished to appoint some BSc to a teaching post because he had one more letter after his name than his rival with a mere BA ... These Tom, Dick and Harrys, these butchers, bakers and candlestick makers in their navy Sunday suits had no means of judging the qualities of a candidate ... They had been told by their leader, a man as ignorant as they were ... the best lack all conviction, while the worst are full of passionate intensity.
>
> (Middleton, 1986, p. 70).

Even where councillors could not be classified as ignorant, CEO dominance could still emerge. A Professor of Government became deputy chair of the Leeds Education Committee in the 1970s and 'the greatest surprise he had was to find that all development, all impulse to innovation and change, came from within the office' (Bush and Kogan, 1982, p. 123).

An example of this impulse was seen in West Ham in the late 1950s. This LEA had a working party deliberating over six months on the future shape of secondary schooling in the area. Having passed to the CEO the information it had gathered, 'it was [then] ready to receive the final recommendation of the CEO' (Peschek and Brand, 1966, p. 27). Mason, in Leicestershire, similarly dominated the decision-making on the form of secondary education the LEA adopted in the 1960s. He did not remember any opposition to his plans from councillors and remarked that, 'the Education Committee were absolutely wonderful but maybe I say that because they took my advice' (Jones, 1988, p. 49). Mason also felt his task was facilitated by the lack of party politics in his LEA. There were many Independents and those who were party members did not sit in party groups nor meet in caucuses nor vote according to a party line. Education Committees of the 1960s could then be described as 'deliberative, not policy making' (Birley, 1970, p. 136).

During the 1970s, the evidence still indicated CEO and officer dominance of the decisions to be made on strategy although it was somewhat equivocal. All agreed that officers dominated in policy execution and that this often led to new lines of strategy but the councillors might influence the lines chosen (David, 1977, pp. 33–8, 71). In turn, CEOs affected those with influence by briefing the chairs of education committees and preparing documents, ostensibly offering choice but perhaps indicating that only one solution was possible. (Taylor, CEO Leeds, 1972 interview recorded in Bush and Kogan, 1982, p. 119). The CEOs' influence could then be described as 'determining policy' (Lenney, CEO Haringey in Bush et al., 1989, pp. 124, 125).

It was in the 1970s, however, that local parties began to operate more on party political lines and this affected the role of CEOs. 'Ten years ago, my job was thoroughly educational', said one CEO, 'Now, I'm sitting here waiting for Labour to put out its manifesto' (Jennings, 1977, p. 115).

Another stated that 'I don't bend with the political wind to get my ideas accepted. I do, however, act as a broker between members of different parties or the same party' to get agreement (ibid.). In that latter statement was the harbinger of the role that was so noticeable during the observations – that of acting as adviser on political tactics to politicians.

Reaching the 1980s, the CEOs' 'role is to judge the health of the service, the quality of it and to help move it forward ... judging what forward trends and forward problems are likely ... a catalyst role, a role to stimulate and to break out of moulds' (Aitken, CEO, Coventry reported in Bush and Kogan, 1982, p. 159). CEOs were much better placed than politicians to lead this mould-breaking, given the CEOs' position at the centre of the information networks (Duignan, 1980, p. 21) and the CEOs' ability to see the whole (Briault, Inner London CEO; Bush and Kogan, 1982, p. 172). There was, perhaps, greater equity of strength over the determination of strategy than had appertained earlier, as Boulter, CEO for Cumbria mentioned. 'I think colleagues in my position must expect politicians to hunt them occasionally' (Bush *et al.*, 1989, p. 106).

The politicians' role

Politicians hunting CEOs are not revealed in written histories. The intricacies and intimacies of the day-to-day tactics are not often recorded. Instead, local government events are followed largely from documents or at council and committee meetings which are open to the public. Politicians have a vested interest in publicizing their effect on educational policies in order to win votes. CEOs have a vested interest in not publicizing their effect on educational policy or they might lose their jobs or, at least, their backstage influence. In the 1920s, for example, Lowestoft LEA was in dispute with central government about teachers' salary scales. In the 1950s, Durham LEA was in dispute with central government because Durham was insisting on all its teachers being union members. In the 1970s, Surrey LEA was in dispute with central government over the introduction of non-selective education. Studying these disputes from published sources reveals the enormous importance of councillors. There is no mention of officers or CEOs (Thody, 1976, 1988, 1991a).

CEOs' views could always be overruled by politicians and if CEOs' attempts at dictation were discovered, there would be a 'thorough going rumpus'. Councillors who let themselves be controlled by CEOs had only themselves to blame (Cole, 1956, p. 159). An example of the effectiveness of political initiative came from 1950s West Ham where, 'Mr David Penwarden ... the rising young star of the Liberal revival, published his outspoken attack on the local system of secondary education'. This had tremendous repercussions and hastened a full review of the LEA's policies(Peschek and Brand, 1966, pp. 26–7). A less happy view of the same type of leadership was noted in Griffith's (1966, p. 534) study of school building policies 'Some chief education officers ... when they have given their committees the best advice of which they are capable, may find that advice departed from for what they regard as irrelevant or prejudiced reasons'. Stewart Mason discovered this in the late 1960s, towards the end of his time as Leicestershire's CEO. The Education Committee could no longer be manipulated so easily and he was expected to defend his policies at full meetings of the County Council (Jones, 1988, p. 185). A less jaundiced opinion of the same circumstances emanated from Claire Pratt, CEO for Hillingdon, who thought that political considerations should outweigh educational ones since, 'you've got to accept the fact that you can't always be right' (Bush and Kogan, 1982, p. 101). Another CEO found that party political control simplified his job since he 'only had to sell an idea once; then all we do is work out the details' (Jennings, 1977, p. 115). The theatre of action for selling the ideas moved from the open Education Committee to the closed briefings for politicians before their caucuses met. The CEOs' role *per se* had not changed but its place in the policy chain had.

Councillors have been deemed important in monitoring officers to ensure efficiency (Sylvester, 1957, p. 187) since officers could be 'needlessly obstructive ... bristling with precedents' (Cole, 1956, p. 116). Only the existence of a political committee to which they must report could stir some officers into action (Birley, 1970, p. 129).

A joint role

The truth about whether it was CEOs or councillors who dominated decision-making no doubt lies somewhere between the two situations outlined above. That 'somewhere between' is filled by the 'polycentric process' of interactions between CEOs and the chairs of their Education Committees (Peschek and Brand, 1966, pp. 67–8). These changed during the 1960s when occasions for discussions between the two grew and began to include day-to-day matters as well as strategy planning (Browning, 1972, p. 10). Chairs became political advisers to CEOs according to Jennings's (1977) study and the relationship with the chair was regarded as very important. It was sensitive, delicate, equal and important (Birley, 1970, p. 129; Bush and Kogan, 1982, pp. 89, 101, 115, 138–9; Griffith, 1966, p. 118). Those CEOs who achieved status as the all-time greats of the golden age of CEOs, discussed later in this chapter, were recorded as having had very close relationships with their chairs of Education Committees. Mason, for example, endorses the value of his chair who was 'wonderful ... he would not allow any snide comments about officers who could not defend themselves in committee' (Mason, 1981).

Together, the CEOs and their chairs of Education Committees could see the whole and so be 'a major influence' (David, 1977, p. 38) but much depended on the personality of the incumbents (David, 1977, pp. 38–40; Griffith, 1966). Most CEOs appeared much circumscribed by local and national demands leaving only a small degree of choice to the incumbents (Pratt, CEO Hillingdon, reported in Bush and Kogan, 1982, p. 97). A few CEOs became famous nationally as well as locally for their achievements and it is the records of these few that have created an image of what a CEO ought to be. The dominance of this image invites investigation.

Emerging personalities: the great and not so great CEOs

The years 1924–74 have been delineated as the period during which major CEOs emerged (Heller and Edwards, 1992). Several personalities dominated the local and national scene and from these examples a belief developed that there was what might be termed a 'golden age' for CEOs. Almost all of the CEOs observed for this research remarked that they wished they had served during the great times of men like Morris or Mason. Exploring the characters concerned indicates that first impressions support the notion that CEOs in the past could exert great power. Revisiting the evidence, however, reveals that all that glistered was not gold.

Positive first impressions

Brockington, Director of Education in Leicestershire, 1903–47, was a legend for his vigour and abilities, a 'key figure in ... complex negotiations' (Seaborne, 1968, p. 203). Locally, he ensured the advancement of technical education despite financial retrenchment, created an effective administrative system and 'laid the basis of ... striking educational experiments' (p. 222). His national reputation arose from his involvement in the securing of national salary scales for teachers and in secondary examination systems. Brockington wrote lengthy reports for committee and circulated them to all staff and governors. They 'show how Brockington increasingly imposed his ideas upon his Committee and the teachers in the County' (p. 204). During the inter-war period, he established a national reputation, through memberships of the Burnham Committee on Teachers' Salaries from its inception in 1919, the Consultative Committee of the Board of Education and the Secondary Schools' Examination Committee. He became identified with particular policies, notably the expansion of technical education on which he 'successfully maintained a high level of expenditure in spite of the economic difficulties' (p. 214). His obituary in *The Times* described him as 'the most eminent director of education in the country' (pp. 222, 223).

Morris (Director of Education for Cambridgeshire in the inter-war years) was noted for his 'masterly probing' (Ree, 1973, p. 3), and his 'fascinating personality, extraordinary strength of feeling about the value of the arts, the village college concept' (Mason, 1981). He developed the idea of the community college, bringing it to fruition in Cambridgeshire and producing an example for others to emulate. His routine management was as effective as his strategic visions.

> From 9–9.30, in the office, there would be desultory air ... but at about 9.35 someone would look out of the window and say; "He's here" ... and backs would straighten, footsteps quicken and voices became quicker and more alert. Mr. T [might] say, "The Great White Chief's in. Look out, Mr H., he'll be at Elementary today. He tore me to shreds yesterday" ... invariably a masterly probing and a pursuing through questioning until each ... fault or inadequacy was brought to light.
>
> (Ree, 1973, p. 3)

Morris had a fascinating personality, stimulating and caustic, with extraordinary strength of feeling about the things in which he believed (Mason, 1981).

Graham (chief education officer for Leeds, 1907–31), a champion of local against central control, was a major force in the Burnham Teachers' Salary Committee. He developed secondary and technical education, a teacher training college and 'an almost ferociously efficient system of administration' (Meyer, 1991, p. 163).

Amongst post-1944 CEOs, Newsom (Hertfordshire) was renowned for his leadership of the national Newsom Commission, Clegg of Yorkshire developed middle schools (Bush *et al.*, 1989, pp. 122–3), Alexander (Sheffield), Frank Barraclough (Yorkshire) and Lionel Russell (Birmingham) were all 'outstanding' (*Education*, 1990a, p. 161). Percy Taylor (Reading) 'was an efficient administrator and had a great gift for getting people to like him and accept his way of looking at things' (Peschek and Brand, 1966, p. 95). Brooksbank (Birmingham) integrated staff from the junior training centres into the education service, jointly authored *County and Voluntary Schools* (1982) and is remembered as 'absolutely unflappable, utterly unperturbable, cool, calm and analytical in any crisis. [He had] the total confidence and administration of ... the education committee ... [and] complete loyalty and affection [from staff]' (*Education*, 1990a, p. 161)

Mason (Leicestershire, 1947–71) had 'missionary zeal' (Jones, 1986, p. 48). He established Leicestershire's community colleges, reorganised secondary education, inaugurated Leicestershire's schools' modern art collection and developed music services for schools. Only 'people with the kind of power that Mason had can make this kind of thing work [establishing a county youth orchestra]. It was an example of real vision' (p. 76). Mason's strategic leadership eschewed detailed guidance for heads who, thereby, felt more involved in policies which left them choice in the intricacies of implementation (p. 180). Mason's successor, Fairbairn (1971–84), adopted a charismatic and single-minded approach to strategy, developing community education, the modern art collection and the conversion of a local stately home to a teachers' centre. He also encouraged links abroad, and wanted Leicestershire at the forefront of educational change.

All these were the creative, individualistic leaders whose heroic model tends to dominate expectations of what CEOs should be. The belief in the charismatic image survives. A USA study noted with approval that 'the

superintendent was described as a "mover", a "shaker", a "visionary"'
(Roberts, 1985, p. 1041).

The negative views

The movers and shakers amongst past CEOs appear to have had some
disadvantages; heroism was achieved at the expense of other things.
'Directors of education who so wished could create what amounted to their
own cultural baronies' (Jones, 1988, p. 86) becoming idiosyncratic even
when praised for their vision (Heller and Edwards, 1992, p. 106). The
careers of Frank Barraclough (Yorkshire) and Lionel Russell (Birmingham)
illustrate this idiosyncrasy with their associations of being 'wilful and patro-
nising' (Heller and Edwards, 1992, p. 140). They were 'outstanding and
demanding chiefs ... [but] to meet their standards and to survive their idio-
syncrasies required nerves of steel, a cool head and unremitting hard work'
(*Education*, 1990a, p. 161). Morris was not 'a good day-to-day administrator'. He interfered too much in the village colleges and got very upset over
minor things such as a dead flower arrangement and this was 'terribly
aggravating' to the principals (Mason, 1981). Brockington was 'ruthless and
pragmatic, and neglected curriculum issues' (Seaborne, 1968, pp. 219–20,
223). Brockington's successor, Mason, exhibited similar 'high handedness'
(Jones, 1988, p. 88), refusing, for example, to accept any one for appointments other than those he himself favoured, often in the teeth of opposition
from the remainder of appointing panels (ibid., ch. 2). On other issues,
Mason did not consult school principals. He alone, for example, allocated
pictures from the county art collection to schools. When he had an idea,
nothing must stand in its way. He promoted change for the sake of change
rather than for the well-being of the teacher and had a 'bee in his bonnet'
about open plan classrooms (Jones, 1988, p. 132). Taylor was depicted as
monarchical (Peschek and Brand, 1966, p. 95). Fairbairn was regarded as a
remote patrician. A local school principal commented to the author: 'We
always thought of Andrew [Fairbairn] as the last of the breed – he talked to
people as if they were right down there – and the arguments he used to get
into with politicians!' He was regarded as *laissez-faire* with officers and
remote from teachers.

Autocratic behaviour was a regular accompaniment of CEO greatness
(Cubitt, 1987, p. 43) but a chief officer should not be autocratic 'because he
offends the senses' (Hill, 1938, p. 140). Middleton's (1976, pp. 110–11)
fictional 1970s' CEO gave offence with his depotism:

> On his biennial visit ... he accused the principal of lack of ideas, failure ... to
> improvise courses that were different. [He explained that] 'I have the politi-
> cians on my back and so I have to defend you from time to time.' They would
> spend perhaps half an hour like this with niggling complaints ... then they'd
> walk round the place with the king-pin becking and smiling at staff and
> students and rubbing his hand in dust on cupboards or radiators ... Curzon

liked his underlings to have time for squirming and then he would descend
with a prepared list of questions which he claimed had been put to him by some
of the desperadoes of the education committee.

The golden age for CEOs?

The myth that there was a golden age for CEOs persists despite the realiza-
tion that there were, in reality, few great CEOs and that these could be
awkwardly autocratic. The years 1924–74 are the period when CEOs'

> charismatic command of local and national constituencies [which] enabled them
> to develop curriculum and institutional innovation on a wide scale ... It may be
> claimed that this talented group used the LEAs to dictate the educational
> agenda ... While many of the embryonic ideas may have come from universi-
> ties or abroad, the group had the talent and enterprise to facilitate their
> implementation.
>
> (Heller and Edwards, 1992, pp. 12–13).

Even within this glowing tribute, however, the dictatorial nature of successful CEOs is noted as is the fact that they may not have been original
thinkers. 'Not many [CEOs] have excelled themselves' concluded David
(1977, p. 44). Hopefully, few achieved the description of one chief education officer as 'reactionary and mediocre' (Meyer, 1991, p. 163) but most
were probably satisfactory and competent rather than bold visionaries.

The few outstanding CEOs gained their reputations in contexts that more
readily facilitated the emergence of the dominant personality than does the
zeitgeist of the late 1980s and 1990s. Central policy-makers welcomed past
CEOs into their counsels (David, 1977, p. 44). National and local consensus
on the goals of education, 'traditional deference' and the shared identity of
an Oxbridge past with government civil servants at the centre (Heller and
Edwards, 1992, p. 107) facilitated CEO involvement at the centre, a forum
from which CEOs are now largely excluded. One of the CEOs observed for
this research, whose tenure followed that of two nationally famous CEOs,
was expressly enjoined by the LEA's councillors not to concentrate on
national activities. If he wished to join non-authority activities, he had to
have the permission of the chair of the Education Committee.

Other contextual features, which may not apply to present incumbents,
supported the emergence of the past great men. First, their reputations
were built over long tenure. Leicester's Brockington had 44 years
(1903–47); Leicestershire's Mason had 24 years (1947–71). His successor,
Andrew Fairbairn had 13 (1971–84) followed by Wood-Allum who had ten
(1984–94). CEOs now serve for shorter periods than in the past and the post
is no longer regarded as the pinnacle for careers which may proceed to
academic life or to chief executive posts. It takes time to establish a reputation, as Brand noted when reporting on the record of the CEO who
succeeded the legendary Taylor; four years was insufficient for Taylor's
successor to have made his mark (Peschek and Brand, 1966, p. 108).

Secondly, past reputations often rested on combinations of CEOs and outstanding Education Committee chairpersons (Mason, Leicestershire: Jones, 1988) or the converse, the lack of dominant chairpersons to oppose a CEO (Taylor, Reading: Peschek and Brand, 1966). Thirdly, some, though not all, of the past great CEOs served in expansive and affluent times which enabled them to effect their policies. National economic forecasts in the 1960s projected £180 million increased spending on education for 1963-68 (Griffith, 1966, p. 21). This was during the period when the money was delivered as a general grant permitting freedom for local authorities in determining its allocation amongst services of which education gained the largest amount. Mason, who was CEO during this period, was 'fortunate to reach maturity at a time when local government, and the administration of education, provided considerable scope for people with ideas' (Jones, 1988, p. 17). His successor, Fairbairn, was noted for always finding funds for his pet projects. This use of his delegated powers, without reference to committee, was eventually 'outed' and stopped and his successor did not have such 'back pocket' access. Only one of the nine CEOs observed during this research made reference to a similar source of funding to which the CEO would have access for supporting projects personally favoured.[5] All nine had to spend considerable time selecting reductions in education services in order to meet centrally imposed financial cuts.

Within the years 1924–74, the 1950s are particularly remarked on for CEOs' opportunities. A key task was school and college expansion. The Minister for Education, George Tomlinson, stated proudly that 'The Minister knows nowt about curriculum', thus leaving the way open for local initiatives. Resources were plentiful and everyone agreed on the value of education. 'Bliss it was in that dawn to be a CEO' (Mann, 1988, p. 25). Mason (1981) depicted these years as a halcyon period of great hope when, generally, everyone supported the value of education and the 'vicious aspect of politics' did not interfere with educational decisions. The size of the responsibilities was awesome; more children, more schools and more teachers than ever before together with the expanding responsibilities of further education. The school meals service illustrates the scale of 1950s' educational enterprise. School catering in one LEA produced 28,000 meals daily. This exceeded the combined total of the area's cafés, restaurants, hotels, industrial and commercial canteens (Sylvester, 1957, p. 187). In contrast, after these years, came the international oil crisis in the early 1970s and subsequent reductions in national expenditure, the beginnings of a declining birth rate, national recession, central government's involvement in the curriculum and revelations of local lack of control in Tyneside and at the William Tyndale School in North London[6] that precipitated more central government intervention.

There were irritants, none the less, which lessen the reputation of the 1950s as golden years. There were financial 'stop-goes' (Mason, 1981). The list of a 1950s' CEO's responsibilities was long and complex (Sylvester, 1957, pp. 187, 188). CEOs strove to be 'creative and genuine policy makers' but had limited scope for considering and implementing alternative strategies (David, 1977, p. 221). Compared with the 1990s, money allocated for education seems plentiful but there was 'perpetually, not enough money' (Boyle and Crosland, 1971, p. 160).

CEOs' abilities to gain national reputations should not, however, be seen as entirely resting on extensive finances. Inter-war directors, for example, made their mark during the depression years. Morris went to the USA to raise funds to implement his strategies. The inter-war years during which Morris and Brockington flourished were not conducive to dominant strategic leadership, because there was no 'national educational policy behind them nor the same urge to do things better and better' (Sylvester, 1957, pp. 187, 188) and there were negative and quasi-judicial controls and regulations. Statutory requirements and national salary scales throughout the twentieth century have dictated how most of an LEA's educational budget must be spent.[7] Ear-marked percentage grants were the norm from 1918 to 1958, capping has prevented local authorities from raising extra funds locally and there have been centrally imposed controls on borrowing for capital projects.

Perhaps we should be more realistic in our expectations of CEOs. Interviewed on his retirement in 1995, Westerby (CEO, Dudley, 1972–95) stated that he had not been a source of creative ideas but he was good at picking out others' suggestions and making them work (Dudley, 1996). Atkinson (CEO, Northamptonshire, 1986–current) explained in a lecture in 1988 that his job was to keep a few teachers in a few classrooms with a bit of chalk. Despite such realism, the expectations of the CEO myth still resonate. In 1996, Merton Borough advertised for a Director of Education, Leisure and Libraries in the following terms:

> Do you have the vision for the improvement of educational standards and innovative ideas on how education, leisure and library services can be integrated to change the quality of life for Merton residents? ... Are you a manager with exceptional leadership qualities?'
>
> (*Guardian, Education,* 14 February 1996, p. 15)

Perhaps it is only hindsight that delineates golden years. There may be 'greats' amongst the present generations of CEOs but time has not yet lent patina to their work.

Quo vadis?

It appears from the above that dominant personalities may flourish irrespective of context. Perhaps this may happen in the future or perhaps CEOs 'will be ... an inconsequential footnote of educational history' (Heller and Edwards, 1992, p. 113). Chapter 12 discusses further the future role of these strategic leaders.

Notes

1   Of the 119 in 1996, 58 had the title Director of Education, 22 were Chief Education Officers and 12 were County Education Officers.

2   School boards were the local authorities for education from 1870 to 1902. The members were the elected element, deemed to determine a board's policies. Each board appointed a few officials for the day-to-day running of the area's education.

3   Since Morgan was a CEO himself, one might have expected him to mention if a predecessor had been leading the committee's decisions. On the other hand, the author may have been imbued with the prevailing orthodoxy that it was the committees which decided or it may be that he used only documents in the public domain, such as committee minutes, in which officers would not be mentioned.

4   In that year, Enfield LEA was judged to have breached its statutory responsibilities to amend its development plan when Enfield moved to a comprehensive system. The Minister for Education had to issue retrospective approval of their changes and thereafter, LEAs' plans to change the nature of their schools had to be approved by the centre. Circulars 10/65 and 10/66 advised LEAs to adopt comprehensivization and made clear that money would not be forthcoming for buildings for selective entry schools. In the 1970s, the Labour government required comprehensive developments. Successive Conservative administrations since then have gradually changed this requirement but in doing so demonstrate central powers over the format of schooling. By 1996, schools could opt to be grant-maintained, outside of LEA control, or to accept industrial funding as technology schools or City Technology Colleges. Selectivity was reintroduced by the 1990s' Conservative ministries.

5   It is, of course, possible that this is one aspect of a CEO's activities unlikely to be revealed to an observer.

6   Tyneside involved alleged corruption by the local authority. William Tyndale was an inner London primary school deemed so inefficient in the 1970s that staff were dismissed and HMIs took over the school temporarily.

7   National salary scales were adopted in the 1920s amidst local authority objections. In the 1990s, their abandonment has been suggested amidst local authority objections.

CHAPTER 11

Leaders review their days

> The job seemed so important at the time but I look back on it without any nostalgia. I think I agree with Heller's view that we will be just an inconsequential footnote in educational history.
>
> (CEO, cohort one)

This was the first reaction I received when I sent the text of this book for comments to the CEOs whom I had observed. This chapter provides an opportunity for them to speak about their perceptions with little intervention from me. The views were collected from interviews with participants from both cohorts, or from their written comments, after they had read the manuscript. The interviews were almost entirely unstructured and no attempt was made to push the CEOs into commenting on every chapter. It was intended thereby to record what they saw as most important.

Chapter 1: The life in the days

> Your football manager analogy falls down – CEOs don't get recycled to other clubs after dismissal.

The wheel–hub concept:

> I liked your analysis of the different representational roles which you observed CEOs fulfilling, e.g. making the council's case on the one hand, and making the case for teachers say, on the other hand. For my part, I regard as valuable that sort of synthesis of the role. I frequently regarded myself as a broker, e.g. at the time of making the budget, or in dealing with the DES.

Chapter 2: The contexts of the days

> I query your conclusion on the similarities amongst LEAs. There is less commonality than you think. They each have developed unique and innovative policies which have created different flavours of LEAs. There was more scope for LEA initiatives than you imply.

Central government relations

There has been a change since about 1993. Central government civil servants are consulting us again. We've been asked to a lot of 'off-the-record' discussions with civil servants at the DFE.

Recently [1995–96] in private meetings, ministers, civil servants and quangos acknowledge all that has been achieved by local government but they won't admit it in public. It's immensely frustrating.

If you're detached from it, you see a very different future for local government than if you are involved in it. Central government has written off local government. Labour is less supportive of local government even than the Conservatives – but I am absolutely convinced there is a role – at least professionally. I had close relationships with senior civil servants and the chief HMI during the early 1980s but the 1980s' Conservative legislation aimed to destroy local government and to remove Labour's power base in local government. The Conservative government aimed to use CEOs to carry through their reforms but as the Conservatives chose to push their reforms through a head-on clash with local government, CEOs were forced into defending local government. I am convinced that change came about around 1983 when Thatcher's second term started. There was a huge increase in powers for the Secretary of State for Education, in both large and small issues. It was proactive centralization. Prior to that it used to be negative or reactive; the central Treasury had powers of last resort and there were controls on, e.g. buildings and grants, but these were defensive not destructive as they became from the mid-1980s. It was unfortunate that Keith Joseph [the then Secretary of State for Education and Science] was a thinker not a doer.

My discussions with other CEOs showed a complete antipathy to central government. This is different to how you perceived us in the observations. I was one of those who worked with a group of CEOs as 'off-the-record' advisers to the Labour Party on how they might undermine the 1987 Education Bill.

There's been a complete reverse during the 1980s – central government is now dominant whereas it used to be local administration which dominated.

I don't agree with the possible analogy with the French regional inspector. I exchanged twice with French inspectors and found their job totally alien.

Local government

I too query Hendy's contention that urban politics are sharper than county politics. What has happened is that the counties have caught up with the urban areas. I didn't find differences.

I am not sure about the generalizability of some of your descriptions of changes. You state, for example, that the numbers of finance officers in local government declined because of devolution to schools [of powers to organize their own budgeting]. In my authority there was a net increase of finance officers because the schools required so much advice and support but these officers were not necessarily in the Education Department.

Chapter 3: The days begin ... and end

I liked your concept of the warming-up exercises.

If you're in your office early or late, then everyone knows it and makes a beeline for you.

Your idea of the CEO being non-existent isn't quite right. We exist – but the tactics are not to make this apparent. You don't tell people what you want – you get someone else to suggest it. Don't reveal your hand.

Chapter 4: The round of the days

It was fascinating finding out what other CEOs do. You don't know what's happening to others in the same circumstances.

The biggest surprise was finding how similar we all were.

It captures the variety and tensions.

It's all a matter of stamina.

The variety is fascinating but frustrating – you plan the week but then something blows up. But that's the great buzz of the job. Setting time aside to think doesn't work.

Chapter 5: Daily leadership

I'm not sure about the analogy with garage mechanics' supervisors. I suppose I could be said to have supervised teachers but the children they teach are much more varied than cars.

CEOs don't write reports – they edit other people's. Similarly, the reading is done by others too and the analysing of government reports.

Corporateness

The key relationship for a CEO is that with the chief executive – I don't think you brought this out. You have to get on with the chief executive. In my case, the chief executive wasn't interested in education. This is good because you can get on with your own thing but bad because if you want support, it's not there.

My chief executive was very supportive. He made the other departments support education.

Education is a target for the envy of other departments. Central government's undermining of education is frequently alluded to by other departments.

I would say I didn't take it [corporateness] seriously but I would want to be corporate. You need the services to come together and act coherently. But an awful lot of what is corporate is peripheral to education.

You're absolutely right about the offensive arrogance of education departments because in practice we deal with highly qualified professionals with higher degrees and we are highly qualified professionals – but this doesn't apply in other departments. You have more high-powered people than in other departments. There are always tensions about salaries. Education Department officers can get more than other departments' officers since our officers have to be comparable with school principals. I got really fed up with the negative reactions to education from the other departments.

Chapter 6: The days' policies

I get irritated because you didn't bring out the big picture in this research. As a CEO, you certainly carry a clear picture around in your head and you can make big, strategic leaps forward. But I note that you do stress the little engagements and realize their importance. They appear random but it's like a jigsaw – you gradually put the pieces together and make sense of the picture. My big picture, for example, was customer responsiveness. That can come from little things like reminding staff to reply to letters quickly. You have to come down to trivial and multitudinous actions to get change and you have to check that action is being done. You have to keep relating it to the big picture and reminding people of that big picture and of how their actions contribute to it.

My main comment concerns whether you have reached conclusions over the influence or impact that CEOs appeared to have on events either by virtue of the office held or because of individuality. Do you have examples of the presence of the CEO being the crucial factor in determining the outcome of events? This seems to matter since the necessity for the role of CEO is questioned.

Author's note: I did not reach conclusions over general, or differential, influence or impact. It was impossible to assess the CEOs' influence on events without also observing all the others who participated, e.g. councillors, officers, union officals. Concurrent observations by a team of researchers of these others who were involved might enable conclusions to be drawn concerning influence. My general impression was that power oscillated between CEOs and party caucuses locally, with the CEOs more often dominating because of greater knowledge, power and political skill. This local power was, however, overridden by central government's authority to direct.

I think your studies were all of CEOs in steady state – whereas there is a role as change agent. You have to give confidence and optimism and vision for the future.

There's a huge ethical position – and this should be translated into everything – CEOs do this.

Major strategic change takes place about once every five years.

Your description of the CEO as apologist for each group in turn – always speaking for the group that was not present – that's very accurate – it's the essence of strategic leadership – the interactions keeping the strategy on track and reacting throughout the day-to-day.

Chapter 7: Servicing the days

Business service providers

You need to include school cleaning in your list. This is the biggest 'privatized' service and one that was most easy to criticize.

Changing to services means it's much easier to monitor work – if customers don't buy a service, that monitors it.

Principals' appointments

Despite the changes in the powers of CEOs to determine appointments of principals – it is now easier for CEOs to dominate than in the past as school governors look more to the CEOs for advice than did councillors.

Despite valuing governors immensely, I think CEOs should have marginally greater powers over principals' appointments. The right to veto governors' choices of principals only on the grounds of applicants having inadequate qualifications is not enough.

The CEO's influence over principals' appointments is never extensive. You can only appoint when vacancies occur. Last week, I attended a retirement ceremony for a principal who had been in post 26 years and who had worked under three different CEOs.

I think the LEA should have stronger powers to stop appointments when they are really bad.

Principals

I was surprised to note your observation that CEOs seemed uncomfortable with school principals. My perceptions were very different on this point. I identified closely with primary school principals – and secondary ones too. It was all very relaxed.

One doesn't spend as much time with them as in the past but when we do, the meetings are more significant since they're about setting strategies and priorities. Each half-term, I had meetings with each of the primary, secondary and special school principals and these would be about significant strategies. They did influence priorities. This is more important than visiting schools. Policies did change in accordance with principals' views. For example, we increased financial delegation to schools from 70 per cent to 90 per cent after principals' requests.

Teachers

In my time, I had often to do battle on behalf of professional interests so that they could be represented in the corridors of power and in rooms where decisions were taken. Did you find a bias of interest in the approaches the CEOs took to educational administration because of their own backgrounds in educaton? Did you find a predisposition amongst teachers and lay persons to allow credibility to the judgements and opinions of CEOs in the light of the [professional educational] background of the latter?'

Author's note: The amount of time that CEOs spent with teachers compared with other stakeholder groups might suggest a CEO bias towards education professionals but teachers are the largest group of employees in an LEA so regular contacts might be expected. I did not question teachers or others about their attitudes but the monarchical concept I proposed for CEOs suggests that there is a predisposition to agree with CEOs' views.

School visits

I have to agree with you – school visits were infrequent.

Despite the autonomy granted to schools, the invitations to attend events are still frequent. I loved going. One year, I went to almost every carol concert to which I was invited. I never thought it a great imposition to go. You can't just pop in – you need to spend half a day – they want you to see everyone.

Visits don't take much time but they confer a sort of endorsement on a school.

Visits can give very vivid images that influence your thinking. You have to expose yourself to such events.

Officers

I wasn't keen on the senior team idea. Teams can't be responsible – the director has to drive the system.

I was interested to note that we now spend more time with our senior teams. This could be because of our change to customer focus. We have to ensure effective delivery in response to need. If officers don't win the business then they get made redundant and that brings pressure on the service role. Previously, it was just keeping the show on the road.

Chapter 8: Stakeholders in the days

I don't think outsiders realize how varied the job is and how you have to be responsive to outsiders.

The trend to parental and govenor involvement will continue but how will the system ensure that account is taken of the totality rather than the particular? How do you make sure you are hearing what the community wants and not what particular pressure groups want? It's the role of the politicians to assert the total view – and they have a mandate for that even if it is a fragile one.

Business community

They're full of rhetoric but not of real support for schools.

It depends on the area. In my last authority, you didn't get important local business people to education linked meetings and agencies – here, you do.

Parents

There were no parent consultative committees but we had a parent–governor association.

We've always said that parents are best dealt with at school level. I helped encourage the formation of a local parents' action group in my last authority – but it was hard going. We facilitated the group's formation – but we couldn't be seen to be facilitating it – that's not our place.

How do you access parents generally? They're only interested in particular schools.

It's easy to get parents involved with special educational needs. But it's difficult and challenging and tough. The parents who participate are those who are motivated to do so because of bad experiences with the system – it's very emotional. Parents who have suffered are aggressive.

Governors

Governors are an entirely good thing in principle and generally a good thing in practice.

I don't agree with the view that CEOs were reluctant to cede power to governors. I regarded governors as very important. Nor does the passage of power to governors decrease CEOs' power – governors really need CEOs' and LEAs' legal advice and administrative back-up to carry out their roles. They don't feel confident without that.

Governors need support from agents who can help them put their views into effect. And they need advice – they need help in making judgements, e.g. how do you decide what is a good teacher – that's hard enough for the professional. They have to be empowered to feel confident in forming their own views without their decisions being pre-empted by others.

Governors will wield more power than the local politicians – there are far more governors than there are councillors – we have to make alliances with parents and governors.

Some governing bodies need more help than others – they want to be told what to do – but you can't do that.

Good governing bodies have a sharp focus on what their school needs and they are prepared to make difficult decisions like sacking people. They do know what will work and what will not and the power to sack at school level means that specific cases can now be dealt with more quickly than before. When we wanted to sack a teacher, we immediately got involved in major locked-on situations with the unions – it was a big performance.'

Chapter 9: Political days

Dominant CEOs

I think you've underestimated the initiatives created by CEOs. These don't come from councillors – politicians respond to trouble and if there isn't any, they don't emerge.

What won't come out of observations is the number of things CEOs deal with that never go to members. CEOs have to judge what not to send. Officers defuse situations. CEOs are gatekeepers – though we may appear as servants.

I would sometimes suggest the opposite of what I wanted to guarantee that awkward councillors would go for the opposite which was what I really wanted to achieve. Sometimes I just wanted a debate when the members wanted me to give a definitive view.

CEOs are politicians. We use the wiles of politicians especially when there is a lack of political direction.

CEO as political adviser

Leaders in opposition were wont indeed to seek my opinion [on teachers' attitudes] especially during elections!

I did occasionally attend party caucus meetings – at least once a year and sometimes more often – and it got more frequent later in my career especially when there were major financial issues or school closures to debate. The politicians wanted me there and to avoid criticism from the opposition [about using professional advice in political deliberations] they would hold the caucus away from the usual venue.

The majority party wouldn't fall out in front of the officers. If they thought they were going to disagree with each other they would ask the officers to leave the meeting.

CEOs in hung authorities

Being in a hung authority was the easiest time for planning. Where there are parties with large majorities they factionalise and argue so you can't be sure what will go through. Where they are hung, the party members stick to the party line so you can be sure. The leader of the Social Democrat Party,[1] which held the balance, used to come to my office and ask me what my shopping list was and they could get that through the budget debates for me. We fought through a major change in comprehensive reorganization that way.

Dominant politicians

The heart of the issue is that decisions on budget cuts lie with politicians but the starting-point is that members consider a range of options suggested by officers.

Local government officers are more committed to local democracy than councillors. We know that choices on policy rest on value judgements and it's not a professional role to make these – we can't make decisions for the community – the councillors have to do that and the present system of councillor elections is the best we've found so far [to get the community views]. I set the criteria against which councillors can make judgements – the choice amongst the criteria has to be by elected people.

CEOs have confidence to do their job because we're appointed by elected politicians to whom we are ultimately responsible. Some things I wouldn't like to do on professional judgement alone.

CEOs have to give their advice in public at committee meetings. That's an enormous power which civil servants don't have. The public have right of entry to our committees so they can hear our views. You have to stand up and be counted. You can't conceal your views as civil servants can.

I don't think you brought out the power of the leader. Leader power can be very strong.

Relations with chair of the Education Committee

It was easy to get on with my chair – he was a lecturer at a local college of further education and he was very astute and knowledgeable about education. We had shared objectives.

Chapter 10: Past days

The changing title – at first, I was Director of Education, then it was changed to CEO, then back again to Director after a year and then reverted to CEO a year later. The Labour Party did not want a director because it sounded like a Board of Directors concept. I preferred the CEO title – it shows we represent education.

You've hardly mentioned Clegg – definitely one of the greats. I knew Fairbairn and Brooksbank well and Clegg was better than either of them.
Author's note: mea culpa – *unfortunately I did not locate a biography of him. If any readers know of one, please contact me. Sir Alec Clegg, CEO for the West Riding from 1948 to 1974, was greatly influential nationally and locally. Under his leadership, West Riding became internationally known for innovation and sound educational administration. He established the first LEA professional development college for teachers in 1952. He established comprehensive secondary schools through a pattern of middle schools. He led the introduction of locally set examinations for the Certificate of Secondary Education. He visited schools regularly. Nationally, he was president of the Association of Chief Education Officers, member of the Central Advisory Council on Education for England (11 years), involved in the preparation of the Crowther (15–18) and Newsom Reports (Half Our Future) and Chairman of the Governors of the Centre for Information and Advice on Educational Disadvantage for three years. He participated in UNESCO delegations. He wrote four books. All these achievements certainly put him into the 'golden age' of CEOs although one obituary did note that 'Clegg never concealed a certain impatience with the nuts and bolts of administration'. More significantly for the future of CEOs today, another obituary stated, 'Politicians today would soon cut down a CEO who threatened to collect to himself the kind of authority Clegg assumed after a quarter of a century in office' (TES, 24 January 1986, p. 6).*

It's true that the relationship between chair and CEO changed in the mid-1960s in my experience too – but why it changed, I don't know.

Ah – so I was the only one of your eight subjects who seemed to have a little hidden away in an 'earmarked reserve' for projects in which I was particularly interested. I wonder if the others really did have such funds but the issue didn't arise during your observations?

This chapter jars – it's out of place so late in the book.

Chapter 12: Future days

I think you need a charismatic figure but that's not suitable as a post-1988 model.

What will replace it – that directive force is needed.

The CEO is a presence in the background who can come in if needed.

My successor is buoyant and optimistic. I never doubted that CEOs and LEAs would survive.

What do you consider right for the future academic training of CEOs actual and prospective? I spent time at Henley and INLOGOV[2] but I would have liked longer sabbaticals for further academic study ... even though the leave was generous ... We are not as specific about qualifications and experience as is the case typically in Canada, USA and in Australia ... From the point of view of people in this country, to what extent are the qualifications and experience which you note as being associated with CEOs crucial to the successful perfor-mance of the duties which are exercised?
Author's note: I did not consider this issue but it does need debate. I would be happy to help design an NVQ Level Five for CEOs!

The future of local government

If you're detached from it, you see a very different future for local government than if you are involved in it. Central government has written off local govern-ment. Labour is even less supportive than the Tories. But I am absolutely convinced there is a role – at least professionally.

One future scenario is no local government. I can see a much stronger possi-bility of regional strategic government and direct connections between senior professionals at the centre and in the regions – bypassing local politicians.

Councillors are not as useful to central government as are officers and there are equity arguments to consider. Having local authorities does mean that people get different treatment according to where they live.

Central government is beginning to realize the public mistrust of 'big govern-ment'. Central government can't manage all the public services directly and the channels of of accountability are too narrow. So they're turning back to local government. Local government throws up ideas and innovations – and pilots them on a small scale and then central government can poach them for national legislation. Devolution of power to schools, for example, was an idea of a few local authorities who experimented with it. It started small and then moved to being nationally prescribed and has now been successfully adopted nation-wide with few changes. Compare this with the National Curriculum which was nationally implemented without any local trials – the result was many *post facto* changes. Central government is recognizing its vulnerability [in executing policies]. For example, it's all very well failing schools but who is to deal with these schools once they have been identified – it has to be local government.

The monarchical concept

That monarch concept – when I attended school events, they treated it as some-thing wonderful – I was made embarrassingly welcome. Schools felt it was important if the CEO went. I tried to get an even spread of my attendances across the LEA. The schools had presents for me – flowers and framed pictures – people might wonder why this is still important.

I find I'm still unhappy with the monarchical concept. But I did use to see myself as a Princess Di type figure though now it's more of the Queen Mum. I did get bunches of flowers and I was quite good at smiling. CEOs are the cheap and readily available public figure and a visit helped to get a school's name in the local paper. The PR role is very important. I reckon I gave six to eight speeches each week.

Appendix: Studying the strategic leaders' days

Gender issues

It was very demanding and difficult keeping marriage and family going as well.

I think there are male and female styles of management but they can be found in both sexes.

Are there different pressures for women CEOs? You do have expectations from family and society.

It was balancing all the work things with home things.
Author's note: These four comments were from the women CEOs.

Identification

I noticed how you vacillated in your opinions throughout the book – a sort of love–hate relationship – as others commentators noted in similar research.

I seemed to detect a change in your attitude as you moved through the book. Your involvement in the issues seems to change your views. In the Epilogue, you are actively seeking a role for us.

The book is more personal and sympathetic than I imagined it would be.

Documentary sources

I loved that novelist's views you quote [Middleton, 1976, 1986]. He portrays it accurately.

Non-participant observation

I was a touch apprehensive about being shadowed but CEOs need an audience – especially one that can't talk back.

I was self-conscious during the shadowing.

It was unsatisfactory that you weren't allowed to attend everything. I was slightly embarrassed about the chief executive not allowing you to be there. I wanted you to see meaningful things.

Presenting the research

> I liked the style of the book – the balance between the academic and the appealing.

> You made surprisingly entertaining reading of us.

The final curtain

> I enjoyed being a CEO; it was very worthwhile. A satisfying job.

> I'm glad I had the experience of being a CEO.

> I didn't realize how hard it was – and yet I thought I knew what I was taking on.

> We're all prima donnas – and it's expected of us but not too much prima and not too much donna.

Notes

1   The Social Democrats were a short-lived centre party in the late 1970s and early 1980s.
2   Henley Management Centre is an associate of Brunel University. It offers postgraduate qualifications in public and business administration. INLOGOV – Institute of Local Government Studies at Birmingham University.

Future days

Defenestration, defence or deflection are the suggestions in this chapter for the future role of strategic leaders at chief executive level in local education. The choice is dependent principally on decisions taken by central government, secondly by CEOs themselves and by stakeholders and peripherally by councillors and officers. For each of the three possible outcomes, this futurology collates the models suggested in the preceding chapters and discusses the contexts which will support each of the options in their emergence as the dominant frame. The Epilogue describes my preferred model.

Defenestration

Dispatching the CEO out of the window of history is the first possible future.

The non-existent CEO was the first concept in this book (Chapters 1 and 3) and to this may be attached the debunking of the myth of the CEO hero-figure in Chapter 10. Such a solo leader would be out of place in the 1990s with their emphases on collectivity and teams, as the theories in Chapter 2 discussed, yet, as Chapter 5 showed, the CEOs were not committed to corporate management with either internal or external stakeholders. The undemocratically dominant professional CEO, protected by an army of officers, emerged from several chapters as a potential dinosaur in a stakeholder democracy. When this dinosaur CEO has also to spend much time persuading politicians (in Chapter 9) to accept ideas in a system of local political representation which itself has become *passé*, then where is the role for the CEO? Can there be a need for local interpretations of education led by CEOs, when England is a centralized system, small enough to be fully unitary? Can there be justification for the 'vast waste of time and resources amongst LEAs each researching ways of developing the service?' (Hornsby, 1984, p. 119).

A defenestration outcome is supported by those who visualize the demise of LEAs (Brown and Baker, 1991; Pimenoff, 1992; Riley, 1992); or who accept that there are pessimists who foresee it (Morris, 1994), or who can point to a country, such as New Zealand, which can demonstrate that it has survived without intermediate tiers of government (Audit Commission, 1993; Lauder, 1995, p. 25). One may also surmise the imminent death of CEOs because 'institutions which fail to meet the requirements of their environments may suffer the penalty of contraction or closure' (Bush, 1986, p. 119). Some of the evidence from Chapters 7 to 10 showed that CEOs have not greatly reoriented their power pathways despite changes around them. Others might suggest defenestration for the opposite reason; CEOs who have adapted to the changes by, for example, becoming politicized, are reminded that 'when individuals engage in politics, there is a high risk of forced exit' (Bacharat and Lawler, 1980, p. 8).

Such forced exit may be encouraged by the growing influence and potential power of new stakeholder groups. Chapter 7 evidenced CEOs stepping aside as governors, parents and business leaders began to enter the decision-making arenas. These take away CEOs' powers to manage schools and to devise area education plans. Above CEOs is central government which has removed CEOs' powers over the curriculum and teaching methods while CEOs' anti-central government stance will exacerbate their loss of authority to the centre (Chapter 2). The centre is demanding performance measures. These have been found for schools but what is there to prove that CEOs make any difference to the effectiveness of schools? 'The research based literature is virtually silent on the superintendent's influence on the state of effectiveness of America's schools' although there is a general belief that there is a link between what superintendents do and the effectiveness of their schools (Griffin and Chance, 1994, p. 70). This is, as yet, an unproven belief in England too.

Effectiveness has been deemed to be related to the involvement of external stakeholders in schools and this has been pushed by CEOs as Chapter 8 revealed. Like their Canadian counterparts, however, CEOs seem more committed to this in theory than in practice. In Holmes's study of six Canadian superintendents, he found that they tried to include the community in consensual decision-making but also that 'the public interest ... is systematically overlooked, not so much rejected as not considered' (Holmes, 1991, p. 260). This was not done consciously, concluded Holmes, but because the CEOs are part of a professional community with its own mores and determinants to which CEOs automatically defer. Without building up stakeholder support, however professional, CEOs seem rather lonely figures now protection is needed.

Protection is needed in the 1990s when LEAs may have difficulty demonstrating that they have a recognizably useful role. The roles envisaged for the LEAs in the late twentieth century, as set out in a 1989 Audit Commission report, read like the battle orders of some long-forgotten campaign by 1996, as the roles no longer existed by then. LEAs' general roles, according to the Audit Commission report (1989), were to set visions, plan future facilities, raise and direct funds and act as a quality regulator. All these were central government's responsibilities by 1996, whether *de facto* or *de jure*. The Audit Commission also proposed specific roles for LEA leadership but these too had been superseded by central government by 1996. The Audit Commission's suggestions were that LEAs should develop:

- provision for the under-fives. This was pre-empted by central government turning all parents into consumers from 1996 by giving them vouchers to spend as they wished on nursery education.
- careers and adult education. Developing this role was also predicted by Pinchin (1987, p. 331) but by 1996 the two services were largely hived off as commercial enterprises and often down-sized because of users' inabilities to pay commercial rates.
- policy on further education provision. Further education colleges became independent in the early 1990s so precluding this role.
- guidelines for co-operation between schools and colleges. During the late 1980s and early 1990s, tertiary colleges became independent of LEAs; schools operated autonomously within LEAs. As a result, CEOs cannot dictate policy to either schools or colleges (Lomax and Ouston, 1995).
- support, guidance and training of schools for independent financial management. This had been completed by 1996 with little need for continuing LEA involvement.
- 'a clear statement of what the education authority is trying to achieve for school children'. They could do this, but what for? No one has to take any notice of it and it no longer fits with the ethos of the times (Lister, 1991, p. 6).
- themselves as backstops if schools failed to manage their finances. If this happens, then financial delegation can be withdrawn and LEAs take over but this is hardly going to provide major business for LEAs.
- monitoring and inspection. This was one of the key roles predicted for LEAs post-1988 thus giving them and their CEOs a central place in the new order of quality controls (Edwards, 1991, p. 40). OFSTED has, however, subsumed this. LEA inspectors have become private franchisers of OFSTED and there is no particular need for these inspectors to remain in their LEA stables under the direction of a CEO.

Defenestration would complete the death of LEAs envisaged 30 years ago. In 1966, Griffith depicted a powerful central government. Local government could only regain its influence, Griffith considered, if there were a definition of a sphere for local government with precise specification of standards, greater freedom of choice over grant spending, greater consultation of LEAs by central government and enlargement of local authorities (Griffith, 1966, pp. 536-40, 542–7, 558). Only the latter has came to pass but many LEAs were decreased in size again in the mid-1990s. Perhaps LEAs are destined to go the same way as the denominational teacher training colleges to which Lofthouse compares them. The colleges lost their hegemony as society secularized and government centralized; a similar redundancy awaits LEAs (Lofthouse, 1982, p. 497). The profession-alization of CEOs has been suggested as one of the reasons for the successful move of LEAs away from central control from 1902 (Maclure, 1970, p. 5). Will central government allow such a potential power base to remain, espe-cially as it is one that judges its actions either in accordance with professional mores or alternatively in accordance with local politicians who oppose the centre?

Does central government, or anyone else, need CEOs with a role defined by one of them in this research as being an 'advocate of people attending school'. There have been serious doubts about whether schools should exist since the deschooling movements of the 1960s and 1970s. By the 1990s, there were serious doubts that the single model of schooling postulated by LEAs was the right one. Diversification was the 1990s' objective yet LEAs were for equity through standardization. Schools without walls is the promise of twenty-first century technology. Where is the scope for the CEO in all this?

Before defenestrating, a pause for thought occasioned by a 1980s TV sitcom series, *Yes, Minister*, about the relations of a minister and his civil servants in central government. The civil servant head of the minister's department, Sir Humphrey Appleby, ruminates to the minister's private secretary:

> *Sir Humphrey:* Local government may be a dunghill but it grows beautiful roses.
> *Bernard:* And if we try to clean it up, we land in the —.
> *(Yes, Minister,* BBC2, 7 January 1987)

Reasoning such as this leads to the second possibility for CEOs – a rear-guard defence.

Defence

Minimalist. Passive. Partial. Specialist. Incrementalist. Reactive. Profes-sional. Conservative. Safe. Maintenance. Survival. Acceptance. Oppor-tunistic. Instrumental. Transactional. Collegial. These are some of the key words in the defence terminology. The words may sound critical but they represent a realistic assessment of what easily might be achieved. The think-ing behind a defence outcome is that, in order to remain in existence, CEOs need to offend as few people as possible while also not revealing the power of which the role is capable. CEOs in defence cannot threaten other groups.

CEOs in defence need other groups – though deciding just which groups are the best likely supporters is not simple in the expanding stakeholder democracy of the 1990s.

The first of the defence concepts arose from Chapter 1 where the CEOs emerged as hubs of wheels endlessly transmitting and receiving information along different spokes. The hub role reappeared in various guises commencing with the warming-up and warming-down exercises each day as described in Chapter 3. The linking of joint initiatives from different points in the system also centred on the wheel–hub concept. Someone has to be in the centre to see where the common needs are and to liaise so that different groups are not each trying to 'reinvent the wheel'. The hub concept found expression in earlier commentaries on LEAs. In the 1950s,

> I could see that such achievements as there were had come mainly through the fact that I had been able to take the initiative in arranging for groups of people to study problems of one kind or another, to take part in the discussions myself, and to get the results followed up.
>
> (Sylvester, 1957, p.186)

By the 1970s, this had acquired a more modern interpretation with the CEO depicted as a human computer, taking in new ideas and welding them into a system (David, 1977, p. 44). Reworking these ideas into the wheel-hub concept, CEOs are both the effective centre, as the organizers, and the affective centre since their symbolic role in representing the unity of the service must be acknowledged.

The second defence concept is that of a supervisor of garage mechanics. Organizing the structures and processes of management and forcing policies along incrementally were roles explained in Chapters 5, 6 and 7. The most important part of this garage supervisory role is somehow keeping track of all the pieces of the engine while they have been removed from the whole for repair and then making sure that the strategic plan of the engine runs successfully when all the parts are put back again. This role also encompasses good personnel management, the 'jollying the troops' role of Chapter 7 and being a service advocate and developer for the reorganized services of the LEA in its privatized form (Laffin and Young, 1990). This is underpinned by the processes of Chapters 3 and 4 – moving the paper, moving the people, moving the ideas. The ideas were the most complex to maintain amidst the daily routines. The 'Greek chorus' thematizing, described in Chapter 5, demonstrated this with one policy initiative. CEOs have to keep many progressing likewise as Chapter 6 outlined.

The third defence concept is that of the politicized CEO. CEOs support LEAs in their current politicized form but in doing this, they vacillate between dominance and subordination, as Chapter 9 showed. The CEOs therefore operate as mid-1990s hunt followers, watching to see which way the fox will run and not yet ready to organize the kill themselves. Meanwhile, they could be envisaged as preparing for the kill covertly by themselves becoming political advisers and politicians. Is this in preparation for the demise of the political element in local government?

Finally, Chapter 7 unleashed the monarchical concept which remains strongly embedded in public perceptions of the CEOs' role. 'Sometimes, principals get upset if you visit the adjacent school and not theirs' commented a CEO going through the routine of a sovereign's walkabout, shaking hands, offering pleasantries and looking interested in everything. The courtiers surrounded the CEO at head office. Politicians who were able to find their way through the labyrinthine court, came for a laying on of hands. Stakeholders and principals tried to touch the robes at ceremonial passings. All attached importance to the CEO's formal appearances and speech-making. The myth of the great visionary CEO may be a myth but it has a strong hold. This seems at odds with the stakeholder republicanism of 1990s' England and it may be for this reason that CEOs do not play to this monarchical role. It may be time to reconsider its value, however. Perhaps the local education world wants, and needs monarchs.

Rationales for defence roles

These four defensive concepts are built incrementally on what already exists and all are underpinned with belief in the need for a CEO in particular and for local government in general, sentiments supported by the 1991 NFER survey in which half the respondents looked to LEAs for advice and support and 20 per cent saw a planning, resource provision and monitoring role (Brown and Baker, 1991; Edwards, 1991). LEAs continue to look after the weak – those excluded from school, the special education children, the 'at risk' schools. This care can be for these general categories of need or for very specific instances. David Cracknell (1995, p. 9), for example, discussing the causes of increased arson attacks on schools, revealed the care and support which LEAs give to their schools in crises: 'From bitter experience, education officers understand the psychological as well as physical damage.' In order to solve the problem, his LEA commissioned research, took precautionary measures working in conjunction with the fire services and architects, evaluated measures and revised them. Who else would there be to provide such support other than the CEOs and their LEAs?

It is difficult to characterize this background role and even more difficult to project its value in a way that would serve to defend the LEAs as Morris showed. No 'simple taxonomy could accurately set out a comprehensive schedule of what LEAs do ... there is a multiplicity of duties, powers and other functions, plus helpful activities and valuable resources, from which LEA-maintained schools will continue to benefit' (Morris, 1994, p. 21). Given this summary, the complications of replacing LEAs with other agencies would not be simple but it is not always easy to convince people of the value of what LEAs are doing. Convincing people of LEAs' value could come from developing the monarchical role of the CEO as LEA defender.

The monarchical role rests on there being characters capable of fulfilling the expectations of some degree of charisma and of such characters being sufficiently uninhibited to play the game with verve. Brighouse in 1988 considered that the days of the great CEOs were not over (O'Connor, 1988, p. 23). Our growing understanding that beliefs and values are important to the success of an organization could also support the monarchical role since there has to be individualized commitment to these to make them real and realizable (Bates, 1994, pp. 214–227; Thom, 1993). The vision of which a monarch is a personification is still vital according to US and Canadian views of the superintendency (Konnert and Augenstein, 1990, p. 32; Townsend, 1991, p. 69). Leaders must 'proselytise at every opportunity for their beliefs' (LaRoque and Coleman, 1991, p. 96). More prosaically, 'the chief officer must be, and seen to be, in charge, always tacitly, and not infrequently, explicitly' (Mason, 1986).

Defensive concepts slightly move CEOs from their current position just as LEAs are moving slightly too. They have adopted the idea of the 'enabling' authority (Brooke, 1989) rather than that of being a direct provider. This continues the English local government traditions of incrementalism from below, generating services as much as has central government direction (Cochran, 1993, p. 9). The aim has been to create high-quality, cost-effective services which will retain existing adherents (Goodwin, 1995b, p. 9; Maden, 1989, p. 10; Thornton, 1995, p. 20) though the format of service delivery may change.

Incremental maintenance as the linking theme of all these defence concepts does not sound exciting but it is what follows next that may be. The one CEO in this study who was in both cohorts reviewed the changes since 1987 when we met again in 1994. 'The strategy has been to grow old gracefully', he said, 'watching for the windows of opportunity through which the phoenix can be reborn'. The phoenix may like to consider the final suggestions of this chapter as possible windows.

Deflection

> [There is a] lack of will on the part of many LEAs to enter into exploration of this new role. If we could agree this as the joint national and local agenda we could avoid a decade of missed opportunity.
>
> (Du Quesnay, CEO Hertfordshire, 1993, p. 19).

> Chief education officers will be the linchpins of the service for a long time to come.
>
> (*TES*, 1989a, p. 10).

> A superintendency and a central office in public education can still be vitally important ingredients in school improvement.
>
> (Crowson, 1994, p. 24)

[There should be] an interactive LEA ... seeking to find a new and creative role ... rather than being passively buffeted ... This new role ... locates the LEA centrally in the local education arena but also recognises the centrality of other key movers: central government; TECs, schools, institutions and governors ... [it] is concerned with the management of influence.

(Maden, CEO Warwickshire, quoted in Riley, 1992, p. 21)

The concepts

Two developmental conceptualizations emerged from my observations. Both deflect CEOs from previous mainstream roles and meet Du Quesnay's intimations of new roles. The first is that of CEOs as the centre of privatized services, organizing stakeholder influence on those services and conducting stakeholder views further up the government chain to the centre. The corollary to this is the second concept of the CEO as an agent for central government. Within both of these is the idea of the CEO as conductor of local experiments from which wisdom can be gained for national dissemination. The latter is nothing new; it is historically how local services have emerged. This idea would be an important adjunct to either of the two conceptualizations.

The stakeholder leader, emerging from Chapters 6, 7 and 8, is the someone who organizes stakeholders, collects views, puts them to those able to act upon them and then implements them. The central agent concept, first explored in Chapter 2, presupposes the implementation of standardization into which the injection of some varied creativity would be welcome. In both of these conceptualizations, CEOs would become obstetricians, assisting stakeholders and centre to bring ideas into the world.

Such ideas might come from those areas whose spokespersons are least able to articulate on their own behalf. It is possible to argue that CEOs and their LEAs have an important role in providing educational opportunities for those not able to provide these for themselves. This is the historical role from which LEAs emerged and to this are owed many developments in education. The projection of LEAs as protectors promoting the values of 'equality of opportunity ... multi-cultural, anti-racist and anti-sexist education' and therefore of the CEO as chief protector (Mullany, 1994, p. 6) or Lord Protector (Chapter 7) is a seductive one and one into which they may be pushed by central government removing their powers over mainstream education. They can, then, be highly successful providers and advocates for the unusual in education, setting examples and standards to be taken up nationally. The danger is that if they seize opportunities which then become politically important, central government will take them over. If such ideas then decline in political importance, a CEO who protects these will be a King Knut.[1] The CEO needs, therefore, to use the political skills that were demonstrably emerging in Chapter 9 to help ensure the continued importance of particular services and of their local control. This would be part of the role as stakeholder leader.

The stakeholder leader would organize ways in which new interest groups could be legitimated. Consultative mechanisms could be set up for the formal incorporation of such groups using the exemplars of the union consultative bodies of the past. CEOs could increase their informal contacts with new stakeholders thus becoming more comfortable with external stakeholders, as Chapters 3, 7 and 8 indicated was needed. Training for stakeholder democracy might be organized in the same way that governor training has been. Eventually, these initiatives might lead to reconstructed representative bodies. In such ways CEOs might make common cause with groups and individuals currently outside the system. The Labour Party nationally in 1996 spoke of a stakeholder democracy as the next stage in the development of the State. Perhaps CEOs could start the education and structures that will support this before they are ordered to do so by central government.

Orders from central government may be viewed differently if the concept of the CEO as a central agent is adopted. Local governments should be seen as franchisers from central government, putting into effect a standardized, nationalized product under a common logo and with a common mission statement. The CEO would be the linchpin of this system but this could only be if central government participates in their appointment and employment and, more significantly, keeps them informed and consulted. CEOs should know exactly how central government wants its laws and regulations interpreting and should not need to fight over the interpretations locally. This concept might result in the politicized CEO of Chapter 9 becoming a party politicized CEO to match the party in power at the centre. Equally, it could mean that the leadership roles of Chapters 5 and 6 gain in significance. With services privatized and schools autonomous, CEOs would no longer necessarily need to be educationalists. Any background in senior management might be acceptable. Such a generalist would have to take a view wider than that of education professionals.

Rationales for deflection concepts

The background to these ideas lies in the view that 'there is still scope for LEAs to exercise new forms of influence' (Riley, 1992, p. 3). Du Quesnay (1993, p. 17), CEO for Hertfordshire, expresses this in practice: 'We are excited by the new relationship which is based on respect for the school's governors and managers as equal partners.' She envisages a continually improved listening skill for her own LEA to find out and then meet the needs of citizens. We must respond to individual citizens while offering schools a club fostering 'co-operation and sense of community so that schools can support each other and make common cause when their pupils' ... interests demand it' (Du Quesnay, 1993, p. 18). A CEO turned academic notes similarly: the CEO 'is identified with the needs and aspirations of whole community, over a lengthy period of time, in which the fashions of politics are an important but not an overriding rhythm' (Tomlinson, 1985, p. 495)

Identifying overtly with the community would enable CEOs operating this system to amass personal power bases by empowering those at lower levels in the organization (Rudolph and Peluchette, 1993, p. 18). Even before the major changes of the mid-1980s in education governance, it was recognized that in order to achieve leadership, CEOs might have to undertake 'activities which go beyond the formal education system' (Finch, 1984, p. 191). Chapters 7, 8 and 9 show that they have not greatly espoused this advice. External stakeholders have been little legitimated but they must gain near equality with local politicians who would themselves become one group of stakeholders amongst others.

The changing character of stakeholders makes this development necessary. Until 1970, citizens were depicted as conformist (during which period the CEO was a director or controller). The 1970s and 1980s produced the critical citizen created by the success of the education system in producing articulate voters (during which period CEOs empowered others and became political manipulators) (Dale, 1989, p. 103). The model for the 1990s and the next century is that of the active citizen who as a volunteer must take over some of the jobs which the State can no longer afford to have provided by paid functionaries. In this last development, the CEO links these volunteers into the system and into the line which begins with central government direction. The CEO does not disappear. 'Paradoxically, the recent evidence [USA] is that managerial change from hierarchical to bottom-up and self-governing structures leads often to an *increase* in overall organisational control' (Crowson, 1994, p. 17).

Stakeholders want a greater share of the action and for this CEOs could be coaches, not players (Leithwood and Musella, 1991a) though they may also have to be referees mediating in disputes between parents and schools, acting as education ombudspersons, 'as channels for accountability and as the faces of regional authorities which have to be intermediaries between the DES and the schools' (Pimenoff, 1992, p. 21). The value of being a proactive coach in improving relations with stakeholders was demonstrated at a 1996 meeting for school governors concerning the possibility of opting into grant-maintained status. A new governor enquired of a school principal at the meeting why there was diminished interest in becoming grant-maintained. 'The recent very marked improvement in LEAs' attitudes', was his answer, 'and the impossibility of getting back into the local authority once you've opted out'.[2] This statement augurs well for stakeholder acceptance of the LEA as enabling 'the community to define and then to meet the needs and problems it faces' (Clarke and Stewart, 1990, p. 4).

CEOs as stakeholder leaders would fit the development of the local, corporate state (Cochran, 1993, pp. 120–4), linking together numerous non-governmental organizations. The recognition of the need for this linking, intermediary role was noted by Lomax and Ouston (1995, p. 159) who discovered that autonomous schools were considering setting up group administrative facilities thus returning to something akin to the LEA. The wheel-hub concept, suggested as a defensive model above, is a starter for this deflection role, as demonstrated also in Canadian and Australian research (Allison, 1991a, p. 36; Macpherson, 1985a, p. 185). This community governance model would meet our traditional attachment to local government and our belief in it as a political educator (MacKenzie, 1961, pp. 14, 18). It is one of the models suggested by Cordingly and Kogan (1993) who also proposed, though with less enthusiasm, the central agency model discussed below.

CEOs as central agents would fit the twentieth century's continuing system centralization. Welfare statism 'made central government very concerned with the quality and quantity of local services but indifferent to whether these are provided by democratically elected bodies' (Hill, 1974, p. 38). CEOs should 'welcome this ... positive leadership by central government, and use [their] influence to ensure that it is promoted swiftly and effectively' (Hornsby, 1984, pp. 120–1). James Pailing, CEO for Newham, left his job following disagreements with his local councillors but the advice he had given them (to which they objected) 'was only following clear and repeated advice from the Secretary of State' (Sloman, 1985, p. 38). Chapter 2 indicated that, publicly, CEOs pursue an anti-central government stance but perhaps this is because they are currently tied to teachers and local councillors as their power bases and these two groups oppose central government. Hence the remark I noted at one meeting, when a 1995 CEO was asked why a particular policy was being adopted, the reply was a weary, 'Because legislation requires us to'. In private, however, one 1994 CEO stated that although hating to admit it, most of the government reforms did seem to be having the desired effect of raising standards but 'please don't quote me on that'.

Suitable CEOs for deflection models

If CEOs are going to take on the deflection roles projected, then there needs to be a strong CEOs' professional association. Cracknell (1995, p. 9), CEO Cheshire, proposed 'a determined national initiative led by the local authority associations and central government' but this was using existing pathways. These existing pathways of the current associations have been strong in the past to the extent that they became a part of the constitution of the country (Griffith, 1966, p. 33). By the 1990s, this was restricting their influence since they failed to realize that they no longer had the privileged status they previously enjoyed. These associations must accept that they are a 'domesticated pressure group' (Rhodes, 1988, p. 325) like other stakeholders and must change their tactics. They remain in existence but is there a possibility of their uniting to counterbalance the centre or is a national association of local government associations a contradiction in terms?

While local governments as an effective collectivity may be difficult to achieve, a collectivity of CEOs should not be. There was such a professional body in the 1960s but it decided to coalesce with the wider profession in the Society for Education Officers. In the mid-1990s, a specialist professional body for CEOs was proposed. It will become a small, highly focused group with strong links and with the capacity to respond quickly to central government changes and to make public comment on these. It should rapidly become a legitimated group for central government consultations and as a conduit through which detailed interpretations of information can be rapidly channelled for dissemination to principals and governors. It might further strengthen itself by acquiring the position of being a professional regulator as is, for example, the League of Educational Administration, Directors and Superintendents' Organisation in Saskatchewan, Canada, which controls entry to the profession.

To achieve either of the two deflective concepts, what type of CEO is needed? Business management theory in the 1990s is suggesting a return to the visionary leader concept (Useem, 1996) and this might collate with the mythical expectations that CEOs must be great people. If so, would CEOs be Nutt's model, as proposed for senior business leaders? These would be those with 'a flexible style ... aggressive decision-makers with a high tolerance for ambiguity and uncertainty' (Nutt, 1993, p. 695). Should CEOs be the Crows, Graces, Snakes, Dragons or Spiders of Starhawke's (1994) philosophy? Crows have long-term vision by flying high and seeing from above. Graces help maintain others' energy by providing enthusiasm. Snakes cultivate awareness of emotions; they glide along, seeing conflict and bringing it to the surface. Dragons are nurturers. They keep the group realistic its resources. Spiders keep people connected. Perhaps CEOs should be Isenberg's beachcombers who discover flotsam at low tide and decide whether or not to keep it or throw it back. Alternatively, they might be much more passive as frogs on lily ponds, waiting for flies to buzz by and only collecting the slowest and the fattest (Isenberg, 1994, p. 129). The more proactive amongst these analogies should be selected for deflection style. These are underpinned by positional power, achieved by having status, expertise and an appropriate personality with 'charm, intelligence and a silver tongue' (Paton, 1994, p. 193)

This charming personality could also be set in a deflected version of a local authority in which the whole service is privatized, including the CEO. Both New Zealand and the USA had versions of this model in operation by the mid-1990s. New Zealand's councils (though note that these do not include education in their remit) have a single employee – a chief executive on a five-year performance contract. The chief executive then employs the other employees, a formation like that already in use in England for OFSTED, and there are small, directly elected political leadership councils and community bodies. The political element remains, but as Clarke and Stewart (1990, p. 16) suggest, there must be new ways of incorporating it. The New Zealand system has dysfunctions but the 'most profound message

... is its current vitality ... From time to time, all systems must benefit from shock' (Audit Commission, 1993, p. 19).

Moving to the USA models, Graves (1995) reports:

- *Philadelphia.* (214,000 students). The superintendent will lose $8000 per year if students fail to make sufficient gains in academic achievements. The superintendent sets goals each year with the school board and the superintendent's pay is linked to whether or not these are achieved. There is a bonus of up to ten per cent for meeting them and a penalty of a five per cent cut for failure.

- *New York.* Superintendents have annual evaluation against goals although so far, this has not been tied to pay.

- *Texas.* One of the criteria which school boards are expected to use for evaluating superintendents is student achievements. One Texas school board has interpreted this to mean offering bonuses for meeting specific targets, e.g. graduation rates.

- *Minneapolis.* This has a corporate superintendent – Public Strategies Group Inc. – which is paid according to successes. Various incentive payments are offered including $65,000 for improved student achievement. Other incentives include increasing parent involvement ($5000), challenging racism ($20,000) and providing leadership development ($20,000). The total earnable is $400,000. Each target has measurable objectives.

- *Ohio – Fairborn – Dayton.* The superintendent there began by making his own pay rises contingent upon students achieving better results (90 per cent in elementary and junior high had to reach their expected or higher results). Then he persuaded other staff, teachers and support staff to do likewise. Unfortunately, he failed to persuade the taxpayers and they protested when the merit rises were due. However, he then moved on to making his own pay rise dependent upon all 12 schools in his domain raising student achievements and getting 96 per cent attendance. Eleven schools raised achievements but one did not so the pay rise was not achieved.

- *Ohio – Swanton.* The superintendent promised to offer his resignation if the percentage of Swanton's ninth graders passing all four sections of Ohio's proficiency examination did not improve by ten per cent. He felt he must do this in order to demonstrate his commitment to academic progress. Disbelief and amazement greeted his announcement and some board members said they would not accept a resignation should it be shown to be necessary. His officers felt unduly pressurized. Other superintendents thought he was crazy or fed up with the job.

- *Baltimore.* This has a collective corporate superintendency –

Educational Alternatives Inc. It runs nine schools in Baltimore, one in Miami and 32 in Hartford, Connecticut. The company looks after the buildings, trains teachers and improves the curriculum. They are paid 50 cents of every dollar saved.

Adding to these performance-related scenarios are questions of the size of the units to be led by CEOs and how these might be led. LEAs might be much smaller so enabling more personal, and direct control. This is happening in the mid-1990s in some areas. Alternatively, the LEAs could be considerably larger. They will have no or few services to provide directly so the CEOs could relatively easily perform the personalization of the post even in larger, regional authorities. Within these larger authorities, the CEOs' influence might be through having appointees on boards of service providers, through being a purchaser of services or through having some sort of regulatory powers through licensing controls (Brooke, 1989, pp. 10–11; Cochran, 1993, pp. 119–20; Cracknell, 1989, p. 227; Edwards, 1991, p. 40). Freed from the minutiae of managing schools and school support services, CEOs would be well placed to use their time to organize the incorporation of stakeholders into influence and the transmission of central government ideas to schools.

The idea of CEOs as prefects of large regions finds echoes in Australian developments. There they are experimenting with devolved administration to give a real role to the regions. This has to grow from systems in which past regionalism consisted only of relieving state departments of administrative chores and where autonomy was limited to being allowed to spend up to £25 on repairs without consulting head office (Sarros and Beare, 1994, pp. 6–7). Using Queensland as an example, the new regions are responsible for development, evaluation and co-ordination. These regional bodies, unlike English local authorities, are the nominated sub-offices of the state department, its 'human face' and the 'pay-off is measured in terms of immediacy, responsiveness and efficiency' (Sarros and Beare, 1994, p. 9).

Finale

In the mid-1990s CEOS are agents, in all but name, of central government and this chapter suggests they should acquire formal accreditation in this role. In contrast, CEOs are also individualist entrepreneurs with a potential new role conducting the stakeholders' orchestra. An orchestral analogy is not new. Hill's (1938, p. 149) vision of the local government administrator was of one who must bring 'human desire and need into perfect harmony as satisfying as a full orchestral symphony'. It is not immediately apparent to the listeners why conductors, or CEOs, are necessary but the public appearances are just window-dressing. The real work is in the rehearsals. The orchestra will play without a conductor but differently, less in time, less in tune, with less force and with less originality. When new instruments are introduced, they need welding in with a conductor's skill. So it is with CEOs and their LEA orchestras.

Perhaps a more prosaic analogy would be that of the bus conductor. In England, this role is becoming obsolete with the advent of one-person buses in which drivers perform the tasks of conductors. The buses operate successfully but they are less friendly than the two-person versions, have slightly more difficulty keeping the passengers under control, are rather more dangerous at night and are held up longer at stops while the driver takes the fares and makes change. Defenestrating CEOs would have the same effect on education services. Being defensive and allowing CEOs to stay with only incremental alterations in their roles would mean the buses will continue to run but on routes that no longer need them. Deflection into new roles could keep the buses on the roads, finding bypasses and new main thoroughfares and keeping the passengers on board. CEOs collectively cost the country around £9 million a year at 1996 money values – a small price to pay, provided they deflect.

Notes

1   King of England, Denmark and Norway during the early years of the eleventh century. A myth arose about him that, tired of the sycophancy of his courtiers, Knut proved his fallibility by sitting on the beach commanding the tide not to come in. The tide did not obey him.
2   Comment collected from a 1996 research project, directed by the author, on school governors from the business community.

Epilogue

'Go with the flow' or 'Align with the praxis of system coherence'

Imaging the future is always risky but fun to try and more fun for those who read it years after it is written. A quiet smile, for example, must greet the 1984 prediction that 'it is unlikely that centralised control of education in this country would be acceptable' (Hornsby, 1984, p. 119). Quiet smiles may greet my final predictions too.

'I'll woluff[1] you back to your space craft' offered the Managing Director, Education, (MDE) to my profound relief. The English region of planet Earth, 2300 hours in November, 2096 was not my usual beat. Not so unusual though for this senior executive of a regional franchise operation for the provision of publicly subsidized education. Being the MDE's shadow, I followed whither she woluffed, noting the surroundings, the events, the people and her role in it all. I was in the first months of non-participant observation research on developments in strategic leadership. I was recreating research done by one of my ancestors at the end of the twentieth century (Thody, 1996) to assess changes in the MDEs' roles. These MDEs were the inheritors of a post once called a chief education officer. My research was to ascertain what these MDEs did each day.

On this first day of my observations, the MDE considered the applications for franchises for operating the core business of education. Today there were three: one from a Year 9–13 private tutorial college specializing in public examination intensive courses and resits,[2] one from a primary school which had had a brief and unsatisfactory flirtation with grant-maintained status and one from a further education cluster of nine colleges who the director knew intended to offer University of Minnesota degrees once their clustering was officially approved.[3]

The MDE had almost completed the core business franchise awards for the next five-year period; next week there would be the bids for the

.es to whom the coveted regional logo meant
 ᴅ guarantee orders from the officially franchised
 ᴧDE discussed with me the valuable new companies
 ɔcutive-technicians to undertake marking and report
 ɹld greatly relieve the master-grade teacher employees
 ɹization for teachers.
 ᴧe logo required a provider not only to undergo major
 ʂ but also to pay a substantial sum of money to the MDE's
 ᴧchise business (known as a school board). This paid the MDE's
 ʂ only employee. The charges also covered the annual monitor-
 ɔr inspections from OFEDBUS,[4] the MDE's appointees to quality
 posts who were legally the managing director's own employees. In
 ɔe, the MDE was a separate company.
 ᴧe MDE holographed the school board parent representatives, local
 ɹsiness leaders and community group members into the room. She
 ɔhecked the pupil brain monitor to ensure that all pupil's views were regis-
tered. Together with the board members, the community groups perused
the screen detailing the agreed policy on franchising established by the full-
time advisory council, elected and paid for by the local tax payers. There
were obviously substantial vested interests in the franchising issue and the
community consultative subject panels had all been involved in establishing
the policy. The community panels each represented one of the stakeholder
areas of interest – finance (local banks, building societies ...), parents (PTA
reps from each school in the area ...) etc.

The franchise policy was central to the financial success of the school
board. All 20 English and Welsh school boards offered franchises and the
credibility of each logo was eagerly discussed and merits hotly debated.
Initially, of course, the core business of teaching had tended to stay in the
geographical areas of each accrediting company but within a few years the
old loyalties had disbanded and the entrepreneurialism of the MDEs had
spread each logo variously across the nation.

The MDE chuckled as she suggested to the school board that they ought
to consider franchising suppliers based in other countries. The chair had
not quite realized the implications of EU membership for primary and
secondary education. Officially, the EU had little direct influence at Phases
I and II of core education provision but it was partly the single market that
had precipitated the National Curriculum at the end of the last century
(Bongers, 1990, p. 42). The MDEs had collectively taken over the Centre of
European Education for England and Wales and had used this as a leader
offering a joint MDE (England) logo for schools with a European dimension. No other EU country had done this and hence the English MDEs had
monopolized the award-granting powers and now spread their influence
into at least eight of the EU countries. The MDEs had used this to become
the centres of information on European vocational training, a confusing
field with which few further education colleges had the time or the staff to

become fully conversant, hence the MDE local information service proved extremely valuable. This MDE initiative had brought the further education colleges back into the regional school board after almost a century of independence. The universities had long since returned to MDE direction. Each university had wanted the coveted regional logo without which central government would give no grants. The MDEs had each selected one university for this award, thus removing surplus capacity and the power of academia, at a stroke.

During the discussion with the school board, the MDE recounted the successes of the logo campaign and how they had been able to continue to corner the market in special needs' provision and specialist sports and math schools. Such efforts to pursue a market segmentation came easily to this MDE, with a first degree in accountancy, a DBA and years in a multi-national biscuit company. Her registration with the General Council for MDs (Local Government) patterned on the late twentieth-century Saskatchewan registry and Scottish General Teaching Council, had assisted the self-conscious professionalization of the MDE career and given it a credibility which neither central nor local government politicians could affect. Currently, her five-year term as MDE was half complete; another year and she'd be contemplating rotation to – was it housing next ? – it just slipped her mind right then.

What the MDE did not mention to the school board was the collective agenda agreed at the last national MDEs' meeting for discussion at the national forum. It had been decided that the 20 MDE companies would each continue to specialize so eventually creating only one franchisor for each type of provision and then using monopoly power to force up standards (and prices). Central government had been party to that agreement. Indeed, central government had initiated the debate for MDEs and spent much time with them working out the details of the policy and ensuring each MDE would provide to their school boards and employees the same interpretations of what had been agreed. The changes could mean that the paid, party political school board chair and the advisory body would recede even more into becoming window-dressing, with the consultative panels replacing them for wider community involvement. Eventually, of course, the MDEs' professional association would then have created a truly national system of education.

After the school board had been dematerialized, the MDE called up a neighbouring MDE. Collectively they were writing a beamdream[5] – not easy with both of them being such different characters with different interpretations of their roles. Still, reflected the MDE, those different interpretations had ever been the stuff of leadership since the predecessor role of CEO had emerged from the primeval sludge of the clerk to the nineteenth-century English school boards. The book centred around the concept of direct consumerism replacing the indirect democracy of local elected councils. The MDEs were researching the genesis of these ideas and had just located what eventually emerged as the seminal article on New Zealand's schools in the 1990s. This showed how the schools which collaborated least with parents had the closest match of values with parents. The choice of the market had achieved more than the choices operative through democratic mechanisms (Timperley and Robinson, 1995).

The MDEs planned to address such questions as: through what mechanisms could direct consumerism be achieved most effectively? What would be the impact of destroying the forums for local political parties and creating league tables of services bought as indicators of what the public wanted? Would direct democracy through Internet be a preferable alternative ? All MDEs were on the National Commission for Education's Reconstruction and they had been considering how other organisations in sub-central government incorporated accountability. It was important that they, the experts, planned the future.

But it was time for me to go. The MDE's working day had already lasted one hour, ten minutes, much longer than the norm for other workers. It was amazing to see how enthusiastic the MDE was for her work despite these long hours.

Notes

1   For those reading this in the late twentieth or early twenty-first century, before woluffing was invented, it consists of elevated walking on air as if one were a mini-hovercraft.

2   For those who might think the format of schools mentioned is curiously old-fashioned for the late twenty-first century, it is as well to recollect how schools in the later twentieth century retained many features 'invented' in the late nineteenth century, such as age segregation in classes. In education, systems change slowly.

3   The international franchises were renewable on a different cycle, falling due in 2135. The MDE was particularly proud of having piloted the first English franchising of schools into France; once other MDEs had begun to follow suit, she had moved to franchising around the Commonwealth.

4   The Office for Monitoring Educational Businesses.

5   Mental flashes to be beamed directly to the minds of those interested in the topic. Subscribers to this service simply specify the areas in which they are interested and 'books' are sent to them by thought waves.

Appendix: Studying the strategic leaders' days: research methodology

I'll walk beside you through the passing years
Through days of rain and sunshine, joy and tears
And when the great call comes, the trumpets sound
I'll walk beside you to the promised land.

E. Lockton (1936)

Walking beside CEOs over the passing years to record and report their daily activities, was fascinating, time-consuming, tiring, analytically complex, challenging and emotionally involving. To those who would replicate this type of research with senior executives and who might seek guidance from this methodology appendix, I confess, as did Fitz and Halpin (1994, pp. 32, 33) concerning their study of élites, that this study unfolded, rather than being planned. Chances of access dominated decision-making; research methods were made to fit opportunities rather than opportunities being sought to fit predetermined methodology. Methodology thus served, rather than led, this research. What was discovered was also more exciting than how it was discovered, hence the placement of methodology in an appendix. None the less, there needs to be description of the methodology to establish the validity and reliability of the findings and to offer routes for those who might wish to try similar research. This appendix therefore describes the choices of senior managers, approaches to them, and the collection, analysis and presentation of data.

Choosing the people

An opportunity sample is the best description for those observed for this research. Collecting them was 'not a neat process' (McHugh, 1994, p. 54) but it was not difficult. I was amazed, therefore, to read that Macpherson required almost two years to persuade three regional directors of education in Australia to let him shadow them, having done considerable research on how best to approach his intended subjects and suffering refusals along the way (Macpherson, 1987, pp. 151–2). Fortunately, this was not published until after my study had begun or I might have given up at the start. I did not know at the commencement how many CEOs, nor how many years, the research would include. Willingness and proximity were the prime characteristics for selection, as other researchers have found (David, 1977, p. 26; Duignan, 1980; Griffin and Chance, 1994). Such willingness can be encouraged if a researcher has the backing of a major research body, is using conventional methodology or has similar status or background to the élites being studied (Fitz and Halpin, 1994, p. 34). I had none of these and, at the time of the first observations, was a neophyte researcher.

Several factors served to facilitate access. The most important was the 'informal grapevine', as Macpherson (1985a) also discovered. A personal recommendation from my university's pro-vice-chancellor to a CEO colleague launched the first observation, and this access indicated to others the acceptability of the research, a method of 'sponsorship' recommended by Walford (1994a). Secondly, being a woman may have assisted access. A woman observer is deemed less threatening than a male (Silverman, 1993, p. 35). 'In our sexist society, where it is men who hold most of the powerful positions, female researchers may be at an advantage ... being perceived as "harmless" especially if they are relatively young and not in senior positions within their own organisations' (Walford, 1994a, p. 224). I was not young but I was only a lecturer during the first cohort observation. Lest any researcher be now contemplating a sex change, it is as well to report that there were two women CEOs in the group who were as welcoming as the men. Thirdly, access to the powerful may be easier than reported, especially in local rather than central government (Walford, 1994a). Being helpful to newcomers must be one of the pleasures of power and those with power are unlikely to lack the confidence to cope with an observation. Fourthly, it may have been, as Hall (1994a, 1994b) found with the principals who agreed to her observation research, that they felt lonely in their positions and welcomed the possibility of reflection on their own practice for their own professional development. I told the CEOs that I was writing a book but, at the time of the first observation, I did not know when it would appear and I did not think to offer them feedback. This failure certainly lost me a second cohort prospect who complained that I should have provided feedback to the first group. Fifthly, as one of them said, CEOs love an audience, especially one that won't answer back. Finally, these leaders are educationalists for whom encouraging research is part of their role. I was the fortunate beneficiary of their kind acceptance of my presence.

The first cohort of five was all male and the second group was two women and two men. In selecting a majority of males, I was not rejecting the female perspective. There was only one woman CEO at the time of the first observations. She was appointed after the study began (Diana Tuck, CEO for Walsall, appointed October 1986), her LEA was too far for my daily travel and she was anyway described as 'a good honorary chap' (Wilce, 1986, p. 6). By 1994–95, there were 16 female CEOs,[1] from whom I selected two. Given the paucity of research on women in management (Hall, 1994a, p. 2) and the existence of allegations that female CEOs are more harshly treated by local politicians than are male counterparts (Hackett, 1994, p. 6),[2] my lack of a feminist viewpoint and of a gender-balanced sample may seem an opportunity missed. There is great debate over whether or not there are feminine and masculine characteristics in management (Hall, 1994a, p. 3) but this debate was not central to this research nor is it one in which I can claim any expertise. I therefore did not look for gender characteristics nor did I choose to analyse data in relation to gender. None the less, I fleetingly reflected on differences that may have affected my data-gathering: I felt much more comfortable on a personal level with the women (a comfort which Hall (1994a, p. 4) also reports in her study of women principals) but much more comfortable as an observer with the men; the women excluded me from more events than did the males.

Making the first contact: selecting the days for observation

For an example of how not to make the first contact, readers should consult David Lodge's novel, *Nice Work* (1989, pp. 95–6), in which the shadow engages in political argument with the subject at their initial meeting. Instead of this, researchers stress the importance of careful preparatory negotiation with those targeted for observation in order to create solidarity (Hilsum and Cane, 1994; Martin and Willower, 1981, p. 70; Whitty and Edwards, 1994, p. 22). In contrast, my approach seems somewhat casual. To the first subject I wrote a letter describing the research and offering a meeting. The CEO agreed to this. With great trepidation I approached the appointment, having first made myself as completely as possible *au fait* with observation methodology and with that executive's context. I met simply an immediate query about when I wanted to start, great friendliness, a cup of tea, a chat about the weather, the LEA and its achievements. This immediate success must have given me a ring of confidence in approaching other possible subjects. In each case, I phoned and then sent a letter explaining the research with a request for access. The letter noted who had already agreed to participate, related some connection with the LEA concerned and its reputation, requested permission to come and talk to them about the research and suggested they might contact those already being observed.

In each case I offered to come and meet the CEO. Each asked me to do so, although one enquired why I wanted to see him in advance of the observation as he was happy just to set the dates. Three were certain from the start that I could shadow for at least a week; the fourth offered one day initially and at the end of that, offered further days. The fifth was perhaps 'forced' into agreement. He was first encountered while still a deputy and I was observing his then CEO. I asked the deputy if he would allow the observation when he took over as CEO. In the circumstances, it might have been difficult for the deputy to refuse. Gamely he welcomed me within a very short time of his appointment and seven years later as the sole survivor of the first cohort.

The ease of access to the first cohort made me less careful in approaches to the second. I sent each potential subject an outline of the book and requested their participation. I did not schedule further meetings but this proved to be a mistake. All four acceded but at the last minute one withdrew indicating serious doubts about the project (which a visit might have allayed). I trod more warily to find replacements (a second CEO retired just before the observations were due to begin), visiting both although, as with the first cohort, the discussions were more about the dates on which I wished to come rather than an investigation into the project or my credentials. Some of the subjects had been shadowed by other people.

We mutually agreed the dates for the observations. My other commitments restricted my availability. I restricted their dates to those on which they operated wholly within their LEAs with no travel beyond that. They generally tried to include a political committee and a departmental management team meeting amongst my dates.

There are criticisms that observation research can preclude generalizations because the samples are small and the time of accompaniment is short (Kmetz and Willower, 1982). In contrast, studies of even single leaders are valued for 'exploring new themes and for starting to bring alive textures of particular circumstances' (Townsend, 1991, 49). Equally, Macpherson's (1984a) study of three directors concluded that similarities exceeded differences in the data thus allowing some role generalizations. This research produced nine sets of data across nine years and includes references to allied studies. Readers must judge for themselves if this constitutes a valid data base.

Non-participant observation

Preparation and validation

This research relied on one method of collecting data about the activities of nine CEOs over 36 days (380 hours and 46 minutes). This might be regarded as methodologically unsound (Cookson, 1994, p. 128) but 'difficulties of constructing accounts of senior officers in action are so considerable that researchers have tended to accept compromises' (Macpherson, 1985a, p. 64). These observations were 11 days longer than the time over which Mintzberg observed five executives in his seminal, 1973 study, the findings of which have dominated our understandings of how managers operate. Some corroboration of findings can be from others' accounts but studies of CEOs are rare as is observation research at this level. Its corroboration with reality must come from review by CEOs themselves and by other policy researchers. Its validity must come from the rigour with which it was conducted and reported and the care taken to retain proof of activities. I, therefore, hold the original field notes, their disk summaries, raw data analysis and documents collected from the sites, such as minutes of meetings.

Preparation for my observations was minimal other than a pilot observation, following my university's pro-vice-chancellor for two days (Thody, 1989). I decided to present the results non-contextually so did not need to interview. I also avoided studies of other strategic leaders as these might have dictated my expectations. The CEOs differed in the extent of preparation they offered me. I did not ask for any background from them (partly to avoid imposing on their time) but what they gave me provided clues to their attitudes. Some presented me with booklets on their authority and its schools, its budget and its central office staffing structure and gave me information about the political composition of the authority. Others gave me nothing unless I asked. All were unfailingly helpful in responding to any requests for information.

Interviewing was rejected for this study because I wished to present an outsider's view rather than that of the subjects and because it had already been used (Allison, 1991a; Brown and Baker, 1991; Bush and Kogan, 1982; Bush et al., 1989; Edwards, 1991; Jones, 1988; Kogan and van der Eyken, 1973; Macpherson, 1985a; Walker, 1994). I also avoided having discussions with the subjects during or since the accompaniment periods, unlike other observation researchers (Hall et al.,1986, p. 224), as I wanted to disturb the normal course of events as little as possible. Questionnaires were eschewed because they provide subjects' perceptions and because, in order to remain a manageable length, they must focus on only part of executive activities (Brown and Baker, 1991; Edwards, 1991; Griffin and Chance, 1994; Leithwood and Musella, 1991a). I decided not to ask CEOs to record their own activities. Such diaries cannot compete with the detail recorded by an observer, as diary research shows (Austin, 1975; Clerkin, 1985; Hickcox, 1992; Stewart, 1965). Fryer, a 1988 CEO, demonstrated this. He admitted that his record did not include 'all those smaller and unprogrammed events that fitted into the interstices of my diary' (Fryer, 1988a, p. 3). He recorded only 13 events in a week, whereas I recorded an average of 17 major activities daily for the 1986–88 cohort and 18 for the 1994–95 cohort. Keeping a usefully detailed diary would also impose on the subject's time and commitment and would, therefore, alter the course of a day's events. Detailed instructions would be needed to ensure that all subjects recorded the same items.

Affectation?

Did being observed affect how the managers behaved? David Lodge's (1989, p. 247) fictitious hero felt he performed particularly well when being shadowed, even playing to the shadow's 'imagined presence and silent applause' when she was not there. School principals, observed in Hall's

1994 study, believed they behaved differently when she was present. One of the subjects of this research commented that it 'makes one terribly self-conscious of what one is doing'. A subordinate noted of another of the CEOs that 'he seemed more optimistic and positive than usual' at a meeting during the observations. There were also minor observer effects on behaviour since the CEOs sometimes stopped to provide explanations to me or to introduce me to unwitting participants in the research. These may have been affected too. A CEO thought that principals 'might posture' if I were there so he excluded me from a meeting. One of the CEO's deputies felt constrained by my presence which she thought altered the tenor of a meeting. A CEO considered that a meeting of sub-committee chairs was 'more muted than usual' during my observations. Does this mean that 'first hand investigation of people in natural settings is an exercise in futility, since in the face of intrusion ... informants will cease to be natural' (Gronn, 1987a, p. 102)?

During the first cohort study, I asked others encountered during the observations, if they thought the subjects had behaved differently from usual. All said this had not happened, adding that, for example, 'He always works at this pace', 'He always takes time to speak to the children on school visits'. Councillors commented that I had melted into the background and they had not noticed me. I also arranged to be observed myself to see how it affected me. After the first half hour I found I was too busy to be aware of the shadow and certainly did not have time to alter my performance deliberately. One of the CEOs echoed this finding: 'Most of the time, I forgot you were there', he remarked, just as regional directors of education in Macpherson's (1985a, p. 73) research had found themselves oblivious to his presence as a shadow. The subjects had little opportunity to manipulate a day's events as evidenced in earlier chapters; visitors and phone calls arrived without direction; many meetings were scheduled by those other than the CEOs. In large meetings, very few participants knew why I was there or even that I was observing so they would not alter their behaviour. In smaller meetings, the CEOs' concentration on the multiple interactions must have inhibited any tendency to 'play to the gallery'. Those telephoning in were unaware of my presence. On tour with the CEO, people sometimes mistook me for a secretary in tow with a shorthand notebook. Many occasions did not lend themselves to my being introduced and I became an unobtrusive part of the entourage.

Identification

Rather than the subjects being affected, was I affected to the extent that my judgements could have been excessively subjective? I acquired great sympathy with my subjects, becoming a strong apologist for each after observing them since it was difficult to avoid the 'sheer power of a dominant personality' (Gronn, 1987a, p. 107) during such intensive attachments.

Such attuning is considered acceptable (Walker, 1994, p. 27) provided one does not 'go native'. Dearlove (1979) and Dunleavy (1980) criticized local government research in the 1960s and 1970s because its data emerged from too close relations with the major professional and political personnel, thus preventing objective analysis. During observation, 'unconscious feelings whether affectionate or hostile' must be confronted (Gronn, 1987a, p. 101) and identification with subjects is strong, almost to the extent of acquiring 'another life ... another identity ... a *doppelgänger*' (Lodge, 1989, p. 216). I became a temporary clone. The cloning in my case was not so much with these CEOs themselves (which would have seemed presumptuous) but more with local government. For a brief while, I learnt to think and expect as a local education administrator. It made me question my own assumptions when set against attitudes I might previously have criticized. The novelist (1989, p. 216) Lodge expresses the sensation effectively: 'Flitting backwards and forwards across the frontier between ... two zones, whose values, priorities, language and manners were so utterly disparate, [the observer] felt like a secret agent; and, as secret agents are apt to do, suffered occasional spasms of doubt about the righteousness of her own side.' This change in my attitudes became evident to me while recording a meeting of one of the subjects with school governors. Usually, I empathized with governors since they were then my major area of research and I was a governor and governor trainer myself. On this occasion, I found myself annoyed at their incapacity to appreciate the CEO's point of view and to understand the lack of viability of their ideas and the complexities of administration.

This 'kind of love' that develops between researcher and researched is not confined to observation (Kogan, 1994, p. 74) but to minimize its effects in this study, the accompaniment phases were split, analysis was not undertaken until some time after the observations, records were as non-judgemental as possible, discussions during the research were avoided and I adopted neutral, non-participant body language and facial expression while observing. I actually 'kept my head down' to avoid engagement but I valued my co-existence with each subject as a vital tool in understanding their work. It helped to release temporarily 'all preoccupation with self [to] move into a state of complete attention' (Heshusius, 1994, p. 17) and to assist my translation of the activities I observed. Some CEOs recognized the extent of my coexistence since they took the trouble to phone me after the observations to inform me of the conclusions to policy initiations I had viewed.

Confidentiality

The closeness between subject and researcher is vital since confidentiality is important (Fitz and Halpin, 1994, p. 35; Macpherson, 1985a, pp. 75, 186; Walford, 1994a, pp. 4, 5). Watching the game of politics being played for real is a fascinating experience; 'who loses, and who wins; who's in, who's out' (*King Lear*), whose arm is being twisted, who has walked into the trap that has been laid, who has side-stepped it, who did not notice that they were being set up – all this is very interesting to the student of micro-politics but all this is confidential as can be the macro-politics of selecting major policies.

Problems with confidentiality did not, however, emerge as often as they were envisaged. The generalizations which this study produced masked confidential, personal issues. The anonymity of the reporting avoided attri-bution. The time between recording and reporting meant that sensitive issues were not so by the time of publication. Events were insufficiently concluded during each observation to make it possible to reveal a full story. My exclusions were at the same low level as those of Martin and Willower's research – about one per cent of events. There were exclusions from two of the four chief officers' meetings I might have attended (it is not known if this was the wish of the CEO or of the chief executive), from an HMI meeting (at the request of the HMI who then offered to be shadowed himself), from a confrontational meeting with secondary school principals (at the request of the CEO who described them as 'being disloyal'), from personal or social events (a Rotary Club meeting, a union meeting, some lunches), from a political leaders' meeting to change a highly sensitive policy (but I was welcomed to the similarly sensitive follow-on meeting the next day) and from a staff disciplinary issue. Exclusions appeared to relate less to confidentiality and more to the subjects' confidence, their desire not to disturb usual group dynamics, their perceptions of their power in rela-tion to others involved in the events and a desire for a rest from constant observation.

Embarrassment

They may need a rest. 'What the hell was he going to do with this woman every Wednesday for the next two months?' asked David Lodge's hero of the novel *Nice Work* as he contemplated having to cope with a shadow. It is possible that these leaders felt the same way. When asked what it was like to have an observer, one of them remarked, 'Oh, Angela's very good at it. It's just me who finds it difficult'. This person did seem uneasy with my pres-ence but by day three, relaxation was evident as the CEO remarked, 'It's nice to have another opinion around' since by then we were commenting privately on events. By the last day, the subject concerned felt sufficiently comfortable to phone home on domestic matters while I was there; one of the others always went to another office when phoning home. Generally, a certain jocularity smoothed away some of the embarrassment as officers proffered invisible chairs or food for the 'invisible' shadow or asked if they should walk through me or round me. Whatever their feelings, the CEOs did not show them and made me feel comfortably at ease.

I anticipated feeling uneasy especially as simply taking measurements of the private offices of CEOs discomforted two Canadian researchers (Lawton and Scane, 1991, p. 179). Initially, I felt embarrassed following the leaders everywhere, even for short trips into adjacent offices, but embarrassment soon dissipated under the influence of the jocularities and the concentration needed for continuous recording. I took my comfort breaks in a mad dash whenever the executive likewise departed or alternatively during committee meetings when the subjects might be passive for long periods.

Exhaustion

Exhaustion was more common than embarrassment. To my subjects' long days I added my travel time of up to four hours a day and I found boring periods during the observations (as did Wolcott, 1973, p. 16). Intending observers are advised to take a physical training course before attempting tracking. Subjects work at a fast pace, with relatively little sustenance and few breaks. I had to concentrate non-stop to remember names, to orientate to new people, in-jokes and locations where everyone knew everyone else, while trying to keep mental and physical pace with very active and intelligent people. I found myself appreciating the feelings of David Lodge's (1989, p. 120) heroine in *Nice Work*, who, after her first hour's observation felt 'confused, battered, exhausted by the sense-impressions'.

Collecting data: note-taking

Taking notes from observation is a skill that rapidly develops (Macpherson, 1985a, p. 81). I piloted A3 sheets for the observation notes, following my university's pro-vice-chancellor for two days (Thody, 1989). Each sheet was divided into 25 columns enabling me to record and analyse data simultaneously according to its start, finish and elapse times, its location, the number of interruptions, the people encountered and the types of meetings. Separate A4 sheets were for recording, *inter alia*, overt and covert purposes of activities, aspects of schooling or management involved and estimates of an event's importance. I used additional sheets to analyse the paperwork with which the CEOs were dealing. The pilot study revealed all this to be unworkable. No more than one sheet at a time could be used. Flicking through sheets to find the appropriate one was time-consuming and intrusive. An A3 clipboard was unwieldy. The variety of work, its speed and rapid changes of location made concurrent analysis and note-taking impossible.

Simplified A4 size sheets were therefore used for chronologically recording events. Half of each sheet was ruled to columns and half left open. In the columns, I recorded each activity's reference letter, its start, end and elapse times, its location, overt purpose and the people encountered during the activity. An activity was deemed to be an 'identifiable single event with an observable beginning and ending' (Duignan, 1980, p. 10), 'incident' in Guest's 1960 terminology. On the open part of the sheet (about two-thirds vertical) I recorded as much as possible of what was seen and said without precategorization, similar to Townsend's (1991) open structuring. A shorthand notebook was substituted when on the move with the notes later stapled to the original A4 sheets; a small notebook was used for social occasions or other events when a clipboard would have been obtrusive. The much more open recording that became my working mode prevented me from making the data fit prespecified codings and so becoming 'taken-for-granted' (Delamont, 1988, p. 10). No previous observation work matched what I wanted to achieve (Macpherson, 1985a, 1985b; Mintzberg, 1973; Stewart, 1982) so, like Hall (1994a, p. 7), 'my decisions about what to observe were eclectic rather than seeking to replicate any one model'. I took notes in abbreviated long hand, as did Hall *et al.* (1986).

Only three of the CEOs had telephones on which I could hear both the caller and the subject so generally, my phone call notes were one-sided. It was usually possible to infer what the caller wanted and CEOs sometimes explained, even though I did not ask them to. Morning and evening work at home were not included in my notes and one of the managers wondered if any observer could be aware of the full extent of this additional work.

The most difficult situations in which to shadow were the informal premeeting sessions or semi-social occasions such as lunches and dinners. Everyone was milling about; the subject frequently changed contacts; it was impossible to ask who were all the people encountered; balancing a notebook, wine and food, while trying to look casual, was not easy. I developed a routine of standing at an oblique angle to a CEO (or back-to-back) while gazing into the middle distance and trying not to look involved.

Trying not to look involved was important as this was non-participant observation. The course of events must be as little disturbed by the observer as possible in contrast to the effect of the heroine shadow in David Lodge's novel, *Nice Work* (1989). She had regular arguments with her subject, intervened in the action and even finished up in bed with the subject. None of these occurred in this research but it was very difficult not to speak sometimes. Joining in seemed natural as I became genuinely interested and involved or where I had expertise and knowledge. Contacts, other than the people whom I was shadowing, engaged me in conversation about the research or drew me into general conversation. It would have seemed impolite to stay constantly distant. I also became drawn in as participants kindly involved me in the fun of the power plays and personality assassinations that are the stuff of any office politics. The only way to inhibit involvement was to avoid eye contact. This discouraged all but the most determined from pulling me into the action. It did not, however, deter children. Observing the CEOs on primary school visits added the distractions of children keen to show me their work. I was delayed with exhibits of clay snails while the CEO passed out of my sight and was on the climbing frame by the time I caught up. Making precise timings of activities on such occasions was difficult.

Aware that an observer should 'always dress and behave according to the inviolate social canons of the host group' (Gronn, 1987a, p. 104), I generally adopted a costume somewhere between executive woman and female secretary modes. I wore a trouser suit only when with one of the women CEOs who dressed likewise. Finding somewhere to sit required a compromise between being unobtrusive, being able to hear the subjects' public and private utterances and being able to see the their faces. In large meetings, it was usually possible to achieve all of these. Where rooms were cramped, as are principals' offices, it was impossible not to be glaringly obvious but everyone did their best to ignore me.

Unlike other observers, I did not keep a journal nor a running record of analysis as did Spradley (1979). I felt I had enough information without this. I did not analyse my notes on the evenings of the days on which I collected them as had Macpherson (1987) and Mintzberg (1973). I was too tired to do this. I did not clarify items at the end of the day with a subject as did Martin and Willower (1981) and Kmetz and Willower (1982). Subject and researcher were both too tired and I would have had to look through 20 pages of notes to find any queries. I did not use a variety of coloured pens as had Macpherson (1985a) nor a tape recorder like Gronn (1987a) since both seemed obtrusive and complicated. I abandoned attempts to keep impressions and anecdotes separately from the main text as had Kmetz and Willower (1982, p. 64). Only occasionally did I record the mail as Duignan did (1980). The quantity was so vast as to need a separate study.

Documentary sources

My secondary sources were dominated by the few studies of CEOs mentioned in Chapter 1. To these I added international comparisons with Canadian and US superintendents and CEOs and with Australian regional directors of education whose roles are roughly analogous. Of particular value for comparisons were the studies using observation (Macpherson, 1985a, b; Duignan, 1980) or which analysed particular activities (Allison, 1991b; Hickcox, 1992; Townsend, 1991). There is more literature available about this level of strategic leadership in education in these countries than in our own although it is not a major genre. There were, for example, only 38 studies of Canadian superintendents amongst 10,000 leadership studies located in 1991 (Walker, 1994, p. 3). Their literature reflects a belief that CEOs can effect change (Bredeson, 1995; Crowson, 1994; Griffin and Chance, 1994; Musella, 1992; Roberts, 1985). There are, of course, some differences between their systems and ours. US and Canadian superintendents are appointed and employed by their local boards which are education-specific local authorities not multi-functional ones as in England. The Canadian system more directly parallels ours in that superintendents have a mass of centrally specified duties but differs in that, in Ontario for example, superintendents have an examination process through which they must pass. Perhaps England lies between the USA and Canadian traditions. In the USA, the superintendency tradition is 'the pioneering of executive educational administration'; in Canada it is 'privileged selection and service in the interests of high ideals' (Allison, 1991a, p. 234).

Primary documents included committee, working group and council minutes, agenda papers and reports. I found these helpful, though not vital, to remind me of the fullness of events where I had recorded only the CEOs' participation. Two of the subjects provided copies of the letters and memos they sent on one day. They were sufficient to convince me that including an analysis of these would prove too time-consuming.

Data analysis

Not wishing the first researches to influence how I annotated later days, I undertook no data analysis until all the observations were complete. The consequent data mountain at the end was very daunting but did enable me to study all the leaders before analysis categories emerged, as Bryman (1988, pp. 61–66) recommended. Other observers analysed each subject almost immediately (Macpherson, 1985a, p. 82; Mintzberg, 1973), or did partial analysis (Owens, 1982, p. 11) or analysed and reformulated their research in progress (Hall, 1994b, p. 3). I was too tired.

My aims were to quantify some of the material to facilitate comparisons rather than just reporting the events witnessed, the latter being considered a lax form of presentation akin to journalism rather than to research (Walford, 1994a, p. 229). Lax it may be, but it was very tempting as the extent of the precision required for the quantitative stage, and the time it required, became evident. Information had to be controlled without burying vital elements in 'a sea of numerical data' (Martin and Willower, 1981, p. 87). This can create a 'blissfully aseptic' view of managerial roles, unrealistically omitting political aspects (Gronn, 1987b, p. 81). The qualitative analysis had to provide depth and entertainment without becoming lost in ethnographic 'busywork' (Theobald, 1990). The latter is deemed suitable only for 'exotic' settings (Lofland, 1971), not a description that comes to mind in relation to English LEAs.

To achieve these aims, I articulated themes, or frames, similar to Donmoyer's (1985, p. 35–7) 'domains' and to Duignan's (1980, p. 8) 'clusters or constellations'. These partially met Silverman's (1993, p. 29) requirement that qualitative research should be theoretically driven since the frames offer some theoretical stabilization to a largely empirically driven study. I could not standardize the frames in accordance with previous research, as Silverman (1993, p. 148) requires, because there was no similar research. The frames had to emerge from the data. They had to provide a home for every item of information collected. Both of these they did but it was not possible to create entirely exclusive categories so that each activity had only one entry as Haggarty (1995, p. 185) requires. Events frequently served more than one purpose and so were counted for both.

Each sheet of notes was worked through laboriously (there were about 800 closely written pages) with every item annotated according to its category. The idea of using software at this stage was tempting but it would have been very time-consuming to type in all the data before the annotations could be applied. Once the annotations were complete, however, computer analysis would have greatly speeded the collation of data. Were I commencing such a project again, I would use software for qualitative analysis but it had not been invented when I began this study.

Presenting the research

Of all the methodological questions to be answered, how to present the research was the most difficult. How could I convey the appeal of the role while satisfying academic imperatives? The nature of the discoveries lent itself to creating fiction and to a style that could be novelistic. This conflicted with the need to offer full proof of discoveries for scholarly credibility (Lipson, 1994) which lent itself to an immensely detailed, academic style. These two had also to be balanced against the need to be ethical. The needs and rights of the people observed had to be respected; a novel might trivialize; an academic text might bore. Neither could quite serve the fascination of strategic leadership.

I discovered three genres amongst others' efforts to present their observations. None seemed fully appropriate for this study though each offered some possibilities. First, there was detailed, descriptive reporting such as: 'The furrowed brow cleared, he shrugged, grinned, turned and limped into the Department'; 'each item of mail was given between five and eight seconds of attention before a decision was annotated for a subordinate or a brief discussion with his R.E.O. ensued' (Macpherson, 1985a, pp. 136, 236). This revealed the depth of the data but made comparisons difficult. Secondly, there was an almost skeletal approach to outlining routines (Hall et al., 1986). This managed to control the quantity of data well, showing its richness and demonstrating the robustness of records but such an approach for nine CEOs would have been very dull. Finally, there were thematic approaches that quantitatively reduced some data while thematically styling the rest around tasks to facilitate comparisons (Duignan 1980; Mintzberg, 1973).

Fortunately there is now much more acceptance of a journalistic style in the presentation of ethnographic research. Even the shock tactics of pictorial style are recommended (Atkinson, 1990) with 'thick descriptions' so that the reader feels transported to actual locations (Owens, 1982, p. 15). Presentation must do more than just reproduce what happened. It must be an imaginative process but one arising from truth not fiction. The people observed have to be re-created; that re-creation must be faithful, ethical and realistic.

Being ethical seemed to me to include being non-judgemental yet an academic text must compare, comment and conclude and subjectivism must be a valued part of this type of research. Once descriptive analogies are selected, however, they acquire normative overtones even where none are intended. I discovered this early in the process when using some of the findings for a conference paper and I used 'medieval monarch' as an analogy for a CEO. One CEO was incensed by this descriptor; two asked for anonymity as result; one (retired) said it was a perfect likeness. Noting such parallels adds interest to the academic reporting but it can seem presumptuous.

It is easy to be wise from the outside, yet what observation teaches is how difficult and complex are the routes to be selected by the strategic leader. One criticizes at one's peril. As Townsend (1991, p. 49) noted of his observational study of one man: 'Had my findings turned out to be less sympathetic, I might have had to disguise the study's location and persons' and Gronn (1987a, p. 103) reports the difficulties of trying to avoid upsetting one's subject.

It was with great humility that I approached these CEOs who agreed to allow me to shadow, and with great awareness of what I was asking. In all cases, the close observation could not help but lead to admiration for the achievements in such a complex role, but equally, it could not help but reveal possibilities which when written up might appear critical. Offence can be given and I now realize perhaps why the Kogan trilogy (Bush and Kogan, 1982; Bush et al., 1989; Kogan and van der Eyken, 1973) reported interviews verbatim with little comment since comment tends to veer to the critical. This happened in the 1977 David study. She tried to soften the criticism with the almost mandatory concluding plaudits but throughout her book, the criticisms were manifest. Walford (1994a) and Cookson (1994, pp. 127, 129) both feel that the powerful are 'fair game' for criticism. This view does not allow for humanity and for the recognition that the powerful share the same adequacies and inadequacies as the rest of us. It also assumes that the researcher's views are right whereas they are only one more perception of events.

With all these *caveats* in mind, this research is presented.

Notes

1 Currently being studied by Al-Khalifa of the Local Government Management Board. Holders of CEO positions are predominantly male, as are US superintendents (Bredeson, 1995, p. 3; Crowson, 1994, p. 1).
2 Four women CEOs appointed in the early 1990s were rapidly dismissed or suspended.

References

Ackroyd S., Hughes J.A. and Soothill K. (1989) Public sector services and their management. *Journal of Management Studies*, **26** (3), 603–19.

Adler, P.A. and Adler, P. (1994) Observational techniques, in Denzin, K. and Lincoln, Y.S. (eds) *Handbook of Qualitative Research*. Thousand Oaks: Sage.

Agar, M. (1986) *Speaking of Ethnography*. London: Sage.

Al-Khalifa, E. (1989) Management by halves: women teachers and school management, in De Lyon, H. and Widdowson, M.F. (eds) *Women Teachers: Issues and Experiences*. Milton Keynes: Open University Press.

Allinson, C.W. (1984) *Bureaucratic Personality and Organisation Structure*. Aldershot: Gower.

Allison, D.J. (1991a) The development of the position and role of Chief Education Officers, in Leithwood, K. and Musella, D. (eds) *Understanding School System Administration: Studies of the Contemporary Chief Education Officer*. London: Falmer.

Allison, D. J. (1991b) Setting, size and sectors in the work environment of Chief Education Officers, in Leithwood, K. and Musella, D. (eds) *Understanding School System Administration: Studies of the Contemporary Chief Education Officer*. London: Falmer.

Arnold, M. (1852) *Morality*. Reprinted in Tinker, C.B. and Lowry, H.F. (eds) (1966) *Arnold: Poetical Works*, London: Oxford University Press.

Atkinson, P. (1990) *The Ethnographic Imagination: Textual Constructions of Reality*. London: Routledge.

Atkinson, R. (1987) Lecture on the role of the CEO, University of Leicester, University Centre, Northampton, February.

Atkinson, R. (1988) Week by week. *Education*, 5 August, 123.

Audit Commission (1989) *Losing an Empire, Finding a Role: The LEA of the Future*. Occasional Paper No. 10, London: HMSO.

Audit Commission (1993) *Phoenix Rising: A Study of New Zealand Local Government Following Reorganisation*. Occasional Paper No. 19, London: HMSO.

Austin, B. (1975) Time analysis of a local government manager's working day. *Local Government Studies*, April, 61–72.

Austin, B. (1977a) Time is money: but how many managers account for it? *Municipal and Public Services Journal*, 11 November, 1133–4.

Austin, B. (1977b) Marking time can be the best way to make progress. *Municipal and Public Services Journal*, 18 November, 1165–6.

Austin, B. and Knibbs, J. (1977) Pressures of the job. *Municipal and Public Services Journal*, 29 April, 409–10.

Bacharat, S.B. and Lawler, E.J. (1980) *Power and Politics in Organisations*. San Francisco: Jossey-Bass.

Bachrach, P. and Barate, M.S. (1963) Decisions and nondecisions: an analytical framework. *American Political Science Review*, **57**, 632–42.

Bacon, W. (1978) *Public Accountability and the School System*. London: Harper and Row.

Bains Report (1972) *The New Local Authorities: Management and Structure*. Study Group for the Department of the Environment, London: HMSO.

Bates, P. (1994) The impact of organisational culture on approaches to organisational problem solving, in Armson, R. and Paton, R. (eds) *Organisations, Cases, Issues, Concepts*. London: Chapman/Open University.

Belbin, M. (1981) *Management Teams: Why They Succeed or Fail*. London: Heinemann.

Bell, J. and Harrison, B. (eds) (1995) *Vision and Values in Managing Education*. London: Fulton.

Bennett, C. (1994) The New Zealand principal post-Picot. *Journal of Educational Administration*, **32**(2), 35–44.

Bernbaum, G. (1987) Interview with the author for this research, 27 April.

Berritt, L.S. (1994) Aesthetics of understanding research. Paper presented at the American Educational Research Association annual meeting, April, New Orleans.

Bezzinna, C. (1996) The Maltese primary school principalship: perceptions, roles and responsibilities. Unpublished PhD thesis, Brunel University.

Binns, A.L. (1957) The C.E.O. and his task. *Journal of Education*, **89**, April, 140–4.

Birley, D. (1970) *The Education Officer and His World*. London: Routledge and Kegan Paul.

Blundell, P. (1988) Not-so-fat cats who deserve a dish of cream. *Times Educational Supplement*, 28 April.

Boaden, N. (1986) Local education: a case study of Liverpool, in *Module 2, E333, The Policy Makers: Local and Central Government*. Milton Keynes: Open University Press.

Bongers, P. (1990) *Local Government and 1992*. Harlow: Longman.

Boyle, E. and Crosland, A. (1971), in conversation with M. Kogan, *The Politics of Education*. Harmondsworth: Penguin.

Bredeson, P.V. (1995) Superintendents' roles in curriculum development and instructional leadership: instructional visionaries, collaborators, supporters and delegators. Paper presented at the American Educational Research Association annual meeting, San Francisco.

Brighouse, T. (1983) Problems and pressures of today. *Educational Management and Administration*, **11**, 97–103.

Brighouse, T. (1986) The officer willed and the squirearchy agreed. *Education*, 19 September, 257–8.

Brooke, R. (1989) *Managing the Enabling Authority*. Harlow: Longman.

Brooksbank, K., Revell, J., Ackstine, E. and Bailey, K. (1986) *County and Voluntary Schools*. (6th edn; 1st edn 1949) London: Councils and Education Press.

Brown, S. and Baker, L. (1991) *About Change: Schools and LEAs Perspectives on LEA Reorganisation*. Slough: NFER.

Browning, P. (1972) Some changes in LEA administration. *London Educational Review*, **3**, Autumn, 4–12.

Bryman, A. (1988) *Quality and Quantity in Social Research*. London:Unwin and Hyman.

Bryman, A. (1992) *Charisma and Leadership in Organisations*. Newbury Park: Sage.

Bush, T. (1986) *Theories of Educational Management*. London: Harper and Row.

Bush, T. and Kogan, M. (1982) *Directors of Education*. London: Allen and Unwin.

Bush, T. , Kogan, M. and Lenney, T. (1989) *Directors of Education Facing Reform*. London: Kingsley.

Chance, W.C. (1992) *Visionary Leadership in Schools: Successful Strategies for Developing and Implementing an Educational Vision*. Springfield: Thomas.

Chong, K.C. and Low, G. T. (1994) *The School Chief*. Singapore: Singapore Educational Administration Society.

Clarke, M. and Stewart, J. (1986) The role of the chief executive: implications for training and development. Draft paper for comment by SOLACE members.

Clarke, M. and Stewart, J. (1990) *General Management in Local Government: Getting the Balance Right*. Harlow: Longman.

Clerkin, C. (1985) What do primary school heads actually do all day? *School Organisation*, **5**(4), 287–300.

Clough, P.T. (1992) *The Ends of Ethnography*. London: Sage.

Cochran, A. (1993) *Whatever Happened to Local Government?* Buckingham: Open University Press.

Cogley, F. (1995) Week by week. *Education*, 16 June, 10.

Cole, M. (1956) *Servant of the County*. London: Dobson.

Cooke, G. (1986) Week by week. *Education*, 11 July, 31.

Cookson, P.W. (1994) The power discourse: elite narratives and educational policy formation, in Walford, G. *Researching the Powerful in Education*. London: UCL.

Coulson, A.A. (1986) *The Managerial Work of Primary School Headteachers*.

Sheffield Papers in Education Management No. 48, Sheffield: Sheffield City Polytechnic.

Coulson, A.A. (1988) Primary school headship: a review of research. Paper presented at the British Educational Management and Administration Society research conference, Cardiff.

Cordingly, P. and Kogan, M. (1993) *In Support of Education*. London: Kingsley.

Cracknell, D. (1989) Week by week. *Education,* 10 March, 227.

Cracknell, D. (1995) Week by week. *Education,* 8 September, 9.

Crowson, R.L. (1994) Leadership and the superintendency: a reform minded perspective. Paper presented at the American Educational Research Association annual meeting, New Orleans.

Cubitt, H. (1987) Week by week. *Education,* 17 July, 43.

Dale, R. (1989) *The State and Social Policy*. Milton Keynes: Open University Press.

David, M. (1977) *Reform, Reaction and Resources: The 3Rs of Educational Planning*. Windsor: NFER.

Davies, L. (1984) The role of the primary school head. Unpublished MEd dissertation, University of Birmingham.

Davies, L. (1987) The role of the primary school head. *Educational Management and Administration*, **15**(1), 43–7.

Dearlove, J. (1979) *The Reorganisation of Local Government: Old Orthodoxies and a Political Perspective*. Cambridge: Cambridge University Press.

Delamont, S. (1988) For lust of knowing: methods used in the study of educational management and administration. Paper presented at the British Education Management and Administration Society research conference, Cardiff.

Dobie, J. (1996) Week by week. *Education,* 5 January, 10.

Donmoyer, R. (1985) Cognitive anthropology and research on effective principals. *Educational Administration Quarterly,* **21**(2), 31–57.

Dudley (1996) *The Westerby Years*. Dudley: Local Education Authority.

Duignan P. (1980) Administrative behaviour of school superintendents: a descriptive study. *Journal of Educational Administration,* **28**(1), 5–26.

Duke, D. (1986) The aesthetics of leadership. *Educational Administration Quarterly,* **22**(1), 7–28.

Dunleavy, P. (1980) *Urban Political Analysis*. London: Macmillan.

Dunsire, A. (1956) Accountability in local government. *Administration,* **4**(3), 85–7.

Du Quesnay, H. (1993) The search for a new partnership: the impact of the education bill on local education authorities, *Education Review,* **7**(1), 16-19.

Durham, M. (1985) Newham CEO leaves amid new controversy, *Times Educational Supplement,* 11 October, 10.

Education (1986a) Brent CEO resigns. 27 June, 570.

Education (1986b) Patten lends the CEOs a helping hand. 31 January, 103–4.

Education (1988a) Harrowing life at the top. 11 March, 200.

Education (1988b) Mr Baker offers officers and inspectors a seat at the table. 29 January, 61–2.

Education (1989) Avon CEO opts out of the new era. 10 March, 230.

Education (1990a) Birmingham's Mr Standfast. 16 February, 161.

Education (1990b) First trial of strength over powers under the 1988 Act. 16 February, 153.

Education Act (1921) [11 and 12 Geo V. Ch. 51]. London: HMSO.

Edwards, J., Sutton, A. and Thody A.M. (1990) TVEI cluster co-ordinators. *School Organisation,* **10**(1), 39–50.

Edwards, P. (1991) *The Changing Role, Structure and Style of LEAs.* Slough: NFER.

Edwards, W.L. (1979) The role of the principal in five New Zealand primary schools: an ethnographic perspective. *Journal of Educational Administration,* **17**(2), 248–54.

Elcock, H. (1982) *Local Government.* London: Methuen.

Finch, J. (1984) *Education as Social Policy.* London: Longman.

Fisher, A. and Spencer, D. (1988) Kirklees ignored advice of director. *Times Educational Supplement,* 15 July, 1.

Fisher, N. (1957) Training for CEOs. *Journal of Education,* **89**, June, 250–3.

Fisher, N. (1965) *Henry Morris: Pioneer of Education in the Countryside.* Peterborough: Arthur Mellows Memorial Trust.

Fitz, J. and Halpin, D. (1994) Ministers and mandarins: educational research in elite settings, in Walford, G. *Researching the Powerful in Education.* London: UCL.

Fryer, D. (1988a) Week by week. *Education,* 1 July, 3.

Fryer, D. (1988b) Week by week. *Education,* 25 June, 523.

Gedling, P. (1986) Week by week. *Education,* 24 January, 71.

Glass, T.E. (1993) Exemplary superintendents: do they fit the model? in Carter, D.S.G., Glass, T.E. and Hord, S.M. (eds) *Selecting, Preparing and Developing the School District Superintendent.* Washington: Falmer.

Gleick, J. (1987) *Chaos: Making a New Science.* London: Cardinal.

Goodwin, C. (1995a) Week by week. *Education,* 14 July, 9.

Goodwin, C. (1995b) Week by week, *Education,* 21 July, 9, 21.

Graves, B. (1995) Putting pay on the line. *School Administrator,* February, 8–16.

Greenwood, R., Walsh, K., Hinings, C.R. and Ranson, S. (1980) *Patterns of Management in Local Government.* Oxford: Robertson.

Griffin, G. and Chance, E.W, (1994) Superintendent behaviours and activities linked to school effectiveness: perceptions of principals and superintendents. *Journal of School Leadership,* **4**(1), 69–86.

Griffith, J.A.G., (1966) *Central Departments and Local Authorities.* London: Allen and Unwin.

Gronn, P. (1982) Methodological perspective: neo-Taylorism in educational administration. *Educational Administration Quarterly,* **18**(4), 17–35.

Gronn, P. (1984) 'I have a solution …': administrative power in a school meeting. *Educational Administration Quarterly,* **20**(2), 65–92.

Gronn, P. (1987a) Notes on leader watching, in Macpherson, R.J.S. (ed.) *Ways and Meanings of Research in Educational Administration.* Armidale: University of New England Press.

Gronn, P. (1987b) Obituary for structured observation. *Educational Administration Quarterly,* **23**(2), 78–81.

Gronn, P. (1996) From transactions to transformations. *Educational Management and Administration,* **24**(1), 7–30.

Guest, R.H. (1960) Categories of events in field observation, in Adams, R.N. and Preiss, J.J. (eds) *Human Organisation Research: Field Relations and Techniques.* Chicago: Dorsey Press.

Hackett, G. (1994) Top women fear macho backlash. *Times Educational Supplement,* 25 February, 6.

Haggarty, L. (1995) The use of content analysis to explore conversations between school teacher mentors and student teachers. *British Educational Research Journal,* **21**(2), 183–97.

Hall, J. (1984) Education fights back: management styles in local education authorities. *Educational Management and Administration,* **12,** 83–7.

Hall, V. (1994a) Changing the subject: some methodological issues in studying gender and headship. Paper presented at the British Educational Research Association conference, Oxford.

Hall, V. (1994b) Making it happen: a study of women headteachers of primary and secondary schools in England and Wales. Paper presented at the American Educational Research Association annual meeting, New Orleans.

Hall, V., Mackay, H. and Morgan, C. (1986) *Head Teachers at Work.* Milton Keynes: Open University Press.

Handy, C. (1994) The language of leadership, in Armson, R. and Paton, R. (eds) *Organisations, Cases, Issues, Concepts.* London: Chapman/Open University.

Harris, J. (1995) Week by week. *Education,* 1 December, 8.

Harvey, C.W. (1986) How primary heads spend their time. *Educational Management and Administration,* **14**(1), 75–80.

Heller, H. and Edwards, P. (1992) *Policy and Power in Education.* London: Routledge.

Hendy, J. (1987a) Week by week. *Education,* 18 September, 227.

Hendy, J. (1987b) Moving from a county to a metropolitan authority. *Education,* 18 September, 227.

Heshusius, L. (1994) Freeing ourselves from objectivity: managing subjectivity or turning toward a participatory mode of consciousness? *Educational Researcher,* April, 15–22.

Hickcox, E.S. (1992) Practices of effective CEOs: a preliminary discussion. Paper presented at the CCEA regional conference, Hong Kong.

Hill, D. (1974) *Democratic Theory and Local Government*. London: Allen and Unwin.

Hill, L. (1938) *The Local Government Officer*. London: Allen and Unwin.

Hilsum, S. and Kane, B.S. (1994) Negotiation of access for observation, in Johnson, D. *Research Methods in Educational Management*. Harlow: Longman.

Hobbes, T. (1651) *Leviathan*, in Macpherson, C.B. (ed.) (1968) London: Penguin.

Hodgkinson, C. (1978) *Towards a Philosophy of Administration*. Oxford: Blackwell.

Hodgkinson, C. (1983) *The Philosophy of Leadership*. Oxford: Blackwell.

Holmes, M. (1991) A delicate balance: leadership or stewardship, in Leithwood, K. and Musella, D. (eds) *Understanding School System Administration: Studies of the Contemporary Chief Education Officer*. London: Falmer.

Hornsby, J. (1984) Leadership by the chief education officer: past, present and future, in Harling, P. (ed.) *New Directions in Educational Leadership*. Lewes: Falmer.

Hoyle, E. (1986) *The Politics of School Management*. London: Hodder and Stoughton.

Hugill, B. (1988) Kent chief to join the growing exodus. *Times Educational Supplement*, 17 June.

Hugill, B. (1989) Quiet man in a mood for change. *Times Educational Supplement*, 3 February.

Humphreys, G. (1989) Week by week. *Education*, 21 July, 43.

Isenberg, D.J. (1994) The tactics of strategic opportunism, in Armson, R. and Paton, R. (eds) *Organisations, Cases, Issues, Concepts*. London: Chapman/Open University.

Jenkins, H.O. (1991) *Getting it Right: A Handbook for Successful School Leaders*. Oxford: Blackwell.

Jennings, R.E. (1977) *Education and Politics: Policy Making in Local Education Authorities*. London: Batsford.

Jennings, R.E. (1983) The deputy director of education: the phoenix of LEA administration. *Educational Management and Administration*, **11**, 29–40.

Johnes, G. (1995) School management: how much local autonomy should there be? *Educational Management and Administration*, **23**(3), 162–7.

Johnson, G. (1989) Rethinking incrementalism, in Asch, D. and Bowman, C. (eds) *Readings in Strategic Management*. London: Macmillan.

Jones, D. (1988) *Stewart Mason: The Art of Education*. London: Lawrence and Wishart.

Jones J.I. (1986) The CEO becomes a damage control contractor. *Education*, 17 January, 58.

Kanter, R.M. (1989) *When Giants Learn to Dance*. New York: Simon and Schuster.

Kirby, P. C. and Colbert, R. (1994) Principals who empower teachers. *Journal of School Leadership,* **4**(1), 39–51.

Kmetz, J.J. and Willower, D. (1982) Elementary school principals' work behaviour. *Educational Administration Quarterly,* **18**(4), 62–78.

Kogan, M. (1975) *Educational Policy Making: A Study of Interest Groups and Parliament.* London: Allen and Unwin.

Kogan, M. (1994) Researching the powerful in education and elsewhere, in Walford, G. (ed.) *Researching the Powerful in Education.* London: UCL.

Kogan, M. and van der Eyken, W. (1973) *County Hall.* London: Penguin.

Konnert, M.W. and Augenstein, J.J. (1990) *The Superintendency in the Nineties.* Lancaster: Technomic.

Laffin, M. and Young, K. (1990) *Professionalism in Local Government.* Harlow: Longman.

LaRoque, L. and Coleman, P. (1991) Transformational leadership and school district quality, in Leithwood, K. and Musella, D. (eds) *Understanding School System Administration: Studies of the Comtemporary Chief Education Officer.* London: Falmer.

Lauder, H. (1995) Educational Reform in New Zealand, 1987–1994. *Celebration Centenary,* Glasgow: University of Glasgow, Department of Education.

Lawrence, B. (1972) *The Administration of Education in Britain.* London: Batsford.

Lawton, S.B. and Scane, J. (1991) Inferring values from the physical culture of the CEO's office, in Leithwood, K. and Musella, D. (eds) *Understanding School System Administration: Studies of the Contemporary Chief Education Officer.* London: Falmer.

Leithwood, K. and Musella, D. (1991a) (eds) *Understanding School System Administration: Studies of the Contemporary Chief Education Officer.* London: Falmer.

Leithwood, K and Musella, D. (1991b) The influence of chief education officers on school effectiveness, in Leithwood, K. and Musella, D. (eds) *Understanding School System Administration: Studies of the Contemporary Chief Education Officer.* London: Falmer.

Lello, J. (1979) *Accountability in Education.* London: Ward Lock.

LGTB (Local Government Training Board) (1985) *The Management of Hung Authorities.* Luton: LGTB.

Lindblom, C.E. (1959) The science of 'muddling through'. *Public Administration Quarterly,* **19**, 79–88.

Ling, P. (1986) The educability of the ordinary man: Eastern Australia 1880 to 1914, in Palmer, I. (ed.) *Melbourne Studies in Education.* Melbourne: Melbourne University Press.

Lipson, J. (1994) Ethical issues in ethnography, in Morse, J.M. (ed.) *Critcal Issues in Qualitative Research Methods.* Thousand Oaks: Sage.

Lister, E. (1991) *LEAs: Old and New: A View from Wandsworth.* London:

Centre for Policy Studies.

Lockhart, A. (1996) Week by week. *Education,* 26 January, 7.

Lodge, D. (1989) *Nice Work.* London: Penguin.

Lofland, J. (1971) *Analysing Social Settings: A Guide to Qualitative Observation and Analysis.* Belmont: Wadsworth.

Lofthouse, M. (1982) The church colleges 1890–1944: teacher training. Unpublished PhD thesis, University of Leicester.

Lomax, P. and Ouston, J. (1995) Inter-school links, liaison and networking: collaboration or competition? *Educational Management and Administration,* **23**(3), 148–61.

Lyons, G. (1972) Patterns of administrative work in secondary schools. *Further Education Staff College Reports* **5**(5), 22–8.

Lyons, G. (1974) *The Administrative Tasks of Head and Senior Teachers in Large Secondary Schools.* Bristol: University of Bristol.

McCabe, D.G. (1992) Beyond brevity, variety and fragmentation: the work of the chief education officer as organisational hero. Paper presented at the CCEA regional conference, Hong Kong.

McHugh, J.D. (1994) The Lords will be done: interviewing the powerful in education, in Walford, G.(ed.) *Researching the Powerful in Education.*

MacKenzie, W.J.M. (1961) Theories of local government. LSE, Greater London Papers, No. 2.

Maclure, S. (1970) *Studies in the Government and Control of Education Since 1860.* London: Methuen.

Maclure, S. (1992) Another endangered species. *Times Educational Supplement,* **3966**, 3 July, 12.

Mcpherson, A. and Raab, C. (1988) *Governing Education: A Sociology of Power Since 1945.* Edinburgh: Edinburgh University Press.

Macpherson R.J.S. (1984a) On being and becoming an educational administrator: methodological issues. *Educational Administration Quarterly,* **20**(4), 58–75.

Macpherson, R.J.S. (1984b) *Ethnographic Research in Educational Administration: An Introduction.* Clayton: Monash University.

Macpherson, R.J.S. (1985a) Being a regional director of education. PhD thesis, Monash University, Melbourne.

Macpherson, R.J.S. (1985b) Problems encountered 'Boswelling' elite educational administrators. *Canadian Administrator,* **24**(4), 1–6.

Macpherson, R.J.S. (1986), Towards biographical and autobiographical research in educational administration. *Educational Administration Review,* **4**(1), 14–28.

Macpherson, R.J.S. (1987). System and structure man, politician and philosopher: being a regional director of education, in Macpherson, R.J.S. *Ways and Meanings of Research in Educational Administration.* Armidale: University of New England Press.

Maden, M. (1989) New networks for old. *Times Educational Supplement,* **1,** September, 10.

Mallaby Report (1967) *Staffing of Local Government.* London: Committee on the Staffing of Local Government, HMSO

Manasse, A.L. (1985) Improving conditions for principal effectiveness: policy implications of research. *Elementary School Journal,* **85**(3), 339–63.

Mann, J. (1988) Why so many education officers say, 'Hello, I must be going'. *Guardian,* 19 April, 25.

Martin, W.J. and Willower, D.J. (1981) The managerial behaviour of high school principals. *Educational Administration Quarterly,* **17**(1), 69–90.

Mason, M. (1986) Leadership in a time of change. *Education,* 23 May, 474.

Mason, S (1981) Interview with Don Jones, University of Leicester, ten years after Mason's retirement. Video in personal possession of the author.

Maud Report (1967) *Management of Local Government.* London: Committee on the Management of Local Government. Vols. 1–4. London: HMSO.

Mercury (1994) It's vital to be a good listener. *Leicester Mercury,* 31 October, 29.

Meyer, W.R. (1991) The archives of the Leeds education authority (1903–60), *Local Historian,* **21**(4), 162–7.

Middleton, S. (1976) *Still Waters.* London: Hutchinson.

Middleton, S. (1986) *An After-Dinner's Sleep.* London: Hutchinson.

Mintzberg, H. (1973) *The Nature of Managerial Work.* New York: Harper and Row.

Morgan, G. (1993) *Imaginisation.* London: Sage

Morgan, T.M. (1986) *Aspects of Monmouthshire Local Education Authority Administration, Volume I 1889–1944.* Cwmbran: Raven.

Morris, R. (1994) *The Functions and Roles of Local Education Authorities.* Slough: NFER.

Mortimore, P. (1988) *School Matters.* London: Open Books/ILEA.

Moulton, H. F. (1919) *The Powers and Duties of Education Authorities.* London: Hodge.

Mullany, P.J. (1991) The changing role of the LEA. *Education, 3–13,* **19**(3), 3–6.

Musella, D. (1992) The impact of the chief education officer on school system culture, change and effectiveness. Paper presented at the regional conference of the Commonwealth Council for Educational Administration: Hong Kong, August.

Nash, I. (1988) The gourmet with a taste for radical change. *Times Educational Supplement,* 15 July, 5.

Northants (1994) *Northamptonshire's Submission to the Local Government Commission for England.* Northampton: Northants County Council.

Novick, J. (1995) Death of the sheepskinned gob. *Maxim,* September (5), 76–9.

Nutt, P. (1993) Flexible decision styles and the choices of top executives. *Journal of Management Studies,* **30**(5), 695–722.

O'Connor, M. (1988) Time for a change. *Education Guardian,* 7 June, 23.

O'Dempsey, K. (1976) Time analysis of activities, work patterns and roles of high school principals. Unpublished MEd Admin thesis, University of Queensland.

Owens, R.G. (1982) Methodological perspective: methodological rigor in naturalistic enquiry: some issues and answers. *Educational Administration Quarterly*, **18**(2), 1–21.

Ozga, J. (1986) The policy-makers, in *Module 2, E333, The Policy Makers: Local and Central Government*. Milton Keynes: Open University Press.

Parkes, C. (1996) Public spirit puts California's schools on-line. *Financial Times*, 12 March, 3.

Parshotam, N. (1987) The fast learner in the hot seat. *Times Educational Supplement*, 7 August, 8.

Paton, R. (1994) Powers visible and invisible, in Armson, R. and Paton, R. (eds) *Organisations, Cases, Issues, Concepts*. London: Chapman/Open University.

Peschek, D. and Brand, J. (1966) *Policies and Politics in Secondary Education: Case Studies in West Ham and Reading*. London: London School of Economics.

Peschkin, A. (1988) In search of subjectivity: one's own. *Educational Researcher*, **17**(7), 17–21.

Peters, T.J. and Waterman, R.H. (1982) *In Search of Excellence*. New York: Harper and Row.

Pettigrew, A. (1983) Patterns of managerial response as organisations move from rich to poor environments: a response to Tim Brighouse. *Educational Management and Administration*, **11**, 104–14.

Pettigrew, A., Ferlie, E. and McKee, L. (1992) *Shaping Strategic Change*. London: Sage.

Pimenoff, S. (1992) Have LEAs a future? *Assistant Masters and Mistresses Association*, **14**(5), 14.

Pinchin, M. (1987) Week by week. *Education*, 23 October, 331.

Prahalad, C.K. and Hamel, G. (1990) The core competence of the corporation. *Harvard Business Review*, **68**(3), 79–91.

Pratt, J. (1987) Education under adversity. *Educational Management and Administration*, **15**, 19–22.

Quinn, J.B. (1980) *Strategies for Change: Logical Incrementalism*. Homewood: Irwin.

Ree, H. (1973) *Educator Extraordinary*. Harlow: Longman.

Rhodes, R.A.W. (1988) *Beyond Westminster and Whitehall: The Sub-Central Governments of Britain*. London: Unwin Hyman.

Riley, K.A. (1992) The changing framework and purposes of education authorities. *Research Papers in Education*, **7**(1), 3–25.

Roberts, N.C. (1985) Transforming leadership: a process of collective action, *Human Relations*, **38**(11), 1023–46.

Rudolf, H.R. and Peluchette, J.V. (1993) The power gap: is sharing or accumulating power the answer? *Journal of Applied Business Research,* **9**(3), 12–19.

Rule, G. (1894) *Mary Gledstone, The Pupil Teacher.* Gateshead-on-Tyne: Henderson and Birkett.

Salancik, G.R. and Pfeffer, J. (1977) Who gets power: and how they hold on to it: a strategic-contingency model of power. *Organisational Dynamics,* Winter, 3–21.

Saran, R. (1974) *Policy Making in Secondary Education.* Oxford: Oxford University Press.

Sarros, J. and Beare, H. (1994) *Australian Contributions to Educational Management: Some Commentaries by Chief Education Officers.* Applecross: ACEA.

Schoemaker, P.J.H. (1993) Strategic decisions in organisations: rational and behavioural views. *Journal of Management Studies,* **30**(1), 107–30.

Schriescheim, C. and Kerr, S. (1977) Theories and measures of leadership: a critical appraisal of current and future direction, in Hunt, J.G. and Larson, L. (eds), *Leadership: The Cutting Edge.* Carbondale: Southern Illinois Press.

Seaborne, M. (1968) William Brockington, Director of Education for Leicestershire, 1903–1947, in Simon, B. (ed.) *Education In Leicestershire, 1540–1940.* Leicester: Leicester University Press.

Sedgewick, F. (1989) *Here Comes the Assembly Man.* London: Falmer.

Self, P. (1977) *Administrative Theories and Politics.* London: Allen and Unwin.

Selleck, R.J.W. (1982) *Frank Tate: Biography.* Melbourne: Melbourne University Press.

Senior, D. (1969) *Memorandum of Dissent* in *Report of the Royal Commission on Local Government* (Redcliffe-Maud). London: HMSO.

Shrivastra, S. (ed.) (1983) *The Executive Mind.* London:Jossey Bass.

Silverman, D. (1993) *Interpreting Qualitative Data.* London: Sage.

Simon, H.A. (1947) *Administrative Behaviour.* New York: Macmillan.

Sloman, P. (1985) L'affaire Pailing in perspective. *Education,* 12 July, 38.

Smith, W.O. L. (1965) *Government of Education.* Harmondsworth: Penguin.

Spradley, J.P (1979) *The Ethnographic Interview.* New York: Holt, Reinhart and Winston.

Starhawke, (1994) Leadership roles, in Armson, R. and Paton, R. (eds) *Organisations, Cases, Issues, Concepts.* London: Chapman/Open University.

Stewart, J. D. and Ranson, S. (1988) Management in the public domain. *Public Money and Management,* **8**(2), 13–19.

Stewart, R. (1965) The use of diaries to study managers' jobs. *Journal of Management Studies,* **2**, May, 228–35.

Stewart, R. (1982) *Choices for Managers: A Guide to Managerial Work and Managerial Behaviour.* Maidenhead: McGraw-Hill.

Stoten, M. (1987) The future for Brent. *Education,* 3 July.

Strength for Chief Officers (1986) *Professional Officer,* **1**(9), 6.

Sydor, S. (1994) Stories and silences in the construction of knowledge.

Paper presented at the American Educational Research Association conference, New Orleans. (Author is at Brock University, Canada.)

Sylvester, G.H. (1957) The CEOs day. *Journal of Education*, **89**, May, 186–9.

Swann Report (1985) *Committee of Enquiry into the Education of Children from Ethnic Minority Groups*. London: HMSO.

TES (1988a) Berkshire scraps race initiative. 19 February, 1.

TES (1988b) Brent CEO 'a racist' – councillor. 26 February, 3.

TES (1988c) Honest advice. 26 February, 2.

TES (1989a) New wave of officers sweeps in. 27 January.

TES (1989b) Getting out while the going is bad ... 21 July, 10.

TES (1990) Row over appointment of 'political' CEO. 18 May, 1.

Theobald, M.R. (1990) The everyday world of women who taught. *History of Education Review*, **19**(2), 15–23.

Thody, A.M. (1968) The Leicester School Board, 1871–1902, in Simon, B. (ed.) *Education in Leicestershire 1540–1940*. Leicester: Leicester University Press.

Thody, A.M. (1976) Central–Local relations in educational administration, 1870–1970. Unpublished MEd thesis, University of Leicester.

Thody, A.M. (1988) Central intervention in local educational disputes, 1902–1944. *Journal of Educational Administration and History*, **20**(2) 71–80.

Thody, A.M. (1989) University management observed. *Studies in Higher Education*, **14**(3), 279–96.

Thody, A.M. (1991a) Central intervention in local educational disputes: the use of Section 68 of the 1944 Act. *Journal of Educational Administration and History*, **21**(1), 59–66.

Thody, A.M. (1991b) Strategic planning and school management. *School Organisation*, **11**(1), 21–36.

Thody, A.M. (1992) *Moving to Management: School Governors in the 1990s*. London: Fulton.

Thody, A.M. (1994) School management in nineteenth century elementary schools: a day in the life of a headteacher. *History of Education*, **23**(4), 355–73.

Thom, D. (1993) *Educational Management and Leadership: Word, Spirit and Deed for a Just Society*. Calgary AB: Detselig Enterprises.

Thornton, Sir M. (1995) There is still a role for local authorities. *Times Educational Supplement*, 6 October, 20.

Tichy, N.M. and Devanna, M.A. (1990) *The Transformational Leader*. New York: Wiley.

Timperley, H. and Robinson, V.M.J. (1995) Achieving shared values between schools and their communities. *Leading and Managing*, **1**(2), 137–49.

Todorov, T. (1984) *Mikhail Bakhtin: The Dialogic Principle*. (trans. W. Godzich), Minneapolis: University of Minnesota Press.

Tomlinson, J. (1985) Leaders of the middle tier. *Education*, 29 November, 495.

Townsend, R.G. (1991) Policy administration as rhetoric: one leader and his arguments, in Leithwood, K. and Musella, D. (eds) *Understanding School System Administration: Studies of the Contemporary Chief Education Officer.* London: Falmer.

Useem, M. (1996) Do leaders make a difference? *Financial Times Mastering Management, Part 18,* March, 5.

Vaill, P. (1978) Towards a behavioural description of high performing systems, in McCall, M. and Lombardo, M. (eds) *Leadership: Where Else Can We Go?* Durham: Duke University Press.

Walford, G. (ed.) (1994a) *Researching the Powerful in Education.* London: UCL.

Walford, G. (1994b) Reflections on researching the powerful, in Walford, G. (ed.) *Researching the Powerful in Education.* London: UCL.

Walker, K. (1994) Perceptions of ethical problems amongst senior educational leaders. Paper presented at the American Educational Research Association conference, New Orleans.

Wallace, M. and Hall, V. (1994) *Inside the SMT.* London: Chapman.

Walton, B. (1987) Week by week. *Education,* 27 February, 177; 6 March, 205; 13 March, 227.

Walton, B. (1990) Week by week. *Education,* 2 February, 103.

Westerby, R. (1987) Week by week. *Education,* 22 May, 445; 29 May, 469; 5 June, 489; 12 June, 513.

Wheare, K.C. (1955) *Government by Committee.* Oxford: Clarendon Press.

Whitty, G. and Edwards, T. (1994) Researching Thatcherite education policy, in Walford, G. *Researching the Powerful in Education.* London: UCL.

Widdicombe Report (1986) *Committee of Enquiry into the Conduct of Local Authority Business.* London: HMSO.

Wilce, H. (1986) Step up for an 'honorary chap'. *Times Educational Supplement,* 26 September, 6.

Willis, D.F. (1980) The work activity of school principals: an observational study. *Journal of Educational Administration,* 18(1) 27–54.

Wilson, R.E. (1960) *The Modern School Superintendent.* New York: Harper.

Wood-Allum, K. (1987) Week by week. *Education,* 24 April, 357.

Wolcott, H. (1973) *The Man in the Principal's Office.* Prospect Heights: Waveland.

Index